Leisure Studies in a Global Era

Series Editors:

Karl Spracklen, Professor of Leisure Studies, Leeds Metropolitan University, UK
Karen Fox, Professor of Leisure Studies, University of Alberta, Canada

In this book series, we defend leisure as a meaningful, theoretical, framing concept; and critical studies of leisure as a worthwhile intellectual and pedagogical activity. This is what makes this book series distinctive: we want to enhance the discipline of leisure studies and open it up to a richer range of ideas; and, conversely, we want sociology, cultural geographies and other social sciences and humanities to open up to engaging with critical and rigorous arguments from leisure studies. Getting beyond concerns about the grand project of leisure, we will use the series to demonstrate that leisure theory is central to understanding wider debates about identity, postmodernity and globalisation in contemporary societies across the world. The series combines the search for local, qualitatively rich accounts of everyday leisure with the international reach of debates in politics, leisure and social and cultural theory. In doing this, we will show that critical studies of leisure can and should continue to play a central role in understanding society. The scope will be global, striving to be truly international and truly diverse in the range of authors and topics.

Titles include:

Brett Lashua, Karl Spracklen and Stephen Wagg (*editors*)
SOUNDS AND THE CITY
Popular Music, Place and Globalization

Oliver Smith
CONTEMPORARY ADULTHOOD AND THE NIGHT-TIME ECONOMY

Karl Spracklen
WHITENESS AND LEISURE

Karl Spracklen
DIGITAL LEISURE, THE INTERNET AND POPULAR CULTURE
Communities and Identities in a Digital Age

Robert A. Stebbins
CAREERS IN SERIOUS LEISURE
From Dabbler to Devotee in Search of Fulfilment

Soile Veijola, Jennie Germann Molz, Olli Pyyhtinen, Emily Hockert and Alexander Grit
DISRUPTIVE TOURISM AND ITS UNTIDY GUESTS
Alternative Ontologies for Future Hospitalities

Udo Merkel (*editor*)
IDENTITY DISCOURSES AND COMMUNITIES IN INTERNATIONAL EVENTS,
FESTIVALS AND SPECTACLES

Leisure Studies in a Global Era
Series Standing Order ISBN 978–1–137–31032–3 hardback
978–1–137–31033–0 paperback
(*outside North America only*)

You can receive future titles in this series as they are published by placing a standing order. Please contact your bookseller or, in case of difficulty, write to us at the address below with your name and address, the title of the series and the ISBN quoted above.

Customer Services Department, Macmillan Distribution Ltd, Houndmills, Basingstoke, Hampshire RG21 6XS, England

Digital Leisure, the Internet and Popular Culture

Communities and Identities in a Digital Age

Karl Spracklen

Professor of Leisure Studies, Leeds Beckett University, UK

First published 2015 by
PALGRAVE MACMILLAN

Palgrave Macmillan in the UK is an imprint of Macmillan Publishers Limited, registered in England, company number 785998, of Houndmills, Basingstoke, Hampshire RG21 6XS.

Palgrave Macmillan in the US is a division of St Martin's Press LLC, 175 Fifth Avenue, New York, NY 10010.

Palgrave Macmillan is the global academic imprint of the above companies and has companies and representatives throughout the world.

Palgrave® and Macmillan® are registered trademarks in the United States, the United Kingdom, Europe and other countries.

ISBN 978–1–137–40586–9

This book is printed on paper suitable for recycling and made from fully managed and sustained forest sources. Logging, pulping and manufacturing processes are expected to conform to the environmental regulations of the country of origin.

A catalogue record for this book is available from the British Library.

A catalog record for this book is available from the Library of Congress.

For my grandparents

Contents

1 Introduction   1

2 A Brief History of Leisure and the Net   11

3 Leisure Studies and the Problem of the Net   32

4 Net Theory and Digital Leisure   53

5 A Theory of Digital Leisure   74

6 Identity-Making and Social Media   94

7 File-Sharing and Net Ethics   113

8 Digital Leisure and Commodification   133

9 Digital Leisure and Communicative Leisure   153

10 Sex and Romance   173

11 Conclusions   193

References   204

Index   227

1
Introduction

I first came across the internet when I saw the famous web-cam set up by researchers in the Cambridge University computing department, which they used to keep an eye on the coffee percolator upstairs while they were working in another room. This was somewhere between 1990 and 1993 (my memory is hazy). I wasn't particularly impressed but my friend Rhodri thought it was cool. He was our house's technological enthusiast and we were all natural scientists, so it was no surprise that we were aware of what was going on in the 'spod shop' (the derogatory name applied to the computing building). But apart from that and some lectures on computing I missed in the first year, the internet had no real impact on my teaching and learning. I was still writing my essays by hand, reading library books and journal articles in hard-bound volumes that smelled of old paper and glue. I left Cambridge without ever seeing anything online or sending any email, though I knew people who were doing both of those things in their leisure time.

I went straight to Leeds Metropolitan University to study for my PhD in the autumn of 1993, after spending a summer thinking I was going to do a PhD at Warwick. I had applied by post, contacted the tutors by telephone and got my acceptance offer through the post. By 1994 (or thereabouts) we had internet access in the library, but it was slow and I didn't use it at all. We did get email around 1995. Then in 1996 we were teaching students about the internet, which they could access all across the IT labs and in the library. It was round about this time that the internet had become the latest new technology to scare the tabloids and impress the broadsheets. I finished my PhD having never looked at a journal or book online: there are no references to websites anywhere in it (I have just searched for the word 'internet' in the Word version of my thesis and found no matches, even though the PhD is about the two codes of rugby and their imaginary communities). When I came back into teaching and researching leisure studies in 2004, surfing the internet was an everyday leisure activity, and the internet itself was an essential instrument of my work. When I lose my internet connection, or the university email server goes down, I feel completely lost and useless.

This research monograph will explore the growth and importance of the internet in shaping the meaning and purpose of leisure and popular culture. I will use the term 'Net' to capture not just the physical stuff of the internet, but the virtual and socio-cultural stuff as well. Journalists used to refer to the internet as the Net with capital letters because they were excited by its novelty and its importance, and it sounds and looks more ominous. I have adopted this usage as I think it is impossible to think about the internet and digital technology without thinking of all the other meanings and resonances surrounding them. Calling it all the Net becomes a useful form of shorthand, as well as a reminder of the strangeness of it. I will show that although we live in a digital age where identities and communities are seemingly in states of permanent transition, leisure remains caught between its communicative meaning for individuals, and its instrumental purpose for governments and global capitalism. This book will draw on the work of Jurgen Habermas, as my previous books have done (Spracklen, 2009, 2011a, 2013a), but it will also synthesize a new theory of digital leisure that draws on the work of Castells, Urry and Bauman and a host of others. It will review leisure theory about liquidity, networks and globalization before creating a theoretical framework that posits a return to a Habermasian account of popular culture. This will be in the first half of the book. In the second half, new research on digital leisure will be introduced to demonstrate the strength of the new theoretical framework.

Central to the theorization of digital leisure is the shift towards postmodernity, global networks and globalization. Globalization has been the focus of a number of key arguments in leisure studies, tourism studies and the sociology of sport. In the latter area, globalization lends itself to helping researchers understand the spread of modern, professional sports around the globe. The global reach of the Olympics and soccer is an obvious example of this trend. Richard Giulianotti (see, for example, Giulianotti and Robertson, 2007) has written extensively on the interaction and tension between the globalization of professional sports and the local ties and cultures of sports fandom. He sees sports such as soccer displaying what Robertson calls glocalization: the nexus of local and national loyalties associated with the local club and the national team being tested on a global stage, where elite athletes routinely travel thousands of miles from their countries of origin to play in the best domestic soccer leagues. Some sociologists of leisure such as Ken Roberts see no problem in accepting the impact of globalization on sports fandom. Roberts (2004) argues that globalization allows the strongest brands in professional sports to prosper and allows the best soccer teams, for example, to have more fans in cities thousands of miles away across the world than in their home country. Globalization is also viewed positively by historians and sociologists interested in the typically English game of cricket, which has been transformed globally by the professionalization of Australian and Indian cricket. The developments in India, in particular, with professional clubs and thousands of fans, cheerleaders and sponsors, have seen the global flows of economic and cultural migration associated with the British Empire reversed – the best English cricketers have taken huge salary increases to sign contracts with clubs in the Indian elite cricket league.

In tourism studies similar arguments have been put forward about the positive interaction between the local and the global. Theorists have argued that the technologies associated with globalization have reduced the size of the world and allow travellers and locals to meet each other as equals (Rojek and Urry, 1997). For example, the rise of the internet has reduced the power of travel agencies and transnational tourist companies and allowed tourists to book direct with hotels in countries on the opposite side of the world. Local businesses can cut out the fees they pay to travel agencies and get bookings directly. This is good for local economies in developing countries, where only a small share of the cost of a holiday booked through a transnational corporation trickles down. Locals can sell their local cultures directly to potential holidaymakers, too – and every region and city has its marketing teams working on websites telling potential visitors about the unique food, climate, landscape, shops, beaches and mountains that can be found there. Globalization also allows resorts and cities that have become unfashionable to find new markets from the growing economies of the East.

However, most theorists and researchers of leisure see globalization as a threat to diversity, and a tool of neo-colonialism. Post-Marxists such as John Horne (2006) argue that modern, professionalized sports and leisure forms are dominated by global capitalism and are vehicles for hegemonic power relationships. Bramham (2006) sees globalized leisure limiting free choices and destroying local pastimes: in a globalized world, everybody watches the same movies, the same sports, and everybody plays the same online games, paying our subscriptions and willingly signing away our ability to think. In the wake of the globalization of leisure, difference and diversity disappear – so traditional sports and games such as kabbadi in India are under threat from the development of American football in the country; and in China, local arts and cultural festivals are at risk of being lost or transformed into commercialized and marketized versions of their former selves. Leisure in globalization, according to Rojek (2010), is leisure that is denuded of its ability to allow people to find meaning: in a world that is globalizing, our choices are reduced and our leisure is increasingly dictated by the benefit-cost ratios of corporations and transnational free trade agreements.

The struggle over the use and meaning of the Net is clear evidence of the commodification of informal leisure habits. When the Net was formalized through the invention of the World Wide Web system in the early 1990s, most early adopters were urban, rich, educated and liberal. These early users saw the Net as a place of free discourse and communication, allowing them to bypass the systems of censorship, commodification and control associated with the entertainment and print industries (Briggs and Burke, 2009). Some early users even believed that the Net would transcend nation states to build a global, international community of free individuals, who would spend their time sharing ideas, spreading democracy and human rights, and creating a free space for artists, dreamers, philosophers and other utopians. This strong belief in the redeeming nature of the digital and the virtual as a free, uncensored site is still prevalent in discourse about the internet, and on the Net itself: Wikipedia, for example, would not exist without its creators giving their time and knowledge to edit the data. However, since the 1990s the Net has become commodified, populated by multinational corporations wishing to sell to us directly (Amazon) or to turn our personal data into a commodity to sell to others (Facebook, Google). Our informal, private digital use is turned into browsing habits and preferences that are bought and sold by marketing companies. Our time on the Net is increasingly used to buy things. There are still millions of websites that give users free material, but even that transaction is one of commodity, buying something for nothing rather than interacting and contributing.

Manuel Castells' (1996) *The Rise of the Network Society* has become a classic text of social theory, charting the rise of the information age and the end of the old modernist social structures. In this book, the first of his *The Information Age* trilogy, Castells argues that the technological advances associated with the Net have disrupted traditional social structures, economics and politics. In this information age, the Net changes the way we consume popular culture, for example. We no longer listen to music on the radio or television and go out to buy it on the high street – instead we browse file-sharing sites and swap recommendations with others. The Net has made all culture popular, and has bypassed traditional arbiters of taste such as professional critics and corporations – there is an anarchic democracy of free choice. However, Castells does not believe that this makes the Net an individualist utopia, a paradise of downloading and sharing. Rather, the Net has become an apparatus of commerce, control and surveillance, with most of this activity hidden behind the discourse of personal freedom. The new corporations work alongside governments to balance the pursuit of profit with the need to limit political action. Popular culture on the internet is increasingly marketized, with every transaction noted and tracked by algorithms so the gatekeeping sites on the Net can target adverts at us more effectively. At the same time, governments are keen to access personal data most of us have placed on social networking sites. We can witness some of these trends in the examples of MySpace and gold farming.

For a number of years in the first decade of the twenty-first century, Myspace.com played a significant role in the construction of modern subcultures. The business models of the pop music industry assumed young people were passive consumers who could be sold one artist after another in a charts system controlled by marketing teams. Big labels made big profits while the labels controlled the supply of information about bands and the availability of music in record stores. All this changed with the creation of MySpace.com, combined with the advance in technology that led to the rise in music-file downloading (legally and illegally) as an informal leisure activity. Bands could now market themselves directly to potential fans without the need for managers or labels; they could sell their music; and fans could find bands they liked through following hyperlinks from one band's page to another band's page. MySpace.com became something that shaped modern pop music subcultures, making underground and extreme music genres and artists freely available and easily accessible to a global audience (Wilkinson and Thelwall, 2010). Some pop music subcultures were invented through MySpace.com's friend connections (such as deathcore in heavy metal, based on the hype of counting thousands of friends). Myspace.com was bought by a transnational corporation seeking to profit from the hype. The pop music industry saw MySpace.com as something to be exploited, playing with hyping and friend-making to try to build fan bases for bands, using online fan networks as they used real-world street teams to hype acts through word-of-mouth. Subcultures drifted away from using MySpace.com as soon as this started to happen.

Online gaming systems such as *World of Warcraft* require hundreds of hours of player time to develop characters. One starts these games with basic characters with little money, basic weapons or spells, and poorly developed skills. It is your initial task to build up your character's profile so that you have enough virtual resources and power to take part in entertaining and immersive multi-character quests. To get to this point means engaging in lots of fights or trivial challenges, taking hours of gameplay. For many online gamers, this is part of the discipline required to be a part of these virtual worlds, and for some there is satisfaction and thrill to be found in killing creature after creature at two o'clock in the morning. But for others there is the option of buying the time of a worker (a 'gold farmer') elsewhere in the world, who will develop a character up to a more interesting and survivable level. Such factories of online character development have emerged to meet the needs of the rich, time-poor gamers of the developed world and are often based in developing countries in Asia. As well as the general task of development, these workers will also do bespoke work, finding particular magic items, for example, which are sorely needed by individual gamers in the developed West. In a world driven by capitalism, it is perfectly acceptable to create these markets – there is a demand from the rich and a supply of gaming talent in developing countries who can meet the needs of the rich Westerners.

About this book

This monograph is an original, new and innovative contribution to leisure theory, internet studies and cultural theory. I will argue that digital leisure, while obviously a novel phenomenon and a novel space, is not something so novel that the structures that govern our world break down before it.

Chapter 2, 'A Brief History of Leisure and the Net', sets out the history and development of the internet as a leisure space. The first section is a relatively brief social and technological history of the Net. The second section of the chapter explores the concept of virtuality and the Net in popular culture from the 1950s to the 1970s. The third section of the chapter examines the growth of bulletin boards in the 1980s and the emergence of the Net as a fully established leisure space. The fourth section of the chapter discusses the World Wide Web and its rapid adoption across rich, Westernized areas of the globe. It will be argued that the leisure possibilities of the Net are limited by the unequal distribution of resources and increasing State control of points of access.

Chapter 3, 'Leisure Studies and the Problem of the Net', is an overview of research and theories about the Net in the subject field of leisure studies – a literature review. It will be shown that researchers within leisure studies who have studied the Net have largely adopted the utopian claims of the founders of the Net, and have used postmodern and post-structural understandings of identity and belonging to argue that the Net is a liberatory leisure space. I will suggest that the claims made for the liquid or utopian nature of leisure on the Net is poorly evidenced and is a matter of rhetoric rather than critical analysis. The first section will explore research papers published in the leisure literature that have the Net as an object of study, either as a primary focus of research or a secondary source of research findings and analysis. The second section of the chapter will concentrate on mapping the internet in the works of key leisure theorists who have tried to make sense of the emergence of the Net: Blackshaw, Rojek, Roberts, Stebbins, Aitchison, Giulianotti and Crouch.

Chapter 4, 'Net Theory and Digital Leisure', focuses on the work of key theorists outside leisure studies who have attempted to understand and critique the development of the Network Society. The first section will discuss the work of Baudrillard, Turkle, Urry, Bauman, Giddens and Delanty. I will argue that the Net is used by each of these theorists as both a metaphor for postmodernity, an agent in the construction and limitation of our social selves, and as proof of the growth of global networks and mobilities. The second section will concentrate on the writings of Castells and his theory of the Network Society. I will argue that Castells was prescient not only about the emancipatory possibilities offered by the Net, but also the hegemonic struggles that would shape the leisure space. The final section of the chapter will explore the Net in the later writings of Habermas to show how his analysis of the Net is tied to his idea of the lifeworld.

Chapter 5, 'A Theory of Digital Leisure', develops a new theory of digital leisure, using Habermas' theoretical framework of communicative and instrumental rationality, along with ideas from Castells, Urry and Bauman. I will argue that for the users of the Net, digital leisure appears to be seamlessly communicative and liberating. Users are given the appearance of being liquid surfers, shifting their focus at the click of a mouse, sharing ideas and cultural interests with people in the global networks. However, the Net itself is a technology that is in reality a form

of instrumental leisure and commodification, based on economic transactions, control and surveillance, and unequal power relations. In this
respect, digital leisure is like any other leisure form. But the effect the
Net has on challenging hegemonies, as well as its unique interactivity
and its speed, makes digital leisure more communicative than sports or
traditional forms of popular culture.

The next five chapters use a combination of original, primary research
by the author, and secondary material from other published research
papers. Statistics on users and content will be collated from professional
monitoring sites. The original research will be a combination of semiotic
analysis of sites, content analysis of sites, discourse tracing on online
discussions and some semi-structured interviews with internet users.

Chapter 6, 'Identity-Making and Social Media', explores the emergence and importance of social media and networks in everyday leisure
time and leisure practices. I will look at the ways in which social networks are used to build a sense of community and belonging, and the
ways in which social networks serve as Goffmanesque public spaces in
which people perform acceptable social identities. I will trace how the
Net has become a social network and communicative leisure space in
more general terms away from the branded and commodified sites such
as Facebook. I will show that fans of sports, music and other forms
of popular culture can use the Net to discuss their private obsessions
with other fans. But I will show that the Net can also be a place where
social activism can be supported, where politics can move from the
online to the offline to build effective protests and campaigns. While
this development is a boon to radical activists on the left, it is also something that can be and is utilized by activists on the far right. Hence the
communicative freedom of the Net, as I will show, is prone to producing
climate-change deniers as much as anti-fascists.

Chapter 7, 'File-Sharing and Net Ethics', examines the practice of
downloading music and film files. The chapter will begin with an
overview of the sociology and anthropology of file-sharing and its
pre-internet equivalents. I will explore the practices around and the
commercialization of YouTube. I will explore the ways in which corporations and governments have reacted to illegal downloading through
the construction of commercial downloading sites and transnational
agreements and legislation on illegal downloading. I will explore Net
users' attitudes to downloading through an analysis of blogs, forum
sites and in interviews. I will look at the ethical arguments for and
against illegal downloading and copyright violation, and will suggest
that users of the Net have lost their ability to make moral judgements,

notwithstanding the anti-capitalist urge to steal from transnational corporations.

Chapter 8, 'Digital Leisure and Commodification', explores commodification through gambling, shopping, sports and gaming on the Net. The first section will concentrate on gambling sites and the increasing professionalization of the corporations that run them. The second section will focus on shopping, comparing big corporations such as Amazon with niche retailers. The third section will explore the availability of sports content on the Net and the increasing use of the Net by professional sports and sports-media corporations to sell content. The fourth section will examine online role-playing games and other games. I will show that all these forms of leisure space and leisure activity on the Net are increasingly being taken over by large corporations who try to hide their ruthless commodification through the adoption of idealistic, individualized Net-speak.

Chapter 9, 'Digital Leisure and Communicative Leisure', looks at the Net and alternative subcultures. The first section is a definition of what alternativism is, which draws on my previously published work (Spracklen, 2014; Spracklen, Richter and Spracklen, 2013). The rest of the chapter explores the ways in which online networks have become safe spaces for alternative subcultures such as goths, punks, extreme metal fans and musicians, with a slight digression to those interested in alternative philosophies. I will show how alternative scenes can shape their own identities and communities in the safety of the Net, away from commercial interests and the rejection and prejudice of mainstream society – especially where alternative subcultures exist in countries that have histories of political, social, religious or cultural repression. In exploring each subculture separately, I will explore how the Net is used by these alternative subcultures as a repository of their histories and their music and their fashions, but how such attempts to provide authentic accounts of their subculture are challenged by people within the community (who pose questions about authenticity and elitism) and by commercial interests looking to co-opt the subcultures.

Chapter 10, 'Sex and Romance', explores the ways in which the Net is used as a source of visceral sexual pleasure and real-world social interactions. The first section of the chapter will examine the growth of pornography online, the commodification of sex and the connection between pornography and pornification of popular culture. I will show that masturbating to pornography is the biggest form of leisure associated with the Net and will explore the debates around censorship and freedom. I will provide a strong feminist critique of the porn industry, but will also suggest that legislation against porn is not necessarily the solution. Instead, I will argue that the gender order has to be challenged across modern society so that men and women are fully equal, and men learn to treat women as human beings and not sexual objects of desire. In the second section of the chapter, I will examine the growth of dating agencies online, and other websites and spaces that offer single people the chance to meet up with other people. I will argue that such sites make communicative leisure choices much easier, but reduce social interactions to an instrumental gender logic.

Finally, Chapter 11 is a short conclusion that sketches out a research programme for digital leisure and for the exploration of the interaction between the Net and other parts of our world.

2
A Brief History of Leisure
and the Net

Introduction

The underlying weakness of many accounts of the Net, popular or academic, is the lack of historical depth. This is not surprising: the Net demands to be understood as a brand new, world-changing, (post)modern phenomenon. Furthermore, academics in cultural studies and leisure studies often fail to be as inter-disciplinary as they should be (Spracklen, 2011a). But to explore the way in which the Net has become an everyday, ubiquitous leisure space, it is necessary to do two pieces of historical analysis: we need to understand how the Net is the latest in a long line of technologies that have changed work and leisure; and we need to understand where the Net itself came from. Despite the crazy ramblings of some inhabitants of the Net, it did not have an immaculate conception, nor did it come from outer space. This chapter, then, will set out the history and development of the internet as a leisure space. The first section will be a brief social and technological history of the Net. The second section of the chapter will explore the concept of virtuality and the Net in popular culture from the 1950s to the 1970s. The third section of the chapter will examine the growth of bulletin boards in the 1980s and the emergence of the Net as a fully established leisure space. The fourth section of the chapter will discuss the World Wide Web and its rapid adoption across rich, Westernized areas of the globe. It will be argued that the leisure possibilities of the Net are limited by the unequal distribution of resources and increasing State control of points of access.

A social and technological history of the Net

Growing up in an age where watching television was a 'normal' part of everyday leisure and a part of mass culture, I found it difficult to envisage what people actually did in their evenings in the days before television and radio were invented (a foolish thought, I know, but at least I was thinking about the meaning and purpose of leisure as a schoolboy). I could not comprehend the world without the leisure of watching television, that little screen which showed me so many different worlds, the technology that brought my family together, and which allowed me to talk to people at school and connect with them. Even now, I use television shows as metaphors or other models to help me make my points in conversation. When I was old enough to read newspapers, they were also filled with discussions about television. For most people born in the 1990s or more recently, the same everyday normality is associated with the Net. When I talk about the Net with my students here at university, I am keenly aware that they seemingly have a very different assumption about what one does in one's leisure time. For these students, the idea of sitting down to watch whatever appears on television seems strangely quaint – they still watch things, of course, but that watching is directed and shaped by their use of the Net, whether informed by blogs or watched on a streaming service, or illegally downloaded from a file-sharing site (Thomes, 2013). For this generation, thinking about the world before the Net makes them as queasy as I once was when I tried to imagine life before television.

But the Net shares many similarities with television and radio. All three are cultural forms that have depended on technological innovation, scientific expertise and the power of corporations and governments. They are all technologies of leisure that owe their existence to the socio-cultural conditions of modernity (Rosa, 2013). They have all emerged from scientific speculations funded by the economic wealth of Western nations and harnessed by governments interested in controlling their citizens, disseminating propaganda and achieving military advantage over their rivals.

These technologies and hegemonic struggles were presaged by the science and the imperialism of the nineteenth century. It was in this key period that modern, Western culture emerged as a consequence of industrialization and urbanization (as I have recounted elsewhere: Spracklen, 2011a, 2013a). This modern culture was constructed as a consequence of the demands of capitalism, and was defined by work and one's relation to work, and one's power over one's own work. New forms of work were created in mills, factories and docks in the Western nations. These new forms of work sharply divided the time of work and the time of leisure, and as a consequence these new workers in their new cities demanded leisure time, leisure practices and freedom to create their own cultural tastes. The ruling elites in Western countries encouraged the growth of organized leisure activities such as sports, in which they retained power and control over subaltern groups. In the Marxist struggle against the capitalists, workers developed networks of libraries, newspapers and magazines to educate themselves and others about the world (Silver, 2003). Unions and radical groups created sports and physical activity associations to organize themselves beyond the official leisure activities provided to them by landlords, politicians and others. Both sides in this struggle over the meaning and purpose of leisure were keen, then, to shape leisure spaces and activities in their own way: on the one hand, as sites of self and social advancement, and on the other hand, as sites of control and surveillance.

In the first half of the twentieth century, radio, telegraph and telephone technologies had already brought different parts of the Western empires closer together. London could receive news in an instant from Moscow. A stockbroker or a general could send instructions to anyone anywhere in the world. These developments created mass media and nurtured popular culture and trends, such as the growth of jazz and the spread of celebrity (Briggs and Burke, 2009). As well as exchanging messages and news about wars faster, people wanted to know more about the actors in movies, or gold-winning athletes (Rojek, 2006; Turner, 2013).

At the same time that this web of communications and popular culture was becoming a part of everyday lives in the urban West, mathematicians and engineers were working out how to build computers. The theory behind such machines had been established by pioneers such as Charles Babbage in the nineteenth century, but practical designs for computers needed the technological development of valves (Mahoney and Haigh, 2011). These devices could be lined up in circuits to act as logic gates. Valves were a key part of early computers such as the ones used in the Second World War to make and break codes. After this war, the arms race of the Cold War and the rise of the American military–industrial complex saw billions of dollars invested in computer science and related technologies. This led to the invention of the transistor, a solid-state version of the valves, then ultimately the silicon chip, which has an enormous number of transistors etched on it. Computers moved from the military into everyday use in corporations and other scientific disciplines. Scientists found ways of increasing the processing and storage capacity of silicon chips and computers, making them useful and cheap enough to be used in a range of applications. By the 1960s, the American military and key computer laboratories were being connected to one another through a primitive form of what came to be the Net, allowing users and computers to share information (ibid.).

Towards the end of the 1960s computers were becoming something that could be constructed by amateur engineers and hobbyists. Information was shared through magazines and books, and a common, tacit knowledge was being created by these enthusiasts. People were beginning to see computers as a source of leisure, both the hardware and software of the computer designs and the games that were soon constructed for personal use. At the same time, universities and corporations were appointing specialists responsible for researching computing and constructing computing systems. A number of organizations started to build networks of linked computers to help reduce processing time and costs, but also to protect data if one computer in the network failed. A number of key inventions were made around the world by different people: the modem, a way of connecting to a network from a computer; email, a way of sending personal messages to other users; and .html (HyperText Markup Language), the language that helps shape the way information is passed through computer networks. Another key invention was the home or personal computer (PC), which was pushed onto the market in the 1970s in a number of countries by a number of organizations, with Apple being possibly the most famous of those. The PC was sold as an aspirational way of saving time and managing work, but companies were soon established that used PCs to run 'video' games, alongside other companies that built the games into the machines and sold them as gaming consoles (Donovan, 2010).

By the beginning of the 1980s, the Net was already in existence, connecting people who had a working stake in being connected to one another – scientists and military engineers, for instance – alongside enthusiasts, gamers and the first generation of people brought up with PCs. Online bulletin boards, as we will see later in this chapter, were a key part of people online, digital leisure experience. Mailing lists were becoming available through email, and people were exploring online gaming and pornography (Briggs and Burke, 2009; Donovan, 2010; Mullany, 2004). The invention of the World Wide Web in 1992 allowed the Net to become manageable and easily searchable, and led to a second generation of Net users using PCs at home with dial-up modems, or using their PCs at work (which were linked to work servers with faster modems and more memory capacity), to create their own web pages, browse web pages and interact with one another on message boards and by email (Mahoney and Haigh, 2011). The Net became a place of leisure, though using it involved a lot of work and time. Net use began to be promoted in the mass media, governments started to invest in technologies to speed up the Net, and people actively used the Net for work and in their leisure time. This was the age of Castells' 'Network Society', where the utopian ideals of the Net's first users were becoming challenged by the rapid commodification and commercialization of the Net (Castells, 1996; Rosa, 2013).

By the late 1990s the Net had become a part of everyday life for most office workers in the West, and for most school pupils, learning about and using the Net was a key part of the curriculum. The proliferation of internet service-providers of the early 1990s was being reduced through corporate takeovers (Dahlberg, 2005). Having access to the Net had become a matter of taste and distinction among the urban middle classes across the world, especially among the university educated. Millions of websites appeared, built in increasingly garish and animated styles, and companies started to sell adverts and build online retailing sites (Zeff and Aronson, 1999). Politicians in the West, and journalists and other cultural trend-setters, started to talk about the profits to be made from the Net, which led to the first 'dot-com' boom and bust and the end of many corporate endeavours (Crain, 2014). But the marketization of the Net bounced back and continued growing in the 2000s, especially with the design of various security systems to allow commercial transactions with supposedly low or no risk. A third generation of Net users appeared in the middle of the 2000s, using broadband and other systems that allowed them to download large files. Soon, file-sharing and downloading videos and other large files became easy for any home user (Mahoney and Haigh, 2011). The speed and capacity of these leisure users' systems allowed the growth of social media (ibid.). By the 2010s, access to the Net through mobile devices such as phones became commonplace. These mobile devices had the speed and the capacity of broadband-enabled PCs, but provided both ease of access and subjective fashionableness (Lupton, 2014). All these technologies for accessing the Net have been driven by commercial interests seeking to capitalize on people's leisure needs, but also driven by the interests of governments maintaining hegemonic control over their citizens, as the revelations of large-scale data capture disclosed by Edward Snowden highlighted (Petley, 2014).

The Net is merely a network of computers physically connected to each other, some hosting large databases, with a shared language of sending and receiving communications and a de-centralized sharing of information and processing functions. Many smaller computers are connected to the Net through service-providers: these computers are what we know as our home or work devices, the things we carry around with us when we are on the move. The Net has grown to encompass trillions of pages of information and now most people think of it as something that exists only in a virtual sense, a belief perhaps encouraged by Net advocates and marketing corporations seeking to make us forget the reality of things (Arora, 2014; Lupton, 2014; Mahoney and Haigh, 2011). It is easy to look at the results supplied by search engines, and the rapid evolution of services that store our own data in the 'cloud' and think the Net is some other dimension, some other Paradise, where the information and the connections have no real-world presence. But the Net only exists in the real world. The Net's physicality is present in the physical space of huge servers in Californian buildings, their processors so active that huge cooling systems use precious energy resources, and in the secretive cables and satellites that are involved in global communications (Mahoney and Haigh, 2011). The Net's physicality is present in every office or bedroom where there is an electricity supply and an off switch, in every factory where phones and laptops are made, and in every mine where the vital metals are ripped out of the ground. The Net is something that has been invented, designed and constructed, and it remains something that is developed and contested (Lupton, 2014). But where did the idea of the Net come from? Ideas about the Net as a place of work and leisure come from popular culture from the 1950s to the 1970s (Mahoney and Haigh, 2011).

Virtuality and the Net in pop culture from the 1950s to the 1970s

In popular science-fiction novels, movies and television programmes of the 1950s and 1960s, the idea that computers could become (almost) infinite sources of information became a commonplace notion. Computers were typically crucial parts of the plots of these stories, benevolent experts that guided a spaceship to safety through the vast reaches of outer space, or malevolent spirits twisted by errors in their programming to harm humans (Dourish and Bell, 2014; Rohn, 2013). Writers had noticed how rapidly computer technology was evolving, and assumed that in the future computers would do many of the tasks needed to keep civilization running. Computers were imagined to be controlling all aspects of society and culture: running factories and cars, but also making music and dispensing the law. In the future, it was thought, computers would free people from work, doing the dull jobs of office administration, and this would herald in a new 'leisure society', where people would fill their lives with directed and spontaneous leisure activities and governments would invest huge resources into keeping citizens happy (Landon, 2014; Smigel, 1963). In the 'Stainless Steel Rat' series of novels by Harry Harrison (for the first in the series see Harrison, 1961), the main character 'Slippery' Jim di Griz is one of the few crooks remaining in a culture that allows computer technology and machines to run every aspect of people's lives. He survives as a crook because he is able to turn the technology to his advantage, re-writing programmes so that, for example, false video feeds replace the actual footage from security cameras at banks. The ubiquity of computers led many writers to see the future as a place where everything about our lives was controlled by computers that kept watch on every move we made – this is the dystopian view of the future as a world of surveillance and unfreedom (Landon, 2014).

But computers were essentially thought of as vast libraries, keeping records that could be accessed and analysed by the machine at incredible speeds. In the hands of honest people, such computer databases were seen as tools for human progress, but in the hands of powerful elites such computers were shown to be damaging. In the television programme *Star Trek*, for instance, Captain Kirk and the crew of the USS *Enterprise* relied on the ship's computer to supply them with an enormous range of technical and cultural information, which helped them make sense of the alien planets that they were visiting (Hark, 2008). The ship's computer seemed to know everything anyone could ever want to know about a problem or a situation, though sometimes it would take hours to supply the correct answer, as if it was physically checking filing cabinets stored away somewhere. Furthermore, the ship's computer could access other computers, other memory banks and databases, as long as there was some attempt to make contact with them. The computer was essential to the smooth running and working of the ship and its crew. There was no question that the computer's information was off-limits in any way – the future in this television show was one where democracy and equality prevailed, money had been discarded as a source of many evils, and scientific enquiry and reason had replaced irrational religions. The computer itself was a tool for human development and was not controlling in any malicious way. When other people's computers controlled their lives and abused them, Kirk did not waste time destroying those computers and giving those people the freedom to learn and make mistakes (ibid.).

Use of the computer of the *Enterprise* was not limited to the work of space exploration. It was also able to play music to soothe the crew in their work stations, or in the recreation rooms or their own private cabins. It could play educational tapes and videos of important events, and could bring up the text of any book on its screens, like an early version of a Kindle. The United Federation of Planets (the organization that Captain Kirk represented) also had a large computer database called Memory Alpha, though to access the database it seems people had to travel to the planetoid on which it was built (Bainbridge, 2011). The idea that computers would connect seamlessly through virtual networks was not used in the show. When the crew get a message from their Starfleet admirals or an alien ship, it is always transmitted over 'sub-space radio', and managed by a member of the crew on the bridge who spends half of her time fiddling with dials like an amateur radio enthusiast to get the right frequency.

Virtuality was something that also emerged in popular culture in this period, becoming more visible in the 1970s (Lauria, 2001). The idea that our own world might not be the actual world, and that we are seeing a fake version of reality, is of course a long-standing philosophical problem of ontology and metaphysics. How do we know that what we see is not an illusion given to us by some external force? In Ancient Greece, Plato (2007) described the thought experiment of people in a cave watching shadows cast by puppets, and thinking these things to be real humans. For Plato, there was an ideal, perfect reality that was hidden by the superficial reality that we see and experience around us. For his followers this meant that what we see as reality is only a virtual reality, a fake, a simulacrum of the truth. The problem with realism continued to be discussed through history. Some radical thinkers in religions such as Islam and Christianity argued that the world was not real as we see it, and only meditation, prayer or some other rigorous activity such as dancing could make someone see the true world of God (Habermas, 2002). Writing in the seventeenth century, Descartes summarized the ways in which we might be fooled into thinking the world as we experience it is real when it is actually fake (Descartes, 1998). Firstly, everybody knows when they have seen something or someone then realized they are mistaken: our senses are bad guides. Secondly, we have all experienced dreams that feel as if we are awake in them: if that is so, how can we be sure this is not a dream? And finally, as with the religious ascetics, God or some malicious demon may well be deceiving us.

This philosophical problem led science-fiction writers to explore the power of computers. They were following the controversies that had already emerged in the first half of the twentieth century about popular culture, reality and coercion. Through those earlier years developments such as cinemas, recorded music and television were shaking people's notions of what constituted reality (Briggs and Burke, 2009). Films watched in the cinema seemed to be more real than the mundane reality outside on the streets. Camera tricks, special effects, editing, make-up and careful use of lighting made the cinema screen into a proto-virtual reality (Bottomore, 1999). Recorded music played at home or through the radio offered highly constructed performances, engineered and produced to be *ersatz* live performances: perfectly performed and perfectly reproduced by the technological systems of the day. Radio broadcasts of music and news could stir up feelings of nationalism and provoke anger and despair – when Orson Welles aired a drama about Martians landing framed as a 'live' news story (based on the famous H. G. Wells novel), the broadcast provoked a media outrage at the panic (though the number of people who actually worried is debatable – see Bourke, 2005). Television, the newer arrival in mass media, replicated the ontological problems of the other media: television viewers seemed particularly willing and able to absorb themselves so much in their favourite shows that they wrote fan letters to fictional characters, or spoke of fictional places as if they were real places (Williams, 2013). Cinema, recorded music, radio and television were only ever constructors of partial virtuality – it was easy to look beyond the screen, or be distracted by something in the real world.

But science-fiction writers saw the capacity of computers for constructing virtual realities that would completely fool the user into thinking they were real (Landon, 2014). By the 1960s, the spread of counter-cultural values in the West saw stories about virtual realities become laced with alternative realities experienced in drug use: taking LSD or similar psychoactive substances seemed to reveal the actual reality of the world 'beyond the veil'. If someone could write a letter to a fictional character in a television programme, if someone could fall in love with a movie star, or be moved to tears by a piece of music, what could happen if a computer had the processing power to build a world in which the experience was indistinguishable from the real world? Like Descartes' demons, these constructors of fake realities are imagined as creators of malicious worlds that keep people docile and in chains in the real world. The pulp-fiction archetype of the brains kept in jars on an alien planet was the new narrative of the cave (Plato, 2007). These brains are fed stimuli by computers and made to believe that they are living happy lives on Earth, but in fact they have been imprisoned by some evil alien creatures for some nefarious reason.

In the work of Philip K. Dick, alternate realities and the confusion over which reality is the real one (if any of them are) are at the heart of some of his most famous stories, such as *Ubik* (Dick, 1969) and *Do Androids Dream of Electric Sheep?* (Dick, 1968). In the former, the narrative moves through a number of alternative realities, some artificially constructed and others the product of psychic powers. In the latter, the hero Deckard is tasked with finding and destroying androids, but discovers in them more humanity than humanity, even though they are supposedly computers. Dick's novels were a strong influence on the 'cyberpunk' genre of the 1980s, books such as William Gibson's (1984) *Neuromancer*, in which virtual reality and concepts such as the Net became part of the backdrop to the narratives. Dick's books were (and still are) also adapted as movies by Hollywood studios. Blade Runner was the most famous, but the movie that introduced virtual reality to the mainstream was *Total Recall*, an Arnold Schwarzenegger blockbuster that nonetheless had as a central conceit the notion that memories could be altered by machines to give people the false belief that they had lived other lives or other leisure experiences.

Popular culture in this period was slower to pick up on the potential of the Net, a network of computers working together, allowing access for users wherever they are. Cyberpunk, as already mentioned, brought the concept into the mainstream, but this was in the 1980s. Earlier than that the idea of a networked digital society comes and goes in the fringes of science fiction. In the 1965 story 'Dial F for Frankenstein', Arthur C. Clarke wrote about a network of computers connected through telephony systems which becomes aware of its own existence (Clarke, 2002). Other writers were using networks of computers as backdrops to stories about computer viruses and hacking (Landon, 2014), and sociologist-turned-author James Cooke Brown wrote about a communications network that resembles the modern Net in 1970 (Brown, 1970). Popular science-fiction movies and television shows in the 1970s such as *Star Wars* and *Battlestar Galactica* mention computers and databases, but the idea of a network with virtual or non-local access is not present. In *Star Wars*, Darth Vader is hunting down the Rebels who have stolen information about the Death Star. Princess Leia hides the 'plans' in the droid R2-D2, who then escapes from the Princess's ship. Eventually R2-D2 arrives at the Rebel base and the Rebels put the plans on their computer and read through them. The thrill of the chase would be absent if the Rebels had just hacked into the Imperial computers from their hideout. Similarly, it seems equally incredible now that Obi-Wan Kenobi has to walk through the entire Death Star to find the computer that turns the landing bay shields on and off, instead of just finding the system online somehow.

Bulletin boards in the 1980s and the emergence of the Net as a leisure space

Since the invention of writing, humans have used the technology to connect with others in a non-local way, and to share information quickly and rapidly to a large number of readers. Much of that information has been written and read by people as a clear type of communicative leisure, using time, resources and skills to engage in frivolous, free discourse about all kinds of things (Spracklen, 2011a). When writing was first invented, it was used by royal or religious elites to communicate secretly with one another and their scribal servants. Later, writing and reading became a marker of Bourdieusian distinction for a slightly broader set of upper classes (Bourdieu, 1986; Fischer, 2003). So in some cultures, writing became a way for merchants to keep records of contracts and inventories. In others, such as the city states of the Hellenic world, writing and reading were things that elite men did in their leisure time as a way of demonstrating that they had the time and the knowledge to take part in a shared literary culture. In Republican and Imperial Rome, reading and writing were shared more widely with other classes, such as soldiers and slaves, but the leisure to write and read letters and books was only available for the wealthy (Fox, 2005). The work of Cicero is perhaps an extraordinary exemplar, but it demonstrates the kinds of things men of the elite wrote and read: his works include speeches, philosophical books and letters to a wide range of people. Writing, reading and communication, then, are a key part of human experience, leisure and culture – though the skills and resources to engage in these acts have always been highly contested and controlled (Fischer, 2003).

The social and cultural practices of sharing information, writing and reading, and communicating with others, are not then, new to the Net. But the technological and social advances in the 1980s opened up the Net as a leisure space where such things could happen in a more communicative, democratic way. The technological advance was the advent of home computing and the rapid growth of computing power in interconnected workplaces and universities (Mahoney and Haigh, 2011). This was the time in which a series of protocols and standards on the internet were agreed. The social advance was the rise of the educated, urban middle classes. Reading and writing have often been the preserve of the rich, who have used those skills to maintain their privilege. Conservatives and other traditionalists have discouraged women and girls and other subaltern groups from becoming educated as a way of maintaining their own power (Butler, 2006; Fischer, 2003). Progressive, liberal education policies in the 1960s and 1970s opened up tertiary education to more people; women's rights and the idea of equal rights were spreading across Western countries, and the proportion of people who could not read or write in these countries (and across the globe) was in decline. This resulted in a generation of people with the technological know-how to understand communication systems, and the confidence to write and read using those systems.

Bulletin boards were set up by enthusiasts to share information and to discuss things. The first bulletin boards were established in the 1970s, but they grew rapidly in the 1980s as more people became competent to set them up and as awareness increased (Mahoney and Haigh, 2011). Bulletin boards sat outside the emerging internet but were founded on the same idea of connectivity, and were run on similar software and hardware. Typically, one person would run a bulletin board on their home computer, and others would use dial-up technology to read the posts on the board, and to post their own messages. Many bulletin boards were set up by technology enthusiasts for others wanting to know about or share information about software and hardware. Most of this was legitimate sharing of ideas, which became a fundamental part of the Net's emerging moral policy of sharing ideas and not selling things (Rafaeli and LaRose, 1993). But some of the technology bulletin boards were set up to share programming code that potentially broke copyright laws. These included bulletin boards that attracted hackers: people wanting to acquire or share knowledge about how to break codes and security systems (Lewenstein, 1995).

Other bulletin boards mirrored the spread of the Net in the 1990s and 2000s. Initially, bulletin boards reflected the leisure interests of the young, educated (mainly male) people who had the technological skills to run and access them – so there were bulletin boards that ran text-based role-playing games, that shared pornographic stories, or discussed well-known science-fiction franchises. But as public awareness of bulletin boards grew they soon offered an enormous range of spaces to read and write about all manner of leisure activities, and all manner of political and cultural interests (James, Wotring and Forrest, 1995). There were significant numbers of boards discussing alternative culture (.alt cultures): neo-paganism, the goth scene, alternative lifestyles and alternative sexualities. There were bulletin boards that supported radical political activism, though there were as many extreme right boards as extreme left/anarchist ones. There were bulletin boards for academic subject fields and disciplines, and ones for people who believed in UFOs and Bigfoot (Lewenstein, 1995). The dominant ethos was freedom of choice, communicative rationality and tolerance of others. In these spaces, the democratic rules of Net discussions were established, with an intolerance shown towards those who break those rules (for being racist or sexist, for example, or for being a troll), and much of the language of the Net was also invented in the bulletin boards (Arora, 2014; Mahoney and Haigh, 2011). Towards the end of the 1980s and into the 1990s the bulletin boards became increasingly sophisticated, hosting pictures and other graphics, and some boards became commercial entities charging subscription fees. These pay-sites were usually supplying subscriptions to games, cheats for consoles, or pornographic material (Lewenstein, 1995). With the advent of the World Wide Web, many bulletin boards transformed into website message boards or forums, some carried on for a few years because of the eccentricity of their users and operators, and some ceased to function altogether as they could not compete with the Net.

The emergence of the Net in the 1980s was a result of instrumentally rational policies in various nation states (Lupton, 2014). The demands of the American military and its security agencies were fundamental to the spread of the Advanced Research Projects Agency Network (ARPANET) (Mahoney and Haigh, 2011). At the time of continuing fears of Soviet invasions, nuclear warfare and communist agitators, the United States government wanted to make sure it could respond quickly and effectively to any threat. The intention of the Net as a disaggregated distribution of shared information, a web of computers with few or no central nodes, was to allow the military and government agencies to keep going even if parts of the network had been damaged or destroyed. The protocols and systems developed on the ARPANET were designed in the main by university-based computing laboratories, which meant that access to and use of the ARPANET went beyond military uses to more practical and scientific ones across the world. By the early 1980s scientific endeavours had become the main drivers of technological advances on the Net, and in 1982 the United States government, through the National Science Foundation, started work on what it called the Computer Science Network (ibid.). This spread access to the Net to a wide range of computing facilities and organizations in the United States and around the world.

Personal use of the Net had been in existence ever since the first networked computers. The first scientists and engineers working in the computer labs designed games that they would share with each other, and they would exchange messages and gossip (Lupton, 2014). The technological and socio-cultural advances of the 1980s allowed the Net to emerge fully as a Habermasian communicative leisure space. In popular culture at the time, home computers and game consoles were markers of cool among young people (Donovan, 2010). While Apple sold its Macs to the urban bourgeoisie of the West, other corporations such as Atari, Commodore and Nintendo made huge profits selling digital products to families and their children (Mahoney and Haigh, 2011). Game consoles were and are designed to run only official gaming programmes purchased in commercial transactions. When Atari introduced its gaming console in the West, it soon became a must-have toy (Donovan, 2010). Other corporations followed with consoles of their own, and video gaming became the ubiquitous leisure activity of the 1980s in Western countries – especially when the violence in some of these games led religious leaders and politicians to call for them to be banned (Gunter, 1998). Some video games were excessively violent, but some asked their users to think and solve puzzles. Some video games were text-based role-playing games that allowed the user to interact with various digital characters, and these games seemed to presage the rise of similar games on bulletin boards, where the other characters were other users. Home computers such as the ZX Spectrum or Commodore 64 were marketed as educational devices, and the latter could be used to create bulletin boards, but the main use of these machines was to replicate the video games that had replaced traditional slot-machines in leisure spaces across the globe (Donovan, 2010). Popular films of the 1980s such as *War Games* portrayed young computer-users as serious gamers and hackers, using their knowledge and skills to break into other computers.

In this cultural context, people with access to the Net through their workplace – or through amateur, serious leisure (Stebbins, 1982) – started to use the Net for gaming and for other leisure activities. Various sites were used to share information about software and hardware, but other sites offered online gaming and messaging. Emails were increasingly routed through the Net to discuss personal, leisure-related matters, and workplaces and organizations with access to the Net were trying to restrict use to work-related activities only. Of course, such workplace policies were as futile as the attempts to restrict telephone usage in offices to work-related activities – all technologies in the workplace have been subverted by workers for their own ends (Arora, 2014; Lupton 2014). The first leisure users of the Net found contact with others, gaming and reading trivial information to be worth their while as they worked the long hours associated with late-modern, neo-liberal economics (which had infiltrated higher education by the 1980s, in the same way it had earlier infiltrated corporate R&D labs). In doing this, they were doing what others were already doing on other networks and on the bulletin boards. Corporations such as CompuServe had launched information services that allowed individual consumers to set up accounts and access them through networked computers, though these services were limited to the sites and data owned by the organization supplying them, and did not allow access to the Net proper (rather like AOL in its early years – see Campbell-Kelly and Garcia-Swartz, 2013). The CompuServe Information Service was a bigger version of the bulletin boards, commercialized and with greater reach and capacity. Similar networks expanded through the 1980s, offering individuals an opportunity to take part in games, read and share messages on message boards, access information and do all the things that people do on the Net, normalizing the habit of 'logging on' to find out things rather than buying a newspaper or going to a library. In France, the government had taken a keen interest in controlling and offering such a network, and the service known as Minitel, live since 1978, was accessible to telephone subscribers through a terminal similar to a PC (Palme, 2011).

This habit of using the Net and other networks for communicative leisure led to the launch of the first internet service-providers in 1989 (Mahoney and Haigh, 2011). These companies offered subscribers access to the Net proper through PCs dialling-up and accessing the computer servers owned by the providers. These first providers faced opposition from some users of the Net, especially the United States government, which was fearful of opening up ARPANET and the Computer Science Network to personal or commercial users. The fear at the time was that the sensitive parts of the Net, the military servers and networks, would become open to attack from America's enemies (Campbell-Kelly and Garcia-Swartz, 2013). Other users (including some of the academic users) were concerned that the Net did not have the capacity to allow non-scientific users to access it, that crucial experimental data might be lost if the relatively primitive Net crashed under the weight of conversations about whether Captain Picard was better than Captain Kirk as the captain of the USS *Enterprise*. But such fears were overruled by the commercial success of the first ISPs, the numbers of people choosing to sign-up and the lack of any calamitous crash or attack. Into the 1990s, the number of ISPs and number of people with personal access to the Net continued to grow.

The World Wide Web and its rapid adoption

Personal use of the internet grew exponentially in the 1990s due to the adoption of the World Wide Web structures and protocols, and also the increase in awareness of the Usenet system (Lupton, 2014; Mahoney and Haigh, 2011). The World Wide Web was invented in the period between 1989 and 1990 by Tim Berners-Lee as a means to make using and exploring the Net much simpler than it had previously been on ARPANET and other networks (Berners-Lee and Fischetti, 2000). The new system established a division of labour between web browsers, software on computers and web servers that hosted web pages, databases and other networking software. The new system provided the concept of websites with unique addresses organized in a logical system, alongside the concept of the interlinked web of databases and pages that could be accessed and read by a user-friendly web browser. Berners-Lee adopted the idea of hypertext links, which had been used in other databases and networks, but his version allowed users to make such links much easier. Finally, he established the common language of websites and website publishing, .html, which again allowed personal users to easily make and publish their own websites.

ISPs soon saw the opportunity to make money from offering access to the World Wide Web. Personal consumers in the West started to buy access to the Net, connecting modems to their computers, buying new computers and installing dial-up software (Bainbridge, 2011). The World Wide Web in the early 1990s became a part of hip, urban cultural capital around the world, a fashionable toy for the technically literate (Lupton, 2014). Websites were built in their millions by individual enthusiasts, keen to share their opinions and their knowledge about a diverse range of activities and had already appeared on the bulletin boards. But the new World Wide Web made using graphics easier, even if pages with pictures often meant a long wait as they slowly downloaded. As people signed up to the Net and accessed the World Wide Web, they could explore all the pages other people made, such as the Internet Movie Database (which still exists today – see Dodds, 2006). The World Wide Web allowed the Net to become a simply designed and accessed leisure space, though access to the Net was still limited to those who could afford the hardware, software and ISP (internet service-provider) subscriptions – the early World Wide Web was still dominated by university-educated, young, middle-class technophiles, and a broader demographic (globally and in each country) remained marginalized by a lack of economic, social and cultural capital. As such, the kinds of leisure activities that the World Wide Web supported reflected the leisure needs of that particular narrow urban elite, and the rules of communicative rationality operating reflected the strong belief in individual freedom and individual choice in late modernity (Habermas, 1984, 1987, 1990). These users were the confident identity-making consumers of Bauman (1992, 2000), Giddens (1981, 1991) and Castells (1996). The users of the World Wide Web could also access the Usenet system through their ISPs, which was established in the 1980s but which had grown in parallel to the bulletin boards (Kayany, 1998). Usenet newsgroups allowed subscribers to read posts and make posts themselves about any number of specialized topics. Usenet newsgroups used similar definitional logic to bulletin boards. There were a fluctuating number of hierarchies in the newsgroups, with rec., .alt and talk. being important groups for leisure (though the whole of Usenet could be argued to be a leisure space, even where individuals discussed scientific or technological topics – see Hill and Hughes, 1997). The growth in the number of people accessing the Net to use the World Wide Web, spurred on by mentions of the Web in popular culture, allowed Usenet to renew itself. For most of the 1990s, Usenet newsgroups thrived and user-numbers expanded, but into the 2000s and 2010s newsgroups have declined as discussion forums on the Web, then social media, have become fashionable (Arora, 2014; Mahoney and Haigh, 2011).

In the early 1990s, the World Wide Web system took over the Net to such an extent that it became synonymous for the Net. Older parts of the Net were switched off, re-configured as stand-alone networks or converted to the World Wide Web in this period, such as the original ARPANET (Mahoney and Haigh, 2011). ISPs started to challenge the remaining legal and policy obstacles in various countries over access to the Net. The legal obstacles were overturned through a series of national and transnational agreements about the Net: that access should be encouraged, that privacy should be respected, and that no one could buy special privileges of access (Castells, 1996). These agreements about the Net were underpinned by concepts about individual freedom associated with Western liberal democracy. The policy obstacles were associated with education and infrastructure. Many politicians and policy-makers did not think the Net had a useful, socio-cultural role, and some believed it to be a source of immoral behaviours and content (Hill and Hughes, 1997). The first scare stories about 'bad' leisure activities on the Net had appeared in the 1980s, and by the 1990s the fears had become commonplace – that the Net would stupefy its users, especially the young, through exposing them to immorality and vice (Potter and Potter, 2001). First of all, politicians needed to be convinced that the Net had an educational value and role – once they recognized the potential learning resource the Net offered, they allowed and supported policies to put Web-linked computers into classrooms and university libraries (Castells, 1996; Lupton, 2014). The second policy obstacle was the need to deliver enormous technological projects to improve communications networks. Home computers operating dial-up modems to connect to service-providers used existing telephone wires – users would frequently complain of services crashing and slow download speeds, a result of using telephone technology and sharing it with telephone users (Mahoney and Haigh, 2011). As leisure use of the Net expanded throughout the 1990s around the Western world and beyond, governments and corporations scrambled to fund new cables and telecommunication systems. Some politicians were initially reluctant to fund capital projects that helped private corporations respond to their customers' needs, but many politicians supported such measures as part of vague commitments to modernization or economic development – (hopefully) winning votes and the backing of key funders in the process (Papacharissi, 2002; Tkach-Kawasaki, 2003).

Berners-Lee designed the World Wide Web to enhance scientific research and discussion, but it soon came to be seen as an opportunity to enhance corporate use of the Net. Large organizations and corporations seized on email as a means of making communications easier. Instead of organizing conference calls or sending faxes or letters to multiple offices, email allowed organizations to inform huge numbers of employees or customers instantaneously. Email became the driver of a carefully controlled *panopticon* of the modern workplace, in which managers could instruct subordinates without having to meet them face-to-face (Fuchs, 2010; Lupton, 2014). The Net allowed organizations to find information that gave them an economic advantage over competitors, and to design websites that could sell their products or services. Some corporations were slow to embrace the opportunities to sell directly to customers online, but others were quick to adapt their marketing and sales techniques (Streeter, 2010). At this time, companies appeared that were only on the Net, with no presence on the High Street or in any city centre, selling products from anonymous warehouses where the workforce was cheap and exploitable (ibid.). Transnational corporations also saw the advantage of using the Net to share important data and information between offices distributed across the world (Fuchs, 2010). At the same time, other organizations such as governments, universities, charities, political parties and campaigning groups set up their own websites and started to use the Net in the same way as corporations – as a marketing and sales device, as a data-sharing device and as a management device (Tkach-Kawasaki, 2003).

Email and internet usage could be carefully guarded and controlled through various software systems, so employees were denied the same freedom to use email and the Net as their managers. These systems were applied when organizations worried in public about their reputations and the danger of their workers accessing porn or sending frivolous emails about their love lives. The initial rush to connect organizations up to the Net was inevitably tempered by a concern to restrict and monitor usage; through the age of the Net, newspapers have thrived on scandal stories about politicians or other public figures abusing publicly funded hardware and software by sending scandalous emails or downloading outrageous content. But control of access to email and the Net gave managers and organizations a Foucauldian grip on their workers (Fuchs, 2010; Lupton, 2014). In the telephone age, it was difficult to stop workers reading books and magazines, or phoning their friends – and hence not working every second for the company – unless a manager was physically present to enforce discipline. With email and access to the Net, it was a simple task to disable computers, or to limit access to internal email, or a list of approved websites. Furthermore, even when access was supposedly unlimited, records of every email sent and received, and every website browsed, meant the act of resistance by doing something pleasurable in the time and place of work was always in plain sight of anyone who wanted to look. All organizations that allowed their workers to use the Net developed policies that discouraged leisure use of the Net in the workplace. The sheer size of the databases of cached material meant that such policies were difficult to enforce, especially around personal emails, but the fact that managers could find out what people were looking at meant workers still self-govern their use of the Net, disciplining themselves over what they think might bring them into a disciplinary process.

The Net was also a space in which corporations could target new markets. ISPs were bought up by large corporations, so that access to the Net was limited to a handful of suppliers, all owned by transnational corporations with various media and communications interests (Mahoney and Haigh, 2011). The infrastructure of the Net remained in the oversight of national governments in many countries, and security agencies continued to monitor use, but corporations built, owned and managed a large proportion of the physical Net. There was a wide range of suppliers of computer hardware, though the chips inside PCs were

built by a handful of companies, such as Intel. Office computing software was dominated by Microsoft, and with the launch of Windows 95
the corporation managed to force their own internet browser (Internet
Explorer) to become a default way of using the Net for a generation
of home and work users (ibid.). The global reach of the Net had been
established in the early years of its existence, but in the 1990s and
into the 2000s this was reinforced by the spread and de-centring of the
transnational corporations that controlled access to the Net. Access to
the Net became a political and cultural demand among marginalized
groups and developing countries, and the corporations responded with
new products. The Net did become a space of communicative resistance,
where anti-capitalists or democrats could organize and plan activities,
and the huge range of information on the Net allows for the marginal
and subaltern to find ways of learning about the forces that keep them
enslaved (Papacharissi, 2002). The Net has been a place of community-
making, a space in which alternative identities can prosper, a site of
play and fun and harmless chatter (Seargeant and Tagg, 2014). Like all
human forms of leisure, the Net has the capacity to be of great good,
and there is strong evidence that people take advantage of the Net in
the same way earlier generations joined trade unions, walking clubs and
lending libraries (Spracklen, 2011a). But this freedom to explore the
Net and one's own identity is bounded by the rules and systems that
created it. The Net is not a metaphor for freedom, it is a real place controlled, owned and exploited by others (Hesmondhalgh, 2010). Despite
the dot-com crash of 2000, when the speculative bubble around Net
start-up companies collapsed and commentators joked that the Net was
a passing fad, the Net has continued to grow as a site of instrumental
rationality. Adverts are now everywhere on the Net, and are becoming
more sophisticated in how they target users. Corporations pay for content on the Net that resembles an independent blog or news story, and
it is impossible to spot this. Technological developments have brought
with them new ways to make money, and new ways for corporations
and governments to monitor and monetize use (Fuchs, 2010; Lupton,
2014). In the 2000s and 2010s the growth in broadband connectivity
and smart phones created new opportunities to keep people as passive
consumers of commodified leisure.

Conclusion

The Net is not a new piece of technology. It has older precedents and
has been around longer than many of its contemporary users realize.

Furthermore, the space that it creates for leisure is similar to that of other technologies and cultural products, such as reading and writing, the book, and more recent forms of media like film and television. The Net as a leisure space, and digital leisure more broadly, fall into the realm of human agency and human endeavour that created paintings on the walls of caves thousands of years ago (Spracklen, 2011a). The Net is clearly a space for communicative rationality (Habermas, 1984, 1987), and communicative leisure (Spracklen, 2009, 2011a, 2013a).

At the same time, this history of the development of the Net points to the fact that the Net is a physical space, built and owned by corporations and governments. The early history of the Net is linked to the instrumental rationality of the Cold War and the struggle for American cultural and political hegemony (Mahoney and Haigh, 2011). And the later history of the Net shows that corporations have moved in to impose forms of instrumentality associated with global capitalism (Habermas, 1987, 1990). This leisure space is, then, a space for the contestation of power and of use between dominant groups and those who wish to have free choice and agency. As such, it should be important to leisure studies. In the next chapter, I will explore how leisure theorists and researchers responded to the development of this interesting and important leisure space and activity from the 1990s onwards.

3
Leisure Studies and the Problem of the Net

As I showed in the last chapter, the Net has been known about in the public sphere of Western popular culture since the early 1990s, and this knowledge and experience spread rapidly from the middle of the 1990s onwards. Even if it failed to make an impact on my PhD, I was using the Net as a leisure space by the time the PhD was awarded. One would expect, then, that leisure scholars writing from the 1990s onwards would be aware of this technological development and swift to respond to the issues it raised. This chapter will be an overview of research and theories about the Net in the subject field of leisure studies – not a systematic literature review, but a search, review and analysis of key literature. To undertake a systematic literature review I would need to read everything that has been written about the Net across the broader disciplines of sociology and media and communication studies, and that would be a Herculean task. So the literature review is limited to one part of leisure studies, with references here and there to other subject fields and disciplines, in this chapter and other chapters.

It will be shown that researchers within leisure studies who have studied the Net have largely adopted the utopian claims of the founders of the Net, and have used postmodern and post-structural understandings of identity and belonging to argue that the Net is a liberatory leisure space. I will suggest that the claims made for the liquid or utopian nature of leisure on the Net is poorly evidenced and is a matter of rhetoric rather than critical analysis. The first section will explore research papers published in the leisure literature that have the Net as an object of study, either as a primary focus of research or a secondary source of research findings and analysis. The second section of the chapter will concentrate on mapping the internet in the works of key leisure theorists who have tried to make sense of the emergence of the Net: Blackshaw, Rojek, Roberts, Stebbins, Aitchison, Giulianotti and Crouch.

Research on the Net in the subject field of leisure studies

There are thousands of social science research papers and books about the Net. A quick search on Google Scholar, for example, reveals 646,000 results for 'Internet sociology'. Most of those results are almost certainly sources that mention both words in passing, but there are still thousands of results that are actually discussing the sociological context and problems of the Net – how much freedom does the Net have? How is the Net used to construct identities? How is the Net used to enforce discipline and control? Can the Net be controlled? Does the Net offer a utopian escape or a dystopian nightmare? There are journals devoted to sociological and cultural examinations of the Net, textbooks for students studying the sociology of the Net, and an evolving range of papers and research monographs (see for example Arora, 2014; Bainbridge, 2011; Cavanagh, 2010; Chadwick and Howard, 2010; Cheng and Missari, 2014; Fuchs, 2010; Hine, 2005; Jewkes and Yar, 2013; Lupton, 2014; MacKinnon, 2012; Nowak, 2010; Papacharissi, 2002; Pinch, 2010; Rosa, 2013; Seargeant and Tagg, 2014; Streeter, 2010; Tatarchevskiy, 2011; Wellman and Haythornthwaite, 2008; Witte and Mannon, 2010; Zhao, 2006). In the next chapter, I will examine some of the major theorists used in this wider body of research. But this book is about leisure, and this chapter is about leisure studies, so how has leisure studies fared as a subject field in addressing the development of the Net as a leisure space and a leisure activity?

The engagement with the Net in leisure studies is improving. For example, there have been important books and journal articles, especially since the 2010s (see for example Arora, 2014; Green and Adam, 1998; Jackson, 1999; Kjølsrød, 2013; McGillivray, 2014; Postigo, 2003; Wilson, 2007), which are in the wider subject field of leisure studies. But researchers in leisure studies have been slow to engage with the idea of the Net as leisure, and the idea of leisure research about the Net, even where related subject fields such as media and communications studies and cultural sociology show strong evidence of engaging in research and debates about the impact of the rise of the Net (see above). For the purposes of this literature review, I have limited the analysis to the journal *Leisure Studies*. This journal is the journal of the Leisure Studies Association, the most critically sociological journal focusing on leisure studies. If any journal would be expected to recognize the importance of the Net as a leisure space and leisure activity, it should be this one: its editorial board has always had critical sociologists as members and it has a broad view of what leisure is (unlike many other journals, which see leisure as being equivalent to recreation). Despite its critical edge and engagement with wider social sciences, the journal serves as an example of the slow and unsteady engagement in leisure studies with the Net.

Using the online resource of the journal's own website at its publisher Taylor and Francis, it is possible to search through the journal to see how many papers mention the Net. By typing in 'Internet' I found 123 articles, which appears to be a healthy number of papers. But this figure includes book reviews and editorials, as well as full papers, and the figure covers the whole 34 volume article of the journal. A brief scan of some of the papers included in the list shows that many of the 123 actually only very briefly mention the Net in passing. To better understand how much of the journal's content is about research on the Net, or at least research about leisure that mentions the Net, it is necessary to do an old-fashioned manual read of the journal. I chose to do this from the year 1994, when consciousness of the Net was beginning to slip into popular culture, to 2013, the last full volume available.

In total, 434 full papers or research notes were published in the period, with 15 being the lowest number in one volume (1998), and 34 the largest number (2013, when the journal went to five issues a year). Of these, only seven (1.6%) are only or fully about leisure and the Net (in chronological order: Miah, 2000; Lawrence, 2003; Mattar, 2003; Rojek, 2005a; Brown, 2008; Gilchrist and Ravenscroft, 2008; Stebbins, 2010). There are a further 20 (4.6%) that make mention of the Net, or draw on some research of Net spaces, or use the Net in some way to make a contribution to leisure theory (again, chronologically: Murdock, 1994; Roberts, 1997; Jeffreys, 1999; Shaw, 1999; Rojek, 2000a; Ryan, 2002; Bryce and Rutter, 2003; Sivan, 2003; Bull, 2005; Crawford, 2005; Lincoln, 2005; Rojek, 2005b; Foley, Holzman and Wearing, 2007; Wheaton, 2007; Cohen, 2010; Spracklen, 2011b; Chambers, 2012; Pavlidis, 2012; Rojek, 2013; Spracklen, 2013b). I have tried to identify these through close reading of abstracts, key words, introductions and conclusions, with briefer overviews of whole papers, so I admit there may be a few papers that have slipped through this analysis, but not many. So in the years when the Net became a key site for leisure, and a key focus in sociology, cultural studies and politics, leisure studies has been focused elsewhere: the vast majority of research about leisure in the most critically sociological journal in the field was about sports, physical activity and recreation, tourism and leisure management.

The first paper to discuss the Net briefly is one by Graham Murdock (1994) on mapping out the changes that were occurring at the time in leisure and society. Most of the paper is a critique of the impact of postmodernity, post-Fordism and post-industrialism on the choices and spaces available for leisure lives. But there is a passing reference of note: one of the many emerging issues for leisure for Murdock (1994, p. 245) is 'the digital revolution... emerging cultural industries are based around the convergence of computing, telecommunications and service-based industries'. Murdock sees the future as being one dominated by mediated leisure forms and a blurring of the boundaries between work and leisure as a result of technological changes. This is a theme returned to three years later towards the end of a paper on youth cultures by Ken Roberts (1997), though he is more sceptical about the supposed breach between the generations caused by the increase in digital leisure (see below).

Two years pass before two other papers refer to the Net tangentially to the main focus of their research – and both these papers are about the sex industries. Shaw (1999) is an exploration of the ways in which women experienced and perceived pornography and the use of pornography. In passing, Shaw mentions the availability of porn on the internet as part of the multi-billion dollar porn industry. Sheila Jeffreys (1999) explores the growth and prevalence of sex tourism, critiquing it from a radical feminist standpoint. On the Net she points out that it is contributing to an increasing global flow of sex tourism and sexual oppression and violence, resulting in increasing objectification of women (Jeffreys, 1999, p. 187):

Currently the international organization of prostitution tourism is facilitated by the internet. Some internet sites are dedicated to the trade in male order brides. This trade is mainly in women from Asia, particularly the Philippines, Thailand, Korea, and Sri Lanka. In the Philippines in 1988–89 there was a 94% increase in the number of Filipino women migrating as fiancees or spouses to Japanese, Australian, German, Taiwanese, British, and US destinations. In the late 1980s and 1990s there has been a growing dissemination and diversification of pornography through cable television, dial-a-porn, home video and computers. Trafficking in women on the Internet in the form of the World Sex Guide, introducing johns to where and how to purchase women and girls worldwide, conversations between johns about using women and young girls, interactive pornography where men can instruct live women through the Internet to strip and perform sexual acts, and websites devoted to buying mail-order brides and to prostitution tourism have aided the organization and global scope of the sex industry.

One year later, the rise of the Net is mentioned by Rojek (2000a), but the journal also sees the first paper to directly discuss the implications of the new technology for leisure and studies of leisure. 'Virtually nothing: re-evaluating the significance of cyberspace' by Andy Miah (2000) reads like a communication from another world in the middle of debates about the professional ethics of leisure managers (McNamee, Sheridan and Buswell, 2000) and the differences between leisure provision in the public and private sectors (Coalter, 2000). Miah's paper articulates the technological developments to the year of publication, along with some of the social and cultural debates about the ethics and practice of using the Net. He is quick to make some interesting predictions about how leisure and work are changing through the growth and potential ubiquity of the Net. For instance, he predicts (Miah, 2000, p. 216):

> Relationships emerging as a result of e-mailing facilities, where people make contact with persons who, for example, have their information and contact details posted on a web-based document, are able to collapse the social barriers of geography and status. Such technology is profound for it makes possible contact with those whom once were inaccessible. Of course, the most celebrated persons are wise enough to remain anonymous in cyberspace. However, certainly within academia, it is possible to seek direct communication with authors of the most authoritative texts. Where once only an interpretation of a reading was possible, one can now confront the author with criticism and points of clarification.

Email has indeed brought people closer together, and changed the nature of friendship. Academics can engage in a true democracy of letters, contacting people in other universities around the world, for instant discussion. And although personal emails are harder to find, especially where people choose to hide behind pseudonyms or paid employees reading and writing emails on their behalf (as is often the case with celebrities), it is undoubtedly easier to engage in informal discourse on the Net than off it. Miah concludes (2000, pp. 222–223) by suggesting:

The kinds of leisure experiences that are found through mediation with a computer screen permit a quite unique approach to understanding lifestyle and identity; one that cannot be treated through the formalism of conventional leisure studies theory. Within cyberspace, not only are the spatial and temporal barriers collapsing, so too are inter-personal ones. Meanwhile, however, new social barriers emerge with unique issues relating to access, understanding, and meaning.

The Net for Miah (2000) is so novel that it demands a new kind of leisure theory. It is something that dissolves structures and identities, giving people enormous potential for self-actualization, play and social connectedness. Ultimately, it is a postmodern form of utopia that has positive moral potential for users, though Miah also warns that the Net's transformative value may be threatened by lack of access and knowledge. The 'giddiness' of Miah's account of the Net is picked up two years later in a paper by Ryan (2002). Like other work of the time, Ryan (2002) is fascinated by Donna Haraway's (1991) claims that humans and machines were hybridizing to form cyborgs. Haraway's thesis is based in postmodern philosophy, but draws its evidence from the growing use of video games and the early 1990s popular cultural trends of virtual reality and artificial intelligence (this was the era of *Star Trek: The Next Generation*'s Borgs, killer cyborgs with hive minds, dedicated to 'assimilating' the peoples of the galaxy – Hark, 2008). Ryan's paper wants to suggest that humans experiencing outdoor leisure and recreation are somehow actually cyborgs in a Harawayian sense. In defending this theory he makes reference to the Net and claims (Ryan, 2002, p. 278):

> Underpinning the whole ontological challenge that cyborgs present is a challenge to what material reality is. For example, technology has reached a point now where physicality is nonessential. The Internet and cyberspace are examples of 'things' that are not really 'things' in a material sense yet still exist.

The Net is real in a material sense, and physicality is essential, even if there is in cyberspace the construction of things that feel unreal (Mahoney and Haigh, 2011). If Ryan (2002) is struck by the novelty of technology and caught making bold statements about the brave new world of virtuality, Bryce and Rutter's (2003) account of digital gaming places the Net in a more mundane reality of commerce and social

interaction. Their paper is not primarily about the Net, but they do provide a helpful summary of the growth and normalization of the Net as
a leisure space (Bryce and Rutter, 2003, p. 10):

> The growth of access to computers in the home and Internet con-
> nections, as well as the recent development of gaming consoles
> which have network capability, has increased participation in online
> gaming and virtual gaming communities. IDC (2000) have estimated
> that during December 2000, almost 24 million Americans (approx
> 28% of Internet users) visited game-orientated web sites (this com-
> pares with 2.4 million UK users), and they predict that 40 million
> US households will be playing games online by 2004. Similarly, the
> rapid rate of diffusion of Internet access is demonstrated by the
> 'Which? Annual Internet Survey 2001' which estimates that cur-
> rently 36% (approx 16 million) of people in Britain have accessed
> the Internet in the last year.

This confidence in the normalcy of the Net, and awareness of its
importance as a site for both commercialization and social interaction
is also present in the second paper in *Leisure Studies* that focuses entirely
on the Net. Unlike Miah (2000), Yassar Mattar (2003) ('Virtual communities and hip-hop music consumers in Singapore: interplaying global,
local and subcultural identities') is based on traditional, sociological,
empirical research about subcultural identity formation. The novelty
of the paper is the way in which it threads its account of its respondents' identity-making through a discussion of virtual communities.
This needs to be defended by Mattar right at the start of the paper from
those critics who might think the Net is an inappropriate site to study
such things, or indeed from those critics who might not fully understand the Net. Mattar begins by citing Castells (1996) and situating the
paper in established social theory before making the novel claim that
virtuality allows subcultural identities to break free from local cultures
(Mattar, 2003, p. 283):

> This paper provides an alternative view of subcultures in this era of
> the 'informational society' (Castells, 1996). In this paper, it is argued
> that a relatively new Information and Communication Technology
> (ICT) – the Internet – has allowed subcultural identities to tran-
> scend their reliance on local cultures. Looking at the case of hip-hop
> music consumers in Singapore and their participation in virtual

communities, this paper shows how subcultural identities assume a fluid nature based upon the specifics of interaction.

The 'new' technology for Mattar (2003) is a liberating one, as it allows for the formation of fluid, hybrid identities that challenge local norms and values. Mattar's respondents can share knowledge about their subculture and feel in control of how they shape that subculture. The Net is not seen as some strange, unreal novelty; it becomes another leisure space that is contested and involved in identity work. Mattar (2003) believes this space has the potential to be communicative for its users, though there are social pressures to conform and to buy the right music and fashions.

In the same issue of *Leisure Studies* there is another paper that is primarily about the Net, a happy moment perhaps for the editors of the time. But whereas Mattar (2003) welcomes the Net as a potentially community-making leisure space, Lesley Lawrence (2003) (' "These are the voyages... "': interaction in real and virtual space environments in leisure') provides a nostalgic paean for the decline of 'real' leisure interactions and activities. The focus of Lawrence (2003) is the collapse of community-based *Star Trek* fan club structures and cultures, and the shift to fandom online. For many of her respondents, there is a suspicion that discussions online about the science-fiction franchise are no substitute for conversations at conventions and club evenings. They miss the feel of fanzines in their hand, the long conversations over beers, and for Lawrence (2003), this loss of face-to-face interaction means a loss of communicative leisure. This, she thinks, will have negative consequences: interaction on the Net will always be limited by its abstract nature, and the commercial limits of accessing the Net. As she concludes, this is probably inevitable as more and more people go online (Lawrence, 2003, pp. 312–313):

> Yet, it is suspected that many of us are becoming accustomed to being 'at leisure' in the confined space of cyberspace, rather than getting out there and 'physically' interacting on a face-to-face basis, perhaps being a virtual leisurist rather than a real one? Data are required to test the view of a possible usurping of traditional leisure practices by changing technology. Has abstract communication become the norm and firsthand experience joined the list of endangered species as inferred by Slouka (1995), as more time is spent in front of the computer screen? Over a decade ago, Stone (1991) confessed to spending more time interacting with her computer than she did

with her friends. Just how true is this today? More crucially where interaction within leisure spaces is concerned, in addition to examining its form and environment, we should be investigating the quality of such interaction, something Kelly advocated back in the 1980s (Kelly, 1983) well before the emergence of cyberspace as we know it today.

Another two years pass before there are five papers that discuss the Net and leisure in any significant way, one of which is completely about the Net. Three of these papers belong to the one special issue about popular music (Bull, 2005; Lincoln, 2005; Rojek, 2005a), one is about digital gaming (Crawford, 2005) and the last is another paper by Chris Rojek (2005b) spelling out his action approach to leisure studies (discussed below). The fact that the 'bump' in interest in the Net is associated with a special issue on popular music and leisure is not surprising: the guest editor Andy Bennett had just published on pop music and the Net at the time (Bennett and Peterson, 2004), and pop music studies has taken an interest in the growth of music subcultures online, as well as the impact of the Net on the music industries (Frith, 2004; Hesmondhalgh, 2010, 2013; Jones, 2002). Rojek's (2005a) paper for this special issue, 'P2P Leisure Exchange: Net Banditry and the Policing of Intellectual Property', explores the culture of file-sharing and downloading associated with the 'illegal' trade of music files, which has rapidly become one of the key 'problems' of the Net (see Chapter 7). Like much of Rojek's work of this period, there is an interesting amount of surface detail, and some provocative questions, but little or no research. Rojek (2005a, p. 358) begins by saying:

> P2P is a system of internet exchange that allows participants to make file transfers without the requirement for a central server to regulate the exchange. The technology permits free down-loading of copyrighted materials. The P2P concept is not new. For decades, Ham radio networks employed the technology to exchange analogue voice signals. Similarly, in the 1970s, the DARPA-Net system, from which the Internet emerged, was founded as a free peer-to-peer system of communication exchange between governments and university main-frame terminals. However, the expansion of the web in the 1990s introduced unprecedented levels of de-regulation. It weakened the power of creative producers, and the corporations that represent them, to assert copyright by vastly multiplying opportunities for exchange and reproduction.

Rojek has it completely right. It is the Net that has created the opportunities to engage in 'illegal' downloading on an unprecedented scale, which has led to a decline in the traditional pop music industries. The technology may have been invented in the 1970s, but the huge growth in the Net combined with the digitization of music players (the shift from vinyl to CD), increased download speeds and memory capacities has made it much easier to share music (Sterne, 2012). As I will show in Chapter 7, file-sharing also evolved from practises such as bootlegging, taping and tape-trading, which were common in pop music scenes: music fans and consumers had always disregarded the intellectual property of music labels, bands and musicians (ibid.). For Rojek (2005a, p. 364), the scale of the problem changes the rules of analysis completely; for him this is the beginning of a new way of regulating, controlling and resisting:

> Within the study of leisure, as with criminology, researchers have been working with a legal system based on a strong dichotomy between licit and illicit practice. This dichotomy has always been controversial. A prominent theme in critical criminology is that the division between licit and illicit is often, in practice, a false conceptual dichotomy. Be that as it may, the opportunities for illegal down-loading provided by the web illustrate the difficulties involved in trying to separate net bandits from active consumers. Hitherto, intellectual property has been recognized at the point of sale and confined to the individual value asserted by the copyright holder and assigned to the consumer. A clear division between producers and consumers has been acknowledged. New technologies problematize this dichotomy by making intellectual property an open text and inducing or encouraging consumers to be active.

It is interesting that Rojek takes this fairly strong line against the cultural practice of 'illegal' downloading, when it could be said to be an act of counter-hegemonic resistance against capitalism (see Chapter 7). This theme of the Net as a site for counter-hegemonic resistance appears in the next paper to fully engage with the Net as a leisure space, though again there is a gap of some years before the journal publishes such a paper. In ' "Power to the paddlers"? The internet, governance and discipline', Paul Gilchrist and Neil Ravenscroft (2008) explore how individuals and campaigning groups use the Net to organize and protest about things they are unhappy about, and how organizations respond to such discourse and activity. Gilchrist and Ravenscroft are interested in how the Net makes it easy for people to self-identify with a community of belonging: in their paper, they are interested in particular in people who involved in paddle-sports ('paddlers') and their campaigns to influence policies about access to rivers and other spaces where they can (or cannot) paddle. As they say (Gilchrist and Ravenscroft, 2008, p. 131):

> We argue that the internet has become a primary site for paddlers to discuss and initiate protest, allowing them to generate a collective identity (or, after Parker, citizenry) that would otherwise be difficult to generate and sustain. In dealing with protest, this collectively demonstrates aspects of the carnivalesque (Bakhtin, 1984; Ravenscroft & Matteucci, 2003), in providing a liminality that allows individuals to express thoughts and ideas that they would not necessarily wish to – nor often could – put into action. However, while facilitating a space for a spatially disparate community to communicate, use of the internet in this way has also had a number of unintended consequences. Not the least of these is the introduction of a largely unregulated multitude of voices to a rhetoric of rights that has not conventionally strayed far from (formal) pressure group politics. In addition, individuals become victims of a sleight of hand, believing the internet can produce alliances and momentum for causes, as appeals are made against particular injustices.

This paper is an excellent example of how leisure researchers and theorists should use the Net. Gilchrist and Ravenscroft acknowledge that the Net is central to many people's narrative about their leisure lives, a key space for them to perform the leisure characters they play, and in doing this performance these individuals make the Net a 'primary' site for their leisure. So, for some paddlers, writing about things they are unhappy about in the paddling world gives them as much pleasure – if not more – than paddling down a river. This sounds like the Net as a leisure utopia, a space where anyone can be anything. But Gilchrist and Ravenscroft warn against this, and use their research to show that the Net can be a place where users are controlled, fooled, diverted and constrained by others who have the interests of the powerful at stake.

The final paper that uses the Net as a primary research focus is 'From Friday to Sunday: the hacker ethic and shifting notions of labour, leisure and intellectual property' by James Brown (2008). This paper explores the relationship between labour and leisure, and the ways in which the Net is allowing new forms of cultural production that challenge the monopoly on commodities owned by the media and cultural industries.

Brown is suspicious of those who argue that copying and sharing copyrighted content is theft, because copyright laws have been established to take the labour of someone else and turn it into profit for those who have ownership of the copyright:

> Framing Web labour and leisure in terms of piracy (or, in terms of what Chris Rojek labels 'banditry') may not fully account for the different kinds of cultural production happening on the Web. The rhetoric of piracy is based on the assumption that cultural products (art, music, film, etc.) are definable commodities to be bought and sold like other commodities. I am not arguing that cultural texts somehow resist commodification, but rather that such cultural texts are different kinds of commodities. Culture always builds on previous texts. As legal scholar Lawrence Lessig argues, in some sense, all culture is 'piracy' (Lessig, 2004). The Web, often blamed for creating an intellectual property crisis, seems to instead be merely reminding us of the nature of all cultural products. Recognising this allows us to rethink labour, leisure and intellectual property.
>
> (Brown, 2008, 396)

After Brown (2008), the next and final paper to fully engage with the Net in the period of this analysis is one by Robert Stebbins (2010) entitled 'The Internet as a scientific tool for studying leisure activities: Exploratory Internet data collection'. This has some important theoretical propositions by Stebbins, as we will see in the next section of this chapter, but it is a paper that instructs researchers about the importance of the Net as a leisure space, rather than one that reports on research undertaken (it was published as part of a special issue on research methodologies).

Between 2009 and 2013, then, there is a slow but steady stream of papers that engage with the Net significantly, but which are not just about the Net. My own papers published in the journal in this period are good examples of how the Net is used to think about leisure spaces and practices. Spracklen (2011b) uses the Net as a source of data about how 'serious' single-malt whisky fans demonstrate their knowledge and belonging in the imaginary community of single-malt whisky fans. Spracklen (2013b) uses the Net as a source of data about how fans and musicians involved in black metal and English folk music police boundaries about who does and does not belong within those communities. In Spracklen (2011b, pp. 105–106) I spell out the importance of the Net as a site for identity-making, and how everything posted on the

Net by individuals is an attempt to construct belonging, identity and exclusions:

> There is, of course, an epistemological and methodological debate about the truth-value and utility for researchers of debates on Internet forums (Fernback, 2007). There is no doubt that users of online forums do not necessarily represent the views of a wider population; users of forums are more likely to be passionate, opinion setters (Eynon, Schroeder, & Fry, 2009). There is no doubt also that users of online forums do not necessarily post what they actually feel about a particular topic. These problems, however, should not concern us. On the matter of representation, this paper does not claim to provide a definitive fan 'response'. Rather, this paper explores responses made by those fans who care enough about whisky to post on the forum at www.whiskywhiskywhisky.com – these fans are not representative of all fans, but they are de facto serious and passionate about what constitutes true whisky fandom.

Mapping the Net in the works of key leisure theorists

The first leisure theorist to take any real notice of the Net is Ken Roberts. In Roberts (1997, p. 12) he discusses the changes that he sees happening in leisure, and what might be the conclusion from the nature of that change:

> Virtual Reality technology may soon allow people to experience any situation irrespective of their physical locations. It is claimed that distinctions between the real, imitation and fiction are tending to break down. Disney parks now appear to be treated in the same manner as the Champs Elysee as real places to visit. Soap opera dramas and characters are reported in newspapers and discussed as if they were real. Another manifestation of this loss of grounding is said to be that the (fictional) public images of celebrities, living and dead, exert a powerful hold on people's consciousness. A related feature of postmodern leisure is said to be its chronic instability. Cultural commodities and their meanings change constantly. Everything speeds up and experience becomes discontinuous and fragmented. This, it is said, leaves people feeling insecure and that nothing can be relied on.

At this point, however, Roberts (1997) dismisses the idea that the Net is something that will lead to insecure, unstable, postmodern leisure. He suggests instead that the changes brought about by the new technology will not be so dramatic at all, and the leisure spaces inhabited by young people and the leisure activities they do will not be ontologically different from those of earlier generations. In Roberts (1999), he continues this theme by claiming that the Net is not such a dramatic new leisure technology at all, and its existence will not alter people's leisure lives to such a radical extent.

Other key leisure theorists in this period only discuss the Net tangentially, or not at all, as if the importance of the Net as an everyday leisure space has yet to infiltrate their thinking. Cara Aitchison's (2000) important contribution to leisure theory critiques leisure studies for failing to embrace post-structuralist perspectives, and maps out how leisure scholars might learn from other subject fields. Aitchison believes post-structural leisure studies will allow better understanding of gender, power relations, subcultures and contestations of space. To demonstrate this she says (Aitchison, 2000, pp. 130–131):

> Leisure research undertaken from a poststructural perspective has been more visible outwith, rather than within, leisure studies. For example, in social and cultural geographies we have seen the Mapping of Desire (Bell and Valentine, 1995), the theorization of Body Space (Duncan, 1996), Images of the Street as refracted through leisure and tourism (Fyfe, 1998), and analyses of the inter-relations between Shopping, Place and Identity (Miller et al., 1998). In sociology, we have witnessed increasing interest in Food, Health and Identity (Caplan, 1997), Body Cultures (Bale and Philo, 1998) and Touring Cultures (Rojek and Urry, 1997), and in gender studies and cultural studies we are aware of the significance of Barbie Culture (Rogers, 1998), Nike Culture (Goldman and Papson, 1998) and Internet Culture (Porter, 1997). In all of these disciplines and subject fields, leisure, culture, sport and tourism have been theorized as central sites and processes of identity construction, contestation and negotiation. Engagement with poststructural theory has enabled analysis of both structural and symbolic power through the direction of our attention to what Adkins (1998: 47), writing at the interface of sociology and gender studies, refers to as the 'social/non-social nexus' or what, for the purpose of this paper, could be termed the social-cultural nexus of gender-leisure relations.

This is a brief mention of the Net, a reference to someone else's work on gender and the Net (Porter, 1997). It does show that Aitchison believes the Net is a leisure space where post-structural contestations of power are at work, where identity is created and where intersectionality works to constrain such acts of agency (a theme she returns to in later work – see Aitchison, 2013). As Aitchison draws on post-structuralism to understand digital leisure, others take a more postmodern line in exploring the possibilities for leisure offered by the Net. In his work on football fandom, Richard Giulianotti (1999, 2002) identifies a number of different kinds of football fans. There are fans who have 'traditional' bonds of identity and community to their local club, who turn out to watch their team play at the local stadium. Then there are other kinds of fans attracted to football in the period of heightened commercialization and commodification in the 1990s. Interestingly, in his typology of fandom, one of the 'new' forms of fan is mediated by the Net, someone who follows the team through various 'virtual' means (Giulianotti, 2002, pp. 38–39):

> The cool consumer spectator is a football flâneur. The flâneur acquires a postmodern spectator identity through a depersonalized set of market dominated virtual relationships, particularly interactions with the cool media of television and the Internet... The football flâneur may tend to be more male than female, but not by definition. The flâneur is more likely to be bourgeois and thus in pursuit of a multiplicity of football experiences. The flâneur adopts a detached relationship to football clubs, even favored ones. A true football flâneur, the cool consumer belongs only to a virtual community of strollers who window-shop around clubs. In the most extreme manifestation, national allegiances may also be exchanged on the grounds of competitive successes or mediated identification with superstar celebrities. The adornment of a team's attire is in tune with a couture aesthetic, drawn to the signifier (the shirt color, the shirt design, its crest, even its sponsor logo) rather than to what is signified conceptually (the specific, grounded identity of the club or the nation). The flâneur thereby avoids any personal consumption by the appended signs but instead consumes these signifiers in a disposable and cliché-like fashion, as if adopting a temporary tattoo. Moreover, the football flâneur's natural habitat is increasingly the virtual arena, seeking the sensations of football as represented through television, Internet, or perhaps in the future, the audiovisual bodysuit. Thus, television presentation of football is tailored toward a flâneur-type experience. Television compresses time-space differences, distilling entire matches or tournaments into 100-second

transmissions of blinding, aestheticized action, to an accompanying backbeat that drifts between techno and opera.

Giulianotti has identified the Net as a key way of becoming a football fan, but the kind of fan who follows this route seems to be critiqued at the same time for their weak ties to the symbolic community, and for their bourgeois habitus. The Net has made leisure choices multiply, but the choices made by the flâneur seem to be ridiculed by Giulianotti for their inauthenticity. The flâneur is not a 'proper' fan because their fandom is mediated, and not experienced 'in the flesh' or 'in the blood' (for the discussions and critiques of this typology see Fillis and Mackay, 2014). What is clear in this paper is Giulianotti's own ambivalence about the flâneur and the role of the Net. The ambivalence about the Net, its role as a potential utopia or dystopia while being at the same time the herald of a new age, is a theme developed by Chis Rojek over a number of years. In Rojek (2005b, p. 21) he states:

> Over [this] period, the UK has moved from a system of communications based in a handful of terrestrial news, information and entertainment broadcasting companies to multiple terrestrial-satellite broadcasting offering unprecedented flows of news, information and entertainment around the clock. More education and more news/information create the conditions for allowing active citizens to engage more meaningfully with civil society. They change the character of leisure. For example, the neoliberal notion that leisure is a matter of choice for the individual so long as it respects the confines of the law, and the socialist principle that the state must directly regulate leisure behaviour, are both discarded. Instead the onus for self-regulation comes from the form of information society and the civic recognition that leisure practice is interdependent and carries ethical and physical implications for the self and the other.

The brave new world of the Net is linked in Rojek's analysis to the arrival of postmodern forms of leisure and identity. In his book *The Labour of Leisure*, he presents a world that is increasingly hybrid, post-structural and playful, where capitalism has changed the roles of work and leisure completely. For Rojek, we now work to make our leisure lives work as identity-making spaces, since the traditional spaces of work are becoming erased in a post-Fordist economy (Bramham, 2006; Lyotard, 1984; Spracklen, 2009). In this world, anything goes for those who can pay or navigate their way through the levels of intentionality, and the

Net is at the heart of this neo-liberal anarchy: 'in a wired-up world in which the 24-hour marketplace obtains, the conventional notion of spheres of interest is too restrictive' (Rojek, 2010, p. 42). He continues by claiming that 'the mass media, the internet and other branches of modern communications provide opportunities for consumers to contrast local and national conditions with international and global circumstances' (Rojek, 2010, p. 47).

If the Rojek of *The Labour of Leisure* sees the Net as a potentially liberatory, utopian space for playing postmodern games, more recently he has introduced some Marxist analysis to his work. In a paper in *Leisure Studies*, Rojek (2013) uses the Net in a more measured way, but still sees it as the prime example of magic and agency in twenty-first-century leisure: the Net is still something that sits outside of 'offline', real-world structures and processes. He writes:

> Take the Internet. Today, this is a major leisure preoccupation in Western society. In a society that Marxism tells us is bent upon policing, the Internet cannot be policed. Where the exploitation of labour is supposedly ubiquitous the Internet provides extensive opportunities for expropriating the expropriator. The illegal downloading of intellectual property is rampant. The practice of downloading or streaming recorded music, film and literature that is formally controlled by copyright is normalised (David, 2010). The division between production and consumption, which classical Marxism deemed impregnable, is breached.
>
> (Rojek, 2013, p. 26)

The fairy glamour of the Net also appears in the work of Tony Blackshaw, in particular in the introduction to his crucial contribution to leisure theory, the book *Leisure* (Blackshaw, 2010). Blackshaw is caustically dismissive of the structuralists such as Bramham (2006) who claim that leisure is constrained, and that modern leisure is a product of some form of hegemonic control. Blackshaw wants to use Bauman (2000) to describe a world that has changed so much that it appears to be incommensurable to the old one that we used to live in – this is a world where we are all classless consumers, picking and choosing our identities, drifting through the liquid modern, doing liquid leisure (see also Blackshaw, 2014). The main part of the book does not use any work on the Net in any systematic way. Instead, Blackshaw uses the existence of the Net as evidence for the radical ontological shift Bauman says has happened (Blackshaw, 2010, p. xi):

These processes of de-differentiation have been accompanied by some other key changes in leisure ... underestimated is the extent to which the world of leisure has changed over the last 30 years ... the rewiring of traditional leisure activities and pursuits – cybersex, digital gaming, celebrating watching and social networking – through information technology and the internet ...

There are some truths in this. Of course the forms and spaces of leisure have changed since the 1970s. Fashions have come and gone. Local and global economies have risen and fallen. The West has become truly post-industrial. Globalization has seen the rise of new powers, new sources of leisure and culture. The power of ruling elites, of masculine gender orders and traditional cultural leaders, has been challenged. The Net has allowed some people to act more freely than was possible in the past. The Net has changed the way some kinds of leisure take place, altering both local socio-cultural contexts and economics of various leisure industries. But these changes do not make the leisure world completely changed: the essence – the meaning and purpose – of leisure lives, activities and spaces continues on, even if the human and commercial transactions are altered by the Net. Blackshaw's argument about the importance of the Net as an effect of liquid change is not supported by the evidence: the Net is full of the tensions and struggles that operate in the real world, and digital leisure is not ontologically distinct from any other kind of leisure.

Robert Stebbins has updated his theoretical frameworks of leisure to account for the rise of the Net (Stebbins, 1997, 2009). Stebbins' powerful concept of serious leisure might usefully be applied to people who maintain websites, while casual leisure might be used to think about how and why people surf the web or check their social-media pages. Stebbins himself has mapped out the ways in which the Net might be a useful source of data on leisure. In a paper for *Leisure Studies*, he tries to persuade sceptics of the value of the Net as a subject of leisure research (Stebbins, 2010, pp. 474–475).

The Internet as a source of useful exploratory data on leisure activities is unparalleled in the history of science. Still it is easy to see how many scholars would scorn it, for surely a great deal of it is superficial. Why waste one's time? Moreover, using the Internet as a source of ethnographic data can be time consuming, as the researcher works to separate wheat from chaff ... In the end, this way of gathering data offers a unique opportunity to explore sets of leisure activities and significantly expand our understanding of a very complex domain of modern life, namely free time. Conducting EIDC on leisure activities should not be scorned as the lazy man's approach to scientific data collection. Most of the information found in these electronic sources is unavailable elsewhere, or available only in very limited fashion (e.g. hard-copy newsletters, magazines, organisational constitutions distributed only to members).

Most of this is aimed at some morally driven leisure scholars who might not think the Net is more than a passing fad, a space for worthless and immoral leisure. The Net is certainly not the kind of thing a more traditionally trained leisure and recreation studies academic would think a 'good' leisure site (the only good leisure activity according to this school of thought would be the kind that is physically active and spiritually uplifting – see Kelly, 1983, 2012). Stebbins is making a case for the value of the Net that they might understand. The Net is useful because people who do leisure (who belong to clubs, for example) are using it to store material that we as leisure scholars might find interesting. Stebbins' argument for the value of the Net is correct, but there is much more to the Net that this argument misses. The Net is valuable not just as a free archive of evidence for leisure in the 'real world', but as a continually changing site and space of leisure itself.

Finally, a more cynical note emerges in commentaries written by scholars questioning the turn to mobilities, liquidity and virtuality. This turn is a fashion of epistemology, one that comes from academics becoming excited by the changes in their own lives: the whirl of international conferences, 12-hour flights, jet-lag and checking emails on Wi-Fi-enabled devices in the Yokohama Starbucks. Living this highly privileged (Western, liberal bourgeois) but hard-working life, one can easily mistake the specificity of one's situation for some awe-inspiring generalization about change. Bauman is one of those who have made this error of navel-gazing, but he is not the worst: John Urry has made a number of strong claims about the mobility of lives in this digitally connected world. For him, as we will see in the next chapter, the Net is a harbinger of this new phase of globalization and global capitalism. But others are not so sure about the all-encompassing change. In a review of the book *The Tourist Gaze* (Urry and Larsen, 2011), David Crouch (2011, p. 291) wonders:

How much tourism is about planes, internet, moving technology and so on remains open to serious debate, and already a number of writings have pointed towards stillness, slowness. Lying on a beach, relaxing with a long meal or simply being together offer three balancing examples to the romance of the highly mobile: people may go a long way to stay in one intimate point for 3 weeks.

Conclusion

Leisure studies research and theorizing on the Net has been patchy. There was, as I have shown, an absence of any sustained discussion of the Net right at the time when the Net was a new and popular leisure space. And where research and theorizing has been happening it has come with a strangely uncritical acceptance of the huge claims made for the Net's world-changing, postmodern heralding significance. Now, however, there are people in leisure studies and related subject fields who do theorize and research digital leisure in a more measured manner. In 2014, for example, the Leisure Studies Association annual conference included many sessions and keynotes on digital leisure and creative industries, and had digital leisure as a main theme. In one of those keynotes, David McGillivray has written elsewhere about the impact of new technologies and the capacity they have for shaping and constructing leisure lives. In a paper published in 2014 he states (McGillivray, 2014, p. 99):

> Increasingly ubiquitous, digital technologies are more accessible, affordable and powerful than ever before. However, a cultural gap remains between those that are comfortable using mobile devices, social networks and other online environments to participate in civic life as consumers and citizens and those that are not. This article is interested in the potential of digital tools and technologies to flatten hierarchies, enabling a wider range of citizens to participate in leisure cultures (particularly around mega sporting events) to subvert controlled narratives and created alternative, localised readings outside of established commercial media platforms. Participating in media production is now an everyday leisure culture made possible by the availability of self-publishing platforms and its evolution, and future direction is in need of further critical exploration.

This is powerful and thoughtful scholarship that arrived too late in the journal *Leisure Studies* to be picked up by my analysis (not that one paper would have made much difference to the conclusion about the relative absence of Net research). McGillivray concludes by saying:

> The institutional arrangements that drive and support the mega sporting event circuit actively seek to massage or manage alternative discourses. Yet, the corporate paranoia to assimilate and align themselves within this common web may act as a catalyst for the very counter movements and citizen narratives they wish to control. As digital and ubiquitous technologies and accelerated lifestyles mature, the strategic, directed and institutional message has come under a counter gaze that organises, mobilises and amplifies locally derived content.
>
> (McGillivray, 2014, p. 108)

The work of McGillivray and others such as Garry Crawford (for example see Crawford, Gosling and Light, 2013) shows clear evidence that leisure studies has started to turn an epistemological and methodological corner when it comes to engaging with the Net. Leisure studies as a subject field is becoming more critically mature and competent in assessing the importance and problematic nature of the Net. This book I hope will play a role in helping the subject field do more research on digital leisure. For this to happen, leisure studies scholars need to engage with the key theoretical debates that have been taking place in the wider scholarly community. This will be the subject of the next chapter.

4
Net Theory and Digital Leisure

What do theorists outside leisure studies think about the Net? There are some theorists who have made a name in wider subject fields and disciplines as prophets of the Net. There are others whose theoretical frameworks have been used by those critically exploring the impact of the Net on human society. There are those who are excited about the possibilities of the Net, those prophets who see the technology as a herald of the dawn of a new age and others who see only doom in the Net's entrails. This chapter will focus on the work of a few key theorists outside leisure studies who have attempted to understand and critique the development of the Network Society. It is impossible to engage with everyone who has written on the Net, or everyone to whom the Net is a stepping-point to some deeper social or cultural theory, so I have had to make a selective choice of authors. I have chosen a range of people who have contributed to Net Theory over time as the Net has developed, but also people whose work is useful for us in understanding digital leisure.

The first section of this chapter discusses the work of Baudrillard, Turkle, Urry, Bauman, Giddens and Delanty. I will argue that the Net is used by each of these theorists as both a metaphor for postmodernity, an agent in the construction and limitation of our social selves, and as proof of the growth of global networks and mobilities. The second section concentrates on the writing of Castells and his theory of the Network Society. I will argue that Castells was prescient not only about the emancipatory possibilities offered by the Net, but also the hegemonic struggles that would shape the leisure space. The final section of the chapter explores the Net in the later writings of Habermas to show how his analysis of the Net is tied to his idea of the lifeworld.

Key theorists from Baudrillard to Delanty

There are discussions about the Net in almost every social and cultural theorist who has contributed to the wider subject field since the 1980s. As I discussed above, in this section I could have engaged with a wider range of theorists, and some readers of this book might think my analysis is weakened at this point by a lack of broader engagement with the theoretical literature. However, I contend that the six theorists here are representatives of that broader epistemological terrain, and their work intersects strongly with the work of many others.

Jean Baudrillard

Baudrillard explores the idea of reality and the Net in a number of his essays and books, both academic and popular (1986, 1988, 1994, 1995, 2002). He is interested in how the changing technology of the Net (at the time he was writing in the 1980s and 1990s) was altering people's perceptions of reality. The idea of virtual reality means individuals using the Net become unable to work out what is the real world, and what is the virtual world. That means two things. Firstly, the virtual becomes a *simulacra* of the real. Baudrillard is concerned throughout his writing to explore the ways in which things become copies of themselves, but copies that hold lesser value in some way (Baudrillard, 1994). The Net for Baudrillard, then, is a space where the politics, the morals and ethics, and the identity-making of the real world, the struggles for equality and the struggles against capitalism, all become pale imitations of the real world. This for Baudrillard is already happening, and he cites examples of how French society is changing for the worse (Baudrillard, 1995), but he also anticipates that this direction of travel will continue. In other places he seems to recognize that the Net and the idea of virtuality have transformative potentials (Baudrillard, 2002). He thinks, for instance, that virtuality is a way of constructing post-structural identities and using agency to resist globalization and commodification. But the idea of the *simulacra* is of something reduced of any ethics and politics, so the Net, while offering the potential for transformations (especially where governments do not understand the technological potential), is profoundly limited and challenged by those with power who understand how to control it.

Secondly, the Net and virtual reality are proof for Baudrillard of the ontological shift to what he calls hyper-reality (Baudrillard, 1994, 1995). The hyper-real becomes the only reality we know when the world is sufficiently mediated and filtered through a number of technological and cultural devices – such as the Net. Baudrillard shows how television news becomes the only way in which viewers experience the 'reality' of a foreign war. He argues in a sense that the actual reality of something (such as the first Gulf War, the subject of his analysis) does not exist for television viewers. The mechanics of editing and the presenting of selected versions of the first Gulf War take place inside television news studios, where producers, editors and presenters work within rules laid down by regulators, policy-makers and legislators. The result is that the Gulf War in a real sense does not take place as experienced by the viewers in the West. Instead, they see a 'hyper-real' representation (and re-presentation) of the fighting. This means that for all intents and purposes the war does not exist *for the consumers in the West*. Of course people actually shoot at each other, people die and all kinds of outrages take place, but the reality on the television (or in the newspapers, or on the Net) is the hyper-reality of managed information and the manipulation of emotions: from anger at the evils of the evil dictator, to joy when 'our boys' return home. The Net, then, is a key site for the construction of hyper-reality – sometimes by ourselves as agents in interactions, but mainly as consumers (Merrin, 2005).

Sherry Turkle

Turkle is an influential American scholar who has developed a range of ideas about the rise of the Net. Her work is situated in feminist debates about the Net. In *Life on the Screen: Identity in the Age of the Internet*, Turkle (1995) argues that the Net is a feminine space that offers women both emancipatory potential, but which is governed by democratic, communicative ideals that spring from how women talk to one another. Turkle was one of the first sociologists of the Net, anticipating its growth and impact on globalization and post-structural identity-making. Drawing on Foucault, Turkle believes that the Net has the potential to be a utopia of sorts, or a heterotopia or third-space (see Foucault 1986, and discussions in Hetherington, 1997; Johnson, 2006), where the structures and constraints of the real world are diminished or removed altogether. Turkle is concerned to counter contemporary work on the Net by radical feminists (for example, Shields and Shields, 1996), which portrays the Net as a masculine space. This is a claim based on the reality of the preponderance of pornography and violent games that were already present in the early 1990s. It is also a claim based on the assumption that people involved in the Net's construction and maintenance are generally men. Turkle recognizes that there are websites filled with pornography, and there is a dominance of men in the IT industry, but she believes that the Net's moral values have been shaped by the women users of bulletin boards, message boards and forums. She argues that there are women technologists, as well as women users on the Net. These women users bring with them co-operation, manners and respect for others – all of which are key building blocks of the Net's communicative democracy.

Turkle's argument has been attacked by a number of radical and post-structural feminists (Travers, 2003; Wajcman, 2002; Zoonen, 2001). One of the biggest flaws in her argument is the essentialist assumption that there are a set of feminine values associated with stereotypes of nurturing (which are then contrasted with essentially masculine values of competition and individualism). There are no essentially feminine traits, but there are culturally conditioned behaviours that construct gendered differences in public spaces such as the Net (Lupton, 2014). The anonymous nature of the Net encourages some people to play with gender roles and stereotypes. However, it seems most people use the Net to reaffirm and normalize culturally conditioned behaviours – so men go on the Net to learn how to be men, trolling and flaming, while women go on the Net to find safe places to learn feminine belonging. Turkle is right to point out that the Net has the potential to be an emancipatory space for women, and there is more to the Net than pornography and violent games. She has been influential in the development of cyberfeminism and other movements that have tried to make the Net become more open to diversity, while challenging head-on the masculine dominance of some parts of it (Travers, 2003). More recently, Turkle (2011) has become concerned about the ways in which digital technologies and their saturation in leisure life are damaging human social interactions in the real world.

John Urry

Urry's work has already been mentioned in the previous chapter. He has been a key figure in the development of critical tourism studies, the sociology of tourism that explores the ways in which the tourist creates and consumes the exotic Other (Rojek and Urry, 1997; Urry, 1990, 1995, 2000). The tourist's gaze according to Urry is analogous to the male gaze described in radical feminism: the tourist objectifies the people and the places they encounter, changing them into a limited range of acceptable stereotypes. Out of this work on tourism Urry has progressed into a wider critical programme of mobilities research (Elliott and Urry, 2010; Urry, 2003, 2007, 2011). The idea behind this programme is that the world has become more closely and densely interconnected. More and more people travel into other countries, not just for holidays, but as part of their working lives. Transnational corporations, states and non-governmental organizations (NGOs) co-operate to ensure there is movement of capital, ideas and culture. For some people working in the global cities and elites, there is the necessity of movement around the world; for others who sit outside the elites, such as the global poor of the South, there are state-led restrictions on movement (Urry, 2007). The Net is just one part of the discourse of mobilities and shrinkage of borders and distances. It enables people and ideas to be globalized, to be global travellers without physically moving – but the Net also allows the work of the elite, cosmopolitan workers to take place. The academic and manager crossing time zones relies on the Net for buying tickets online, for staying in touch with work, and staying in touch with their leisure activities – so long as there is Wi-Fi, the global mover remains in the centre of their networked, mobile world (Elliott and Urry, 2010).

Urry is too careful a sociologist to let his ideas lead him into embracing the new world as a good thing. He is strongly critical of the damage caused to the climate because of this huge rise in international travel. The environmental costs are not just in terms of global warming, they also impact on the regions around airports and global hubs (Urry, 2011). Urry is also keenly aware that the fluid, mobile agents of the global elites are not as free as they might seem. They are as trapped as the migrants from the South behind the barbed-wire on the real borders – trapped by their lifestyles and the modern work ethic that makes them work long hours and travel to strange places thousands of miles from their families and friends (Urry, 2003). The Net here is a system of control as much as a system of freedom: the Wi-Fi is on but there are emails from line managers to deal with before one can check Facebook (Fuchs, 2010). Others in the mobilities programme are more susceptible to the myth that this new form of work and leisure is actually a transformative one (Davis, 2010; Mcquire, 2010). Urry's ideas are used to claim that the world is becoming postmodern, post-structuralist, a place where the Net allows anyone anywhere to transcend borders, nation states and social structures. The cost of living this life, the powers of the State and transnational corporations in shaping it, is elided into a footnote, or quietly overlooked.

Zygmunt Bauman

Bauman is strongly influenced by Marx and the Frankfurt School of Horkheimer and Adorno, though he also owes a debt to Gramsci and Foucault for their respective theories of the operation of power in modern society. In the latter half of his academic career he realized that the trends towards postmodernity and globalization were indeed happening (Bauman, 1992, 2000, 2002, 2003, 2004, 2005, 2006a, 2006b). He noticed that the logic of capitalism, which had led to a global marketplace dominated by faceless corporations, led also to two contradictory states of being for human actors. First, social structures were weakened or dissolved completely by changes in the politics and economics of each Westernized nation state. This was because capitalism demanded individual consumers as rational actors. But capitalist marketing also needed to be able to predict consumer behaviour, so alongside the gradual dissolution of social structures and the social bonds that tied people together collectively, new ways of thinking about people as groups emerged. In places of work, for example, the new market economics demanded that collective action by unions on behalf of the working class was reduced: anti-union laws were passed by governments in Western countries, flexible working hours were introduced to help corporations increase their profits, and a strong part of the working-class Labour movement lost its community, identity and solidarity.

But the new flexible labour force, individualized, atomized and powerless, was quickly segmented into new consumer groups by the market, which replicated the power relations of modernity to some extent. Those consumer groups are reinforced through the Net, where subcultures become audience segments. Solidarity is therefore fragmented by the rise of virtuality and digital leisure. The Net increases the speed in which these liquid trends occur, making most of us into individualized actors, de-humanized and cloven from collective action. Bauman says in this period of modernity a new elite class emerged that was global in outlook, educated, confident and happy to move from project to project. Propping up the new elites was a range of middling classes in variable states of security, with enough disposable income to be segmented and targeted by corporations. Underneath those were the failed consumers who did not have the steady incomes to be able to afford the fashions and lifestyles of the other classes. However, in this new modern world, individuals could move up and down more easily – with weakened social structures and traditional hierarchies of family, 'race' and gender unnecessary for the success of global capitalism, social identity and status became fluid. This is the liquid modernity that Bauman describes in the eponymous book (Bauman, 2000), the new, late version of modernity in which he claims we still live, where technological change – such as the rise of the Net – and globalization have increased the speed in which modern nation states become part of the global, Westernized, liquid modern society. Bauman has been attacked for his

lack of evidence-based argumentation, and has also been accused of plagiarism and use of other people's ideas as if they are his own (see Best,
2013). These are serious charges. But they do not stop us from reading Bauman and reflecting on the influential contribution he has made
to understanding the world. We can see that the Net, for Bauman, is
evidence of the liquid turn in modernity, the fracturing of collective
belonging and the division between failed consumers and the elites.

Anthony Giddens

Giddens argues that class has dissolved in the West because there are
no longer huge factories, mines and other big industries, and we now
live in a post-industrial, globalized late modernity (Beck, Giddens and
Lash, 1994; Giddens, 1991). Evidence for the post-industrial shift is obvious, and the Net is one place where Giddens (1999, 2005) says such
late modern working practices such as flexible working takes place. But
this is to mistake the absence of a type of working-class community
for an absence of any working-class culture. First of all, the weakness
of defining class through looking at and categorizing occupation has
been commented on by a number of theorists (Scase, 1992; Skeggs,
2013). Changing employment patterns brought about by a shift to a
post-industrialist society have seen a rise in the number of traditionally
white collar, lower middle class jobs in insurance, banking and other
clerical and service professions. However, it is clear that this new class
of workers share a similar heritage and culture to the traditional working class. The miner's daughter is now an insurance clerk, the miner's
son is now a bank cashier. So although it is true to say the occu-
pations traditionally associated with the working class are in decline,
and that the postmodern society has created a wealthy consumer class
where hamburgers and Hollywood films ('movies') are devoured by all
(Featherstone, 1991), there is still a class divide between the ruling class,
a managerial bourgeois class and a working class that is denied control
in the workplace and which still does the work. Now, however, that work
is more likely to be inputting data on policy claims rather than riveting
steel.

   Giddens is stronger on globalization, and the Net is clearly a place
that engenders this trend. Globalization as a process is a direct effect
of increasing commodification and homogenization of culture and the
commercialization of everyday life. Globalization itself is claimed by
Giddens (1990, 1991, 1999, 2005) as one symptom of a shift to the
postmodern in the (current) late or fluid state of modernity, indicat-
ing close affiliations with the basis of postmodernism. Some writers see

in globalization an exchange of ideas, values and identities: the hybrid world of multiple identities (Kraidy, 2005). In political and cultural studies discourses, however, globalization is identified as a whirlwind for American values (Appadurai, 1996), leading to claims by Ritzer (2004) that the empty, homogenous values of McDonaldization are becoming de facto the norm for the world of work (and leisure) far removed from Kansas. In the brave new world of globalization, the modernist paradigms of national, class and gender structures are swept away by the hegemonic values of a postmodern free-for-all (Bauman, 2000). Globalization as a process has been happening ever since the first merchants sailed the Mediterranean in the age of the Phoenicians and the Greeks. But clearly the spread and diffusion of culture, power, wealth and ideas has increased exponentially in the last 150 years. Globalization is a process that transcends traditional norms, values and ideologies associated with the pre-modern and modern world, ideologies such as modern nation states (Held, McGrew, Goldblatt and Perraton, 1999), or authentic/permanent notions of cultures and tradition (Williams, 1977). Instead, as argued by Brah (1996) and many others, globalization forces the adoption of universal norms, values and ideologies through the power of transnational processes.

Gerard Delanty

Delanty is in the globalization tradition of Giddens and Bauman. He is one of the main popularizers of the idea of cosmopolitanism (Delanty, 2010, 2011, 2012a, 2012b). This idea of cosmopolitanism supposes that postmodernity and globalization have accelerated to the point where new transnational, intercultural identities and communities are beginning to emerge. While some of these are reactions against globalization and the blurring of boundaries, cosmopolitanism is a new identity that supposedly recognizes and celebrates difference, hybridity and diversity. Virtual communities, for Delanty, are crucial sites for the construction of cosmopolitan belonging, because they bring different cultures together to create shared identities and intercultural exchanges (Delanty, 2010). Cosmopolitanism is something that is seen as an inevitable product of intercultural exchange and the increasingly communicative discourse of the globalized Net. Delanty is not claiming the Net is something profoundly different from previous sites of community formation. He recognizes that all humans form community with others, and have used a number of ways to find belonging and exclude others. In modernity, however, with the loss of traditional forms of community, ways of belonging such as municipalism, nationalism and citizenship became the norm for nation states. Delanty (2010) suggests that these forms of community remain important ways of belonging today, though the cosmopolitan and the virtual together create postmodern challenges to these communities.

This concept of cosmopolitanism is problematic, and there are a number of challenges to the idea (see discussion in Knight, 2011). Sometimes it seems as if the idea of cosmopolitanism is a political or moral ideal, rather than a social reality, projected onto the world by people desperate to see nationalism and other exclusive forms of belonging disappear. There is no doubt that transnational organizations such as the United Nations place an important emphasis on global citizenship and respect for others, and most if not all academics might feel they would like to live in a world that is fully cosmopolitan. I hope I am a cosmopolitan person myself, comfortable with diversity, hybridity and interculturalism. But how does this moral imperative to be cosmopolitan actually emerge in the real world? Some scholars have questioned whether cosmopolitanism is just another form of elite cultural capital, used to gain status and dismiss others who do not have the wealth to spend on the things that make one cosmopolitan: long-haul flights, long holidays and so on (Lebow, 2012). Others have wondered whether the cosmopolitan truly exists, or whether the idea of the cosmopolitan is actually hiding Westernization or Americanization and the death of difference (Bhambra, 2011). Virtual communities, for example, might in fact be spaces where Western popular culture and norms and values are imposed on others. It has also been suggested that cosmopolitanism is internally incoherent (Robbins, 2012) – how can all differences be respected and privileged in a world that includes radically opposed communities of thought in politics and international relations? On the Net, the cosmopolitan ideal of allowing every voice to be heard equally and fairly is often undermined by the clamour of political enemies whenever there is something controversial to be discussed.

Manuel Castells

Castells was one of the first sociologists to chart the rise of the Net and the changes it was making to society. He has since continued to research the impact of the Net and the ways in which human agency and hegemonic power interact. Castells is interested in what he calls the shift to the Network Society, a development that has occurred alongside the technological progression associated with the Net. His first work on the Net is polemical in nature. He is concerned, writing in the 1990s, that traditional sociology and cultural studies have failed to take account of the ontological changes happening in society. His book *The Rise of the Network Society* (Castells, 1996) has become a classic text of social theory. It charts the rise of the information age through an analysis of how markets were digitized, how workplaces were becoming reliant on digital technology and how the Net itself was beginning to become part of everyday working and leisure life throughout the world. This was bringing people closer together, transcending borders, speeding processes of globalization, speeding up transactions, spreading knowledge and increasing personal freedoms and liberties.

Castells argues that we are also seeing the end of the social structures associated with high modernity. These changes are happening separately from the technological changes associated with the Net. The Castells of the 1990s is keen to show how the global economy, globalization, Westernization, the trends to equality, migration patterns and the spread of liberal democracy all shift power from traditional elites, dissolving exclusionary patterns associated with class, gender and so on. This is the turn to a post-industrial society, a classless or bourgeois society, an urban society where everybody works in an office (Bauman, 2000). This is a postmodern turn that was happening without the technology of the Net. But the two have become interconnected, Castells argues, and the result is the increasing speed of change and the transition to an ontologically distinct Network Society. The Network Society is one that can only be understood sociologically through research that follows the connections between parts of the network. As with Latour's Actor-Network Theory (Latour, 1987), Castells sees this network as a network of things as much as a network of humans or human organizations: the Net is just one part of the network of networks, one of the things that binds humans, computers, offices and other spaces together with nation states and transnational organizations. Castells recognizes that networks existed before the postmodern turn, but the ability to move information and material through them was restricted by the limits of technology: the speed of sailing ships, the payload of a caravan or the reliability of the postal service.

The Rise of the Network Society is the first of his *The Information Age* trilogy (Castells, 1966, 1997, 1998), which concerns itself with understanding how important sociological concepts such as power, structure and agency have been reformulated by the changes to society. In this trilogy and elsewhere, Castells (1996, 1997, 1998, 2000, 2001, 2007, 2009, 2012) argues that the technological and cultural advances associated with the internet have disrupted traditional social structures, economics and politics. Traditional social structures such as the gender order are disrupted by the spread of knowledge and the communicative leisure and rationality that the Net's rules of engagement encourage. Traditional economics is disrupted by the spread of virtual trading in stock markets, and the ability for consumers to have almost limitless choice online. All these challenge traditional politics, as the Net spreads a morality of free and fair discourse. We are living in a new world, with a new sociology to understand what is going on, a type of utopia where the Net bypasses those traditions. As he says (Castells, 2000, p. 695):

> The new society is made up of networks. Global financial markets are built on electronic networks that process financial transactions in real time. The Internet is a network of computer networks. The electronic hypertext, linking different media in global/local connection, is made up of networks of communication – production studios, newsrooms, computerized information systems, mobile transmissions, and increasingly interactive senders and receivers... Governance lies on the articulation among different levels of institutional decision making linked by information networks. And the most dynamic social movements are connected via the Internet across the city, the country, and the world.

This analysis of the impact of the Net and its status as a dynamic social movement is undoubtedly correct. For those who have access to the Net, there has always been the utopian promise of infinite interaction and discourse with a global community of like-minded people, all couched in an ethics of fairness and the freedom to be anonymous, to have fun, to be uninhibited by controls – by legislation, by nation states, by transnational corporations. When it comes to our taste in popular culture, in things such as music and films and television, the Net has transformed what we think is good and how we choose to consume these things. The entertainment industry has tried to make people continue to buy the products it tells us to buy, and to buy them in high-street shops (or online from trusted retailers). We no longer obey the logic of instrumentality the industry has tried to impose on us. We like to think we have risen up against the exploitation of marketing, professional criticism and the logic of the business. We no longer trust what we are told about which things to purchase (Arora, 2014). We no longer listen to music on the radio or television and go out to buy it on the high street – instead we browse file-sharing sites and swap recommendations with others. As Castells explains (2007, p. 246):

> The diffusion of Internet, mobile communication, digital media, and a variety of tools of social software have prompted the development of horizontal networks of interactive communication that connect local and global in chosen time. The communication system of the industrial society was centered around the mass media, characterized by the mass distribution of a one-way message from one to many. The communication foundation of the network society is the global web of horizontal communication networks that include the multimodal exchange of interactive messages from many to many both synchronous and asynchronous.

What Castells is saying is the media and those who controlled it have lost power. The modern media were developed to exchange news and information, but rapidly became ways on which hegemonic power was maintained by elites. Once upon a time, totalitarian or autocratic nation states could censor media and use it to make propaganda, binding citizens to subservience and obedience (Briggs and Burke, 2009; Spracklen, 2013a). The control of communications and the media by nation states was a key element of the construction of modernity, and the process of instrumental rationality that limited autonomy. The use of propaganda to promote nationalism and control the masses is tragically a part of recent European history, but it has happened to a greater or lesser degree in almost every country (for example see discussion in Volcic and Erjavec, 2013). Even in liberal democracies with a strong ethic of press freedom (such as the United States), where control of the media was less obvious, capitalism could still manipulate the media to create audiences, markets and tastes: making people watch sports, making people eat hamburgers, making people buy cars. The Net has made all culture popular, and has bypassed traditional arbiters of taste such as professional critics, nation states and corporations – there is an anarchic democracy of free choice. There is a Habermasian (Habermas, 1984, 1987) communicative rationality at work in how people use the Net to resist the instrumentality of the entertainment industry (as we will see later in this book).

But the extent to which this 'dynamic social movement' is a radical shift or a rejection of instrumentality is questionable. Indeed, Castells has later modified his position on the Net and the radical, communicative potential it offers. Castells does not believe that the shift to the Network Society is necessarily a morally good position for society. He does not think the trends automatically make the Net an individualist utopia, a paradise of downloading and sharing. There is an inevitable struggle between those who wish to use the Net for morally good reasons, to be free and fair, and those who wish to use it for more instrumental reasons. The Net has the potential to be a utopia, but the potential also to be a dystopia, and the reality of the Net says Castells, is that it is the site of a struggle between these two different ethical frameworks. Leisure lives on the Net are free to shape so long as access to the Net is free and un-monitored by security agencies. Leisure lives on the Net are communicative in the way they offer radical politics and social movements a way to organize and resist (Castells, 2012). But the extent to which such leisure is free is limited by the ways in which the Net is a product of instrumentality. That is, in his later work Castells (2009, 2012) says the Net has become an apparatus of commerce, control and surveillance, with most of this activity hidden behind the discourse of personal freedom. The new corporations of the Net make huge profits from selling our personal data – with every step we take seen as legitimate fuel for sponsor-driven advertising algorithms (Arora, 2014; Mahoney and Haigh, 20011). The corporations also work alongside governments to balance the pursuit of profit with the need to limit political action – offering security agencies extensive and unfettered access to hardware and databases. This is all in the name of countering terrorism and crime, but the levels of intrusion and the unaccountable nature of it means everything we access or write on the Net potentially makes us a bad citizen or – at worst – an enemy of the State denied legal privileges. As Castells (2007, p. 252) says:

> Media businesses aim at positioning themselves in the Internet-mediated communication realm; mainstream media set up direct links to the horizontal network of communication and to their users, so becoming less one-directional in their communication flows, as they relentlessly scan the blogosphere to select themes and issues of potential interest for their audience; actors striving for social change often use the Internet platform as a way to influence the information agenda of mainstream media; and political elites, across the entire political spectrum, increasingly use the ways and means of mass self-communication, because their flexibility, instantaneity, and unfettered capacity to diffuse any kind of material are particularly relevant for the practice of media politics in real time. Therefore, the study of the transformation of power relations in the new

communication space must consider the interaction between political actors, social actors, and media business in both the mass media and networked media, as well as in the interconnection between different media that are quickly becoming articulated in a reconfigured media system.

As previously noted, the Net is increasingly marketized, with every transaction noted and tracked by algorithms so the gatekeeping sites on the internet can target adverts at us more effectively. At the same time, governments are keen to access personal data most of us have placed on social networking sites. So there is on the Net a political struggle over who gets access to what, how much people pay (if they pay at all) and how much anonymity and freedom of expression are tolerated. On the Net, extreme utopians believe that corporations and governments should have no control over people's use of the Net, that individuals should be allowed to do whatever they like, so long as they abide by the rules of courtesy and engagement laid down in the early years of the Net's formation (Arora, 2014). But of course this extreme utopian view is an ideal, and a dangerous one, since there are many things that are not tolerated on the Net, and many things that should not be tolerated (Lupton, 2014). There is always a struggle over the limits of freedom of expression in any community or society – the Net makes such struggles more pertinent as they are played out against a technology where the advocates of freedom are more technologically skilled than the traditional guardians of morality employed by the State (Morris and Higgins, 2010) (this is a similar problem with plagiarism in schools and universities, where Net-savvy students use the Net to find people to write their essays for them in ways that are undetectable by anti-plagiarism software). Castells (2007, p. 258) continues:

> The twin processes of globalization and the rise of communal identities have challenged the boundaries of the nation state as the relevant unit to define a public space. Not that the nation state disappears (quite the opposite), but its legitimacy has dwindled as governance is global and governments remain national. And the principle of citizenship conflicts with the principle of self-identification. The result is the observed crisis of political legitimacy. The crisis of legitimacy of the nation state involves the crisis of the traditional forms of civil society, in the Gramscian sense, largely dependent upon the institutions of the state. But there is no social and political vacuum. Our societies continue to perform socially and politically by shifting the

process of formation of the public mind from political institutions to the realm of communication, largely organized around the mass media.

There is for Castells a supposed crisis in the construction of civil society, what Habermas (1989, 1990) might refer to as the public sphere. The Net has left nation states and their governments struggling to understand what their citizens are doing, and struggling to control the ways in which popular culture and communicative rationality is constructed. Even though Castells notes that nation states still try to retain hegemonic power over society, he thinks the Net has made this impossible. There are too many spaces and places for individuals to turn to – if the State takes control of or shuts down one website, activists and dissenters can create another ten (McGillivray, 2014). The WikiLeaks affair demonstrates the power of the Net to confuse the attempts by security agencies and bureaucracies to stop information they do not like from escaping into the public sphere of the Net, copied on thousands of servers and distributed widely (Arora, 2014). The Net, then, becomes a new commons, a new site for freedom, free leisure, free politics and action. In this new public sphere, even the hegemonic power of global capitalism is invoked to show how liberating the 'galaxy' of the Net (a term he uses in Castells, 2001) becomes for Castells (2011, p. 784):

Communication networks are largely owned and managed by global multimedia corporate networks. Although states and their controlled corporations are part of these networks, the heart of global communication networks is connected to, and largely dependent on, corporations that are themselves dependent on financial investors and financial markets. This is the bottom line of multimedia business. But financial investors place their bets according to the expected performance of media business in the global financial market – the mother of all accumulations of capital and the dominant network of global capitalism, as analysed in my trilogy on *The Information Age* (Castells, 1996–1998, 2010). The critical matter is that the global financial market is a network itself, beyond the control of specific social actors and largely impervious to the regulatory management of national and international institutions of governance, largely because the regulators chose to deregulate the financial networks and program the financial markets accordingly. Once financial markets became organized in a loosely regulated global network, their standards became applicable to financial transactions around the world,

and therefore to all economic activities, since in a capitalist economy, production of goods and services begins with investment from
capital and yields profits that are converted into financial assets.
The global financial market exercises network power over the global
economy.

The power of the Net has, for Castells, enabled global capitalism to
become better at its job. This in turn has led to global capitalism exert-
ing what he calls 'network power' over the world's economy. So the
technological progression and the freedom to evolve and network and
adopt and adapt leads full circle to hegemonic control. Castells seems to
be both critic and disciple of the Net at the same time. For this he has
been attacked by many people on either side of the ethical debate (see
for example Frost, 2006; Hodge, 2013; Holton, 2005; Webster, 1997).
The Net does offer lots of opportunities to be free and adventurous in
one's leisure, but of course such freedom to explore this digital 'galaxy'
is constrained by a number of realities. First of all, accessing the Net
is not free – someone needs to pay for our access, and many people
in the world still lack the necessary resources. Second, access to the
Net requires the freedom to use hardware and software that is controlled by organizations such as nation states and corporations. This is
clearly a source of hegemonic power for those organizations that can
tap the Net's cables or turn off someone's access. Third, there are still
enormous social and cultural forms of discrimination that restrict people's ability to become Netopians. The potential of the Net to be a new
public sphere depends on its universality and its freedom from controlling powers such as nation states and capitalist corporations. That
universality presupposes equality of access and equality of opportunity,
neither of which is evident in the real world of the early twenty-first
century. Frost (2006, p. 48) describes the limits of the Network Society and Castells vision of the Net as a space of personal freedom and
adventure as follows:

> To constitute a new 'public sphere,' a medium needs to have certain
> qualities; chief among them is true accessibility (Papacharissi, 2002).
> Easily accessible for some, the Internet remains beyond the reach of
> many others. As such, it fails the requirement for inclusivity in demo-
> cratic life. Next is a requirement for participant equality. The Internet,
> however, is not necessarily more equal in its treatment of partici-
> pants than you would find in an offline setting. Instead, because
> offline speech issues and learned linguistic practices can advantage

or disadvantage the online speaker, we have no reason to view the Internet as a space with especially egalitarian communication characteristics (Crawford, 2002)... To the extent that the Internet is merely the leading edge of a broader social transformation, then, Castells's 'Internet galaxy' promises to be a lopsided place.

Jurgen Habermas

In the rush to make the Net a site for the construction of a democratic utopia, the work of Jurgen Habermas on the public sphere was quickly adopted by many pro-Net utopians (Arora, 2014; Bohman, 2004; Lupton, 2014). Habermas uses the idea of public sphere to account for the rise of modernity: specifically secularism, liberalism, modern nation states, capitalism and science (Habermas, 1989, 1990). Habermas shows how the period of the Enlightenment in Europe was constructed by a gradual retreat of feudal autocracy from complete control of cultural life. In place of autocracy came bourgeois liberalism, which propagated a public communicative rationality of democratic-free discourse. This was typified by the rise of coffee shops and newspapers. The public sphere is crucial for the preservation of democracy in late modernity. Habermas fears that the rise of global capitalism, juridification and instrumental bureaucracies undermine the public sphere and the lifeworld on which it depends (Habermas, 1984, 1987). I have followed the line of Habermas' reasoning to make the related claim that leisure is being increasingly instrumentalized, thus losing its communicative nature to the forces of commodification and commercialization (Spracklen, 2009, 2011a, 2011b, 2013a, 2013b).

It might make sense to see the Net as a new form of public sphere where democracy, freedom, equality and communicative rationality are all preserved. This, after all, is the claim made by many of the theorists in this chapter. The Net is a public sphere of sorts. It is democratic. It is based on freedom of opportunity and parity of involvement. It is supposedly capable of transcending national borders, cultural prejudices and structural discrimination. It is supposedly free from state controls. But for a long time, Habermas said nothing about the Net, even as his fame and reputation globally as a critical scholar of modernity paralleled the early growth of the Net in popular culture. Some people speculated that he would one day write favourably about the Net, especially since the Net was explicitly analysed as Habermasian (Bohman, 2004; Dahlgren, 2005; Papacharissi, 2002). However, Habermas has provided a strong critique of the emancipatory, communicative nature of the Net.

His views are first published as a footnote to a longer paper (Habermas, 2006, p. 423):

> Allow me in passing a remark on the Internet that counterbalances the seeming deficits that stem from the impersonal and asymmetrical character of broadcasting by reintroducing deliberative elements in electronic communication. The Internet has certainly reactivated the grassroots of an egalitarian public of writers and readers. However, computer-mediated communication in the web can claim unequivocal democratic merits only for a special context: It can undermine the censorship of authoritarian regimes that try to control and repress public opinion. In the context of liberal regimes, the rise of millions of fragmented chat rooms across the world tend instead to lead to the fragmentation of large but politically focused mass audiences into a huge number of isolated issue publics. Within established national public spheres, the online debates of web users only promote political communication, when news groups crystallize around the focal points of the quality press, for example, national newspapers and political magazines.

For Habermas, the Net has some communicative value and potential as a genuine public sphere. He recognizes the way in which the Net can be a space where dictatorships – which operate strict regimes of control over their citizens through censorship of information – can be challenged, resisted and potentially overturned (Arora, 2014; Castells, 2012; McGillivray, 2014). He acknowledges that in some spaces on the Net there can be a true public sphere where a commons of popular opinion and culture is constructed free from instrumental interference – hence his mention of what he calls 'quality press' websites. But too much of the communication and interaction on the Net is between specific communities of interest, which are too isolated from one another to create an authentic public sphere and shared popular culture. For Habermas, the Net is ultimately a disabling device for the public sphere. It makes alienation, isolation and *anomie* easier, and encourages individuals to withdraw from political struggles and debates for the pleasure of token interactions around commodified, commercialized interests (what he calls the 'issue publics'). That is, individuals spend time on the Net talking to other individuals about music genres, books, movies, sports, genealogy and a million other hobbies and pastimes, and in doing so they fail to realize how much power they are losing to hegemonic structures (Gramsci, 1971). Even where political action is engaged in through the Net, it is restricted to particular issues and campaigns rather than a general defence of the public sphere and the lifeworld against instrumentality.

The main body of the paper referred to in the first sentence of the footnote is about the general trend to increasing instrumentality and marketization of the public sphere in the modern media. In his conclusions, Habermas (2006, p. 422) says:

> With regard to the colonization of the public sphere by market imperatives, what I have in mind here is simply the redefinition of politics in market categories ... Under the pressure of shareholders who thirst for higher revenues, it is the intrusion of the functional imperatives of the market economy into the 'internal logic' of the production and presentation of messages that leads to the covert displacement of one category of communication by another: Issues of political discourse become assimilated into and absorbed by the modes and contents of entertainment. Besides personalization, the dramatization of events, the simplification of complex matters, and the vivid polarization of conflicts promote civic privatism and a mood of antipolitics.

These are the trends and deficits in the wider electronic and broadcast media that Habermas sees equally at work in the Net. There is nothing unique about the Net. It is for Habermas another space where the instrumentality of modern capitalism shapes and restricts the ability of humans to be active, communicative agents. The Net becomes a site where the political discourse is reduced to the 'modes of entertainment', where careful analysis is replaced by the 150-character Twitter feed and the 'me too' culture of gesture politics. This is part of the general marketization of the public sphere, and ultimately the Net is a space like any other media space, where communicative rationality is replaced by the logic of the market: the ideals at the heart of the message board culture are replaced by the world of Amazon, Google and Facebook, where huge companies make profits selling advertising space and personal data to others.

Habermas' pessimism about the communicative nature of the Net is repeated in an interview he has given ('Internet and Public Sphere: What the Web Can't Do'), published online at resetdoc.org (http://www .resetdoc.org/story/00000022437). In this interview he is asked whether or not the Net is beneficial for democracy. Habermas (2014, p. 1) first replies neither, then continues:

> After the inventions of writing and printing, digital communication represents the third great innovation on the media plane. With their introduction, these three media forms have enabled an ever growing number of people to access an ever growing mass of information. These are made to be increasingly lasting, more easily. With the last step represented by Internet we are confronted with a sort of 'activation' in which readers themselves become authors. Yet, this in itself does not automatically result in progress on the level of the public sphere. Throughout the nineteenth-century – with the aid of books and mass newspapers – we witnessed the birth of national public spheres where the attention of an undefined number of people could simultaneously apply itself to the same identical problems. This however, did not depend on the technical level with which facts were multiplied, accelerated, rendered lasting. At heart, these are the same centrifugal movements that still occur today in the web. Rather, the classical public sphere stemmed from the fact that the attention of an anonymous public was 'concentrated' on a few politically important questions that had to be regulated. This is what the web does not know how to produce. On the contrary, the web actually distracts and dispels. Think about, for example, the thousand portals that are born every day: for stamp collectors, for scholars of European constitutional law, for support groups of ex-alcoholics. In the *mare magnum* of digital noises these communicative communities are like dispersed archipelagos: there are billions of them. What these communicative spaces (closed in themselves) are lacking is an inclusive bind, the inclusive force of a public sphere highlighting what things are actually important. In order to create this 'concentration', it is first necessary to know how to choose – know and comment on – relevant contributions, information and issues. In short, even in the mare magnum of digital noise, the skills of good old journalism – as necessary today as they were yesterday – should not be lost.

The Net, then, allows too many people to become authors, with no one reading and discussing the work that is published by these authors. There is no critical role played by editors and journalists in sifting through the writing and gathering that which is crucial for advancing knowledge and debate. Instead of a public sphere bounded by a limited shared set of interests and aims, there is an almost infinite space of unconnected sites, or as Habermas describes it, the 'great sea' of islands. We are all too busy talking about our stamps and our problems with alcohol – our leisure interests – to see the gaps that need to be filled if we are to save the public sphere and the lifeworld.

Conclusion

The arrival of the Net has not just had a big impact on (Western, globally Northern, globalizing) society, it has also had a big impact on social and cultural theory. In this chapter I have shown the ways in which various social and cultural theorists have engaged with the rise of the Net. For theorists writing at the end of the twentieth century, the Net was evidence of some sort of progression from or fracture with late modernity. For theorists writing in this century, there is a combination of awe and fear about the ways in which the Net might make or break a new, possibly postmodern society. All the theorists reviewed in this chapter have important contributions to make to digital sociology, or the cultural sociology of the Net, and their work has been drawn on widely across those disciplines and subject fields. In the next chapter, I want to focus on the use of Habermasian ideas to help us define and delineate digital leisure and its study.

5
A Theory of Digital Leisure

There may well be a few older scholars of leisure and culture who agree with the blunt assessment by Habermas that the Net is overrated in popular culture and over-played in contemporary academic literature. But even if we are sceptical about the significance of the Net, we cannot ignore its importance in contemporary leisure lives. We have to have a theory (or theories) of digital leisure to make sense of all this. In this chapter I develop this new theory of digital leisure using Habermas' theoretical framework of communicative and instrumental rationality, along with ideas from Castells, Urry and Bauman that have already appeared in this book. I will argue that for the users of the Net, digital leisure appears to be seamlessly communicative and liberating. Users are given the appearance of being liquid surfers, shifting their focus at the click of a mouse, sharing ideas and cultural interests with people in the global networks. However, the Net itself is a technology that is in reality a form of instrumental leisure and commodification, based on economic transactions, control and surveillance, and unequal power relations. In this respect, digital leisure is like any other leisure form. But the effect the Net has on challenging hegemonies and giving some individuals some freedoms, its unique interactivity and the speed in which digital leisure works, makes it more communicative than sports or traditional forms of popular culture.

Habermas, leisure, communicative and instrumental rationality

I have developed a theory of communicative and instrumental leisure using the work of Habermas (1984, 1987, 1989, 1990) elsewhere (see Spracklen, 2007, 2009, 2011a, 2011b, 2013a, 2013b; Spracklen and

Henderson, 2013; Spracklen, Richter and Spracklen, 2013). For readers familiar with this work, this paragraph and the next one may be ignored. For those unfamiliar with his work, these two paragraphs will serve as a necessary overview. My critical lens is underpinned by Marxist and post-Marxist theories of modernity and capitalism. Marxist political theories suggest that the age of modernity, the age that started with industrialization and urbanization, is the age in which capitalism becomes dominant in society, to the extent that capitalists become the new elites. Marxism originally predicted that capitalism would force a world revolution once the workers realized that they were being used by the capitalists. However, in the twentieth century, when capitalism became global, it seemed to be succeeding without creating world revolution. A number of radical theorists tried to explain why it had succeeded. Gramsci (1971) says modern capitalism succeeded by fooling people into thinking they were free, through the elites' complete control (hegemony) of culture. This is a very pessimistic view of society and of humanity but one that captures a truth about how modernity works, and how elites retain control of political systems. We do not see that popular culture, the media and popular forms of leisure keep us in chains.

Jurgen Habermas (1984, 1987, 1989, 1990) has taken the Gramscian idea of capitalist control and has argued that this is in the form of instrumental rationalities (reducing everything to profit or to material gain) that constrain our ability to think for ourselves. Habermas is also strongly influenced by Adorno (1947, 1967, 1991; Adorno and Horkheimer, 1992), who argued that the culture industry was a way of controlling the working classes, in the same way that the Roman elites quelled popular anger through the distribution of the dole and the arrangement of games. But Habermas, following Weber (1992, 2001), also believes that as humans we have free agency and the ability to think and act in a communicative way, that is, without restraint or control, among others who are free to do the same. This communicative rationality is the logic behind basic human interaction, the construction of the public sphere and the lifeworld, the space in which humans live freely and act freely. That, says Habermas, has been consistently undermined by another form of logic – instrumental rationality – that reduces human interactions to ratios of profit and loss, the basic ends of capitalism, and the logic of bureaucratic efficiency. In my own research and writing on leisure, I have applied these Habermasian ideas to understanding leisure, culture and sport (Spracklen, 2007, 2009, 2011, 2013a, 2013b). I have argued that leisure is a communicative act – that is, an act that is undertaken freely, often in free interaction, agreement and discussion with others. Leisure has served as a space for the maintenance of the public sphere and the lifeworld, both historically and in the age of modernity. But such communicative leisure is under threat – the space to be communicative is being reduced as the hegemonic elites take control of more and more leisure spaces and activities. So the communicative leisure of play is replaced by the instrumental leisure of professional sports, which serves both capitalism, the gender order and nationalism; or the communicative leisure of singing and playing music is replaced by the pop music industry. Leisure then is an essentially human act in its communicative nature, which is at risk of being taken over by corporate, instrumental leisure.

My theory of digital leisure extends the Habermasian framework of leisure I have previously developed. It builds on Bauman's (2000) idea of liquid modernity by noting that such liquid identities can be constructed as ways of resisting the instrumentality of commodification, but more often than not such liquid identities are a consequence of the instrumentality of modern society, as Bauman himself suggests. Digital leisure, leisure on the Net, is no different to any other leisure activity or leisure space. It is the site of resistance and challenges to hegemony, a site for the construction of communicative lifeworlds, but a site where instrumental leisure is gaining ground, colonizing those lifeworlds and replacing them with instrumental systems. Digital leisure then is potentially humanizing, life-affirming and self-actualizing, as Urry suggests (Elliott and Urry, 2011; Urry, 2007), but more often than not it is a pastime useful only to the capitalist system and the hegemonic power of the late modern nation state.

This theory of digital leisure challenges the theoretical frame in the recent work of Castells (2009, 2012). As I showed in the previous chapter, he suggests that the Net is becoming more controlled by nation states and by corporations, though he claims that they are unable to completely take over the entire Net. He has faith in the capacity of human actors who are 'Net-savvy' users to overcome the systems of control and surveillance and to find spaces in which they can resist hegemony. He believes that the Net offers endless opportunities for new social movements to keep their discussions and plans hidden, enabling them to be effective in their actions in the real world: he cites activist-organizations in the Arab Spring and in the Occupy Movement as examples of successful campaigners able to use the Net to improve their campaigning (Castells, 2012). However, while some counter-hegemonic moves are always possible, and the lifeworld's boundaries can always be pushed back by communicative action, online or offline, the Net's structure makes it difficult to resist the tide of instrumentality. To use the Net one has to pay money, sign contracts, hand over personal information, all of which binds one to a capitalist system that monitors our every move. Nation states and other hegemons are then able to track our use very simply, through various surveillance techniques. So the balance of the Net is heavily weighted towards instrumentality, though of course communicative leisure does take place in every corner of it. The consequence of this dichotomous relationship is that the Net, like the Roman God of Janus, is two-faced. That is, it is capable of being, at the same time: a space for freedom while being a space for control; a space for constructing and de-constructing identity and belonging; a space for serious leisure and a space for inconsequential leisure.

The Net is a space for freedom

As we have seen, the Net's technological and cultural history has left it with a set of moral values around fairness and freedom. The way in which the Net was initially designed as a centre-less cluster of nodes, each sharing information and passing information around the system, lends itself to arguments that the Net is designed to give parity of access and parity of control. That is, fairness is hard-wired into the Net (Mahoney and Haigh, 2011). It is claimed that each user of the Net is treated equally by the systems that make it work, and as such there is no hierarchy of use and access. This in turn has given rise to a culture propagated by early adopters of the Net of treating each other user as an equal with the right to use the Net and pass comment on things on the Net (Arora, 2014).

The ethics of fairness has continued to be built into the interactions that take place online, and into the hardware and software of the Net's structure. The structure of the Net is still designed in a way that does not privilege corporate or State users over individual users. Everyone is equal in their transactions through the Net. For the interactions that take place online, there are rules of behaviour written explicitly into the terms and conditions of some sites, which create moderators who work to ensure that interactions are civilized (polite, respectful and so on – see Arora, 2014) and everybody has the same chance to be involved in interactions. Where moderators are not employed by the creators of the website, users take it upon themselves to moderate the language and behaviour of others who use a website (Lupton, 2014). In other words, people work collectively and communicatively to decide the rules of engagement and interaction on the Net, and nearly always come up with something that replicates a Habermasian public sphere (Papacharissi, 2002) – where everybody in the public sphere is allowed to take part in discussions and decisions without the threat of attack or sanction, so long as they in turn respect the different opinions of others. Of course, in practice, many of the Net's users abuse such privileges, using chat rooms and social media to bully ('troll') others, to engage in flame wars and to be sexually and racially abusive. The fact that these attacks create outrage among other users and lead to the sharpening of sanctions does not mean that the public sphere has failed. Rather, the public sphere has used its communicative rationality to redefine who belongs in the particular space, and what happens when people use their freedom of speech to behave unfairly and unethically towards others.

The ethics of fairness is closely related to the normative ideal of freedom. The Net's early adopters believed that the Net would be a space where information and data could be accessed and used freely by anyone (Mahoney and Haigh, 2011). There was a culture that drew heavily on American law to argue that users of the Net had complete freedom of speech, which led to arguments that the Net allowed users to freely access whatever they liked, even if that thing broke copyright laws or laws against pornography, for example (Drushel and German, 2011). As well as being able to say what they liked, to access what they liked and to explore what they liked, users were also allowed to hide behind pseudonyms and avatars that gave them anonymity. This was connected to the radical utopianism of the Net: users argued that they did not want others to know who they were because they might be accessing the Net from countries with strict laws of morality or strong and limiting censorship controls (Arora, 2014). But anonymity also gave others the freedom to do things away from the gaze of their families, their work colleagues and their local communities. Again, this was Habermasian communicative rationality at work: the understanding of freedom that allowed anonymity along with freedom of access and freedom of speech was developed by the public sphere of Net users in the 1980s and 1990s (Papacharissi, 2002).

The Net is still a space where such freedoms are valued and defended. Anonymity is still valued by many users of the Net. Anonymity is not just about being able to troll on a chat forum, it is also about not having one's personal use of the Net being made public. The argument that only the guilty have something to hide is of course an egregious one. Yes, we all have something to hide, but often that something is quite innocuous – we should all have the freedom to have private lives. This is a mark of communicative rationality at work, the ability to distinguish between public and private spheres, recognizing that we play a number of roles in our lives that do not necessarily all need to connect: for example, being a manager in an office, a mother, a human with a range of private interests and friends. Anonymity is under threat: the opportunities to be anonymous are shrinking with the rise of corporate-controlled social media such as Google, and State monitoring of information (metadata) on a wholesale basis. That so many users of the Net object to these attacks on anonymity is evidence that such anonymity is valued in the public sphere.

Freedom of speech and freedom of access are also still important aspects of the Net's public sphere, still part of the communicative discourse that shapes polices about how the Net is developed. Net users want to be able to access all parts of the Net, and do not like being told by governments and corporations that they are not allowed to access parts of the Net that might be 'bad' in some way. Limit the ability to access pornography, the argument for freedom of access goes, and the next thing to be limited will be access to radical politics, then scientific knowledge (Kim and Douai, 2012). Similarly, freedom of speech is still seen as a given in the public sphere of the Net, even where it conflicts with the ethic of fairness. The default position is still that individuals should be allowed to say what they want, and users should be allowed to access and post what they want. This default position is being strongly challenged, and some ground has been lost on absolute freedom through communicative discourse – people have agreed through discussion to sanction trolls and the circulation and downloading of certain forms of pornography, for example (Arora, 2014). But absolute freedom is also under threat from the growing importance of Habermasian instrumental controls on the Net.

The Net is a space for control

The Net owes its origins to the American military, and the Habermasian instrumentality behind the Cold War. The supposed threat of Soviet nuclear bombs wiping out the command centres of the United States led the Americans to investigate ways in which information could be distributed across a network, so that the destruction of one site would not mean the loss of the information (Mahoney and Haigh, 2011). At the same time as the military was developing the Net and connecting up its primitive databases and computers, the rush to build nuclear missiles that hit their targets and did not blow up accidentally led to an increase in funding for solid-state circuitry research. The American government contracted laboratories in universities and in the private sector to explore new technologies with a military application, and corporations contracted with the government to develop patented and profit-making products (Nowak, 2010). So the Net emerged out of a neat confluence of two forms of instrumentality: the paranoid logic of ultra-competitive international conflict and hegemonic control; and the cold logic of capitalism. At the heart of this development were free-thinking scientists and engineers, taking part in the communicative discourse of submitting papers to conferences and journals that claimed to create new knowledge, getting published and challenging the work of others. But the big science of post-war America was funded by the military–industrial complex (first named by President Eisenhower in 1960 – see Ledbetter, 2011), and the aims and objectives of big science were dictated by the demands of the military–industrial complex: be able to destroy the Soviet Union, be able to keep track of people and agencies working against the West and be able to make profits (Fuller, 2000, 2012). While the Net branched out of big science to become something owned collectively and communicatively by its early adopters, it retained its links to both capitalist industry and America's security agencies (Fuchs, 2010; Nowak, 2010).

As the Communist threat to the West receded at the end of the twentieth century, some political theorists such as Francis Fukuyama argued that the world was coming to the end of global conflict and the politics of history: the West had won, and Western values were in ascendancy (Fukuyama, 2006). The Net was seen as a harbinger for this end of history, as it spread across the globe, taking with it Western liberal democracy, individualism and ethics (Castells, 1996). But the Net remains a space for Western hegemonic control (Gramsci, 1971), where capitalism is normalized and Western nation states routinely keep watch on the activities of their own citizens. Furthermore, it is a space where citizens keep watch on each other's activities, as the communicative rationality of the public sphere is replaced by the instrumental rationality of Foucault's (1991) governmentality.

The Net is a space for the capitalist control of everyday leisure. The anarchism of the bulletin boards and newsgroups has been replaced by marketing strategies, advertising algorithms and the ubiquity of payments for access. The Net was always capitalist in its design, and personal use was always mediated through subscriptions to ISPs. But the extent of capitalism's instrumental control of the Net has grown massively in the first years of the twenty-first century (Arora, 2014; Fuchs, 2010; Lupton, 2014; McChesney, 2014; Ritzer and Jurgenson,

2010). Most popular websites require subscriptions to join them – these are either taken in cash or free, providing users allow the owners of the websites to bombard them with adverts and exploit their personal data for profit. The Net's individual website designers have been largely replaced by transnational corporations: the bulk of the traffic on the Net is dominated by companies that shelter in tax havens and which have an inordinate amount of influence on legislators in nation states and beyond. The communicative leisure of surfing the Net has been replaced by the purchase of apps, pieces of software that limit the potential of exploring and learning to carefully screened pleasures. The Net has become a space for consumption. Shops are closing down in towns and cities across the world as people buy everything online (Harvey, 2011; Satterthwaite, 2001). Even where users are downloading content for free and breaking copyright laws, they are still consuming the content instrumentally – users download pop music and Hollywood movies, not work that has a higher aesthetic quality (Adorno, 1991). In other words, they have taken on board the instrumental messages of capitalism.

The Net is increasingly a space where governments have the power to control what we access, who we interact with and how we interact with them. Since the end of Communism new enemies of the State and right-thinking society have appeared in the West: so-called Islamic terrorists and extremists, and paedophiles (Lumby and Funnell, 2011). While most people might agree such terrorism and abusive behaviour is beyond the pale of the public sphere, the existence of these enemies has led to legislation and permissions for government agents to investigate activity on the Net and to invade the privacy of individuals (Fuchs, 2013). The state of permanent fear about these folk devils leads the State to assume people suspected of being a terrorist or a paedophile are lesser human beings, with no right to be treated fairly like any other citizen. Furthermore, nation states have easily expanded their searches for deviants and enemies online to include legitimate radicals and dissenters. The power granted in the search for terrorists is extended to others who pose a 'threat', then the argument is made that is better just to look at everything, because most people are up to no good – the State quietly intercepts and searches through everybody's data. This is a reality in many countries such as Iran and China, but the West is no lover of freedom: the WikiLeaks affair and the revelations by Edward Snowden show that the United States is routinely sifting through everybody's metadata in the search for 'terrorists' (ibid.). We are now living with a Net that is so under surveillance that we have taken to inspecting other people's messages, and our own, to see if we are doing things that might make us suspects in the dark corridors of secret State power. We have become complicit in our own governmentality, allowing the instrumentality of totalitarianism to make us into the members of the Party in Orwell's 1984: publicly smiling for the spies and the cameras, secretly in fear of saying the wrong word.

The Net is a space for constructing identity and belonging

The Net is clearly a space where people can find community and belonging, and construct their social identity. The Net has become a key leisure space at a time when the economic consequences of post-industrialization are changing the way in which people in the West construct identity and belonging. Following Bauman (2000) and Urry (2007), it can be argued that traditional social structures such as class, and traditional spaces of identity such as work have changed dramatically. People no longer identify with a job as they move through a number of jobs in a short period of life. People no longer identify closely with their class or a particular locality, as moving through those jobs makes them move location and move between classes (Elliott and Urry, 2011; Giddens, 1991). As such, communicative leisure becomes one of the spaces left in the lifeworld where it becomes possible to construct identity and belonging, to feel part of a community of like-minded individuals. This value of communicative leisure has always been present, and this is why people do all sorts of wonderful and strange things in their leisure lives. The Net has conveniently made identity-making in communicative leisure much easier and much more accessible for many people in the West (and beyond), precisely at a time when other ways of making identity are being subsumed by the instrumentality of Weberian rationality and the neo-liberal workplace flexibility of late modernity (Habermas, 1990, 1998, 2000, 2008; Ritzer, 2004).

This communicative identity-work on the Net is obviously associated with the early development of its communal ethics (Arora, 2014; Lupton, 2014). In signing up to the early Net, users found both a sense of symbolic and imaginary community among other users, and a space where they could pursue more tightly knit communities of ritual and belonging. To be a user of the Net was to be someone who aligned themselves with its ethics of fairness and democracy, its utopian beliefs and its suspicion of anyone who tried to limit the freedoms of the Net (Castells, 1996, 2000). There was a strong sense of belonging to a community of other Net-savvy, tech-savvy users, which transcended national boundaries and other social structures. Alongside this sense of Net-community came opportunities to form communities of interest around particular bulletin boards, newsgroups and websites: communities that shared political opinions, tastes in music and clothes, sports or comics or movies and so on (Lupton, 2014). For many users of the Net, this had and still has a profound comforting effect on them. It is still one of the communicative strengths of the Net that it allows people with some otherwise marginal, excluded or unfashionable interest to find each other and talk to each other: whether they are secularists in a profoundly religious society, or psychobilly fans in a town where no other psychobilly lives, or enthusiasts for green living. This community-making is strong and long-lasting and as felt and as legitimate as any kind of community-making in the real world. Even if the actual structures of the Net change (such as the decline of message boards and chat forums), there will still be that communicative leisure act of finding community and belonging through connecting with similar others. The growth of alternative music scenes such as heavy metal worldwide is an example of how the Net has created a sense of community and identity that is realized in this communicative discourse online (Spracklen, 2013b, 2014). The recent expansion of rugby league globally is attributable to fans in countries marginal to the 'homelands' of England and Australia (such as Brazil, Greece and Canada) being able to find each other on the Net. They can then access videos about the sport to show to people in their own countries, who then become fans and ultimately players.

Identity-making is also at work communicatively around gender and sexuality on the Net. Despite the criticisms of Turkle's (1995) work, the Net is a space where women can find belonging and safe third space for exploring their own identities (Consalvo and Paasonen, 2002; Harcourt, 1999; Paasonen, 2005; White, 2006). Women in strongly patriarchal societies can bypass the restrictions that exist in the real world and engage in conversations with women and men online under the security of (relative) anonymity. They can be free to do whatever communicative leisure they prefer. They can discover the work of feminists and liberal democrats more easily, and use these to shape their political struggles for equality. In societies that are not so strongly patriarchal the Net is still a space for women to take control of their lives and form bases to critique hegemonic masculinity, whether through the practice of taking control of one's leisure or engaging in campaigns against sexism and inequality (Harcourt, 1999). Men can learn that hegemonic masculinity exists and can engage with others on the Net about how best to fight it (White, 2006).

For many users, the Net is a key space in their exploration of their own sexuality and the sexuality of others (Holland, 2008). The early communal ethics of the Net respected difference and diversity, and this has continued to shape the way in which non-heterosexual individuals have found a collective voice on the Net. The Net has been crucial in shaping the political struggle against homophobia and for gay rights, providing a place to share information on how to win policy and legal battles in countries around the world (Nip, 2004; Rak, 2005). The Net has been a key resource in giving gays, lesbians, trans and others a space where they can be who they are without facing abuse. It has been a communicative leisure space where they have learned how to belong and identify with others with similar sexualities, a space where they have bonded and played and talked. In a similar manner, the Net has given people with disabilities a platform to be educated about policies and discrimination, a space to meet other people with disabilities to chat and relax, and a tool for organizing campaigns battling to make nation states pass laws that reduce their exclusion from society (Thoreau, 2006). All marginalized groups can find shared community and belonging online, and use those online spaces to engage in informal, pleasurable leisure and play, or to organize and fight for freedoms in the real world.

The Net is a space for de-constructing identity and belonging

While it is true that the Net serves a space for constructing powerful, counter-hegemonic, alternative identities, and is a space for building inclusive communities, any theory of digital leisure has to take into account the evidence that the Net serves to reify and normalize existing social structures and hegemonies. Rather than create a sense of communicative belonging, the Net acts as an agent of instrumental forms of socialization and individuation. That is, hegemonic forms of belonging and identity are imposed on others, supressing difference and diversity, and marginalizing subaltern and alternative social identities (Adorno, 1991; Gramsci, 1971; Habermas, 1987). Where alternative forms of identity and community are not wiped out altogether by the homogenization of the Net, they are transformed into neo-liberal lifestyle choices. Alternative cultures become alternative patterns of consumption and play, with the political edge of the cultures smoothed out in Disneyfication of their practices (Bryman, 2004; Spracklen, 2014). Individuals are socialized into systems of instrumentality and systems of control, not a lifeworld of human endeavour. The instrumental leisure that the Net has become makes all forms of community shallow, the products of economic exchanges, available to those who can afford to pay to be involved. The homogenization of culture, community and identity on the Net, then, is a harbinger of increasing individuation, alienation and *ennui*. Instead of finding community and belonging that is fulfilling, individuals find only transience and trend-following. People flip from one trending form of social media to another, desperately trying to prove they are cool and they belong by joining in the instrumental logic of having more likes or followers or friends than anyone else. In this sense, identity and belonging have become de-constructed, the connection between them and feelings of satisfaction and pleasure fractured by the stress of keeping up with the symbolic market (Fuchs and Dyer-Witheford, 2013; Žižek, 2010). There is no social identity on the Net, no belonging, but there is a chimera of belonging that people chase, hoping to find true community.

On the Net, the gender order is maintained and perpetuated through the toxic nature of trolling, and the normalization of sexual abuse and heteronormative pornography (Nowak, 2010). Rather than transcending heteronormativity, the Net acts as a space for the reification of hegemonic masculinity (White, 2006). In this leisure space, the interests of heterosexual men are normalized partly as a result of the history of the Net, but also as a result of the commercialization and commodification of the Net. In the vast reach of social media, men and boys roam without fear, acting out heterosexual male roles and fantasies, dismissing other forms of masculine behaviour as being 'gay'. The male gaze insists on limiting women and girls to approved roles – as objects of male sexual desire and as objects of male judgement and abuse where they do not play the game of potential sexual conquest.

Marginalization of difference is effected by the ways in which the norms of globally Northern or Western, middle-class culture are imposed on the interactions of others (Ritzer, 2004; Spracklen, 2011a, 2013a). English becomes a default language of interaction, making it difficult for those not able to use that language fluently to be taken seriously. Rather than a global intercultural exchange, the Net becomes a way of imposing American English and American popular culture on the rest. Trivially, this might be seen in the way the word 'gotten' is now used by users of the Net who live in England – so much of the Net is made by Americans that even the creators and users of the Queen's English have succumbed to the American usage. More seriously, this Americanization is the process identified by Stuart Hall at the end of the twentieth century (Hall, 1993), which has only accelerated with the growth of the

Net as an everyday leisure space. It is a process of cultural hegemony, made more difficult to resist by the attractiveness of the Net to aspiring Western-oriented urban elites in many countries (Rankin, Ergin and Gökşen, 2014; Szablewicz, 2010). Such elites have always wanted to buy American movies, clothes, food and drink. Now the Net has made it possible to get all these things and more. While these elites show off their knowledge of American television and hamburgers, others in their countries cannot explore the Net at all: they are too poor, too isolated from the technologies that allow Net use, or are unable or unwilling to learn English to a Net-proficient level.

The gap between the Net-haves and the Net-have-nots is a natural progression from the commodification and commercialization of the Net. Because of its American roots, the Net is an unfettered, unregulated free market. This means that anyone can enter the market and establish an ISP or an online retail website. But the reality of global capitalism is that large corporations have the ability to buy out or undersell their competitors (Ritzer, 2004). The free market does not actually work as a free market. Smaller capitalist ventures invariably disappear, to be replaced by a handful of transnational corporations, and quite often the market shrinks to a monopoly. The Net has demonstrated this logic and trend, and now the big transnational corporations dominate social media, retail, access to the Net and the hardware used to access it. The Net might have its anarchists, radials and file-sharers, but these are increasingly marginalized by big corporations looking to make profits from people's digital leisure. Instead of belonging to a community that shares files and interactions, increasingly the Net citizen is individuated, a model consumer purchasing products from Amazon or streaming movies from a legal, subscription-based source. The capitalist system has fought back and taken control of the Net, turning its potential for inclusion and identity-making upside down. Instead of finding community and belonging, individuals pay to belong to exclusive clubs. There is an insidious form of cultural capital at work, turning people into commodities themselves. The idea of the Net-community has become extinguished by the massification of the Net. Individuals who check their Twitter accounts do not stop to engage in meaningful conversations, nor do they abide by the communal ethics of the early Net. The decline in chat rooms and message boards indicates that even communities of interest are being de-constructed, as people give up talking freely to each other to buy things and advertise their instrumental desires (through liking bands, brands and movies and television programmes on their social media pages).

The Net is serious leisure

A large proportion of the Net has been constructed and maintained by individuals in their free time, after they have finished the paid employment that gives them money to pay their bills. This unpaid effort is not just the work of web-designers and programmers using their special skills and knowledge altruistically; it is also evidenced in the work of moderators in chat rooms and message boards. This is an example of what Robert Stebbins (for example see 1982, 2009) refers to as 'Serious Leisure', which undermines some of the assumptions about leisure, non-work and free time made by other leisure theorists. Rather than establishing clear lines of division between the world of work and the world of leisure, the concept of serious leisure suggests that for some activities and in some spaces, leisure becomes something like work, even if it is not paid work. According to Stebbins, there are two types of leisure: casual and serious (as well as project-based leisure, which does not concern us here). The former is individualistic, frivolous, and often short in duration – watching a television programme, for example. The latter – serious leisure – is typified by individuals dedicating so much time and effort to their chosen leisure activity that it resembles work. College-level athletes are an obvious example of individuals doing a serious leisure activity: their lives are restricted by the rules of training and diet regimens, they spend long hours in the gym and they do this for the brief moment of playing sport. So, increasingly, says Stebbins, leisure resembles work because of the dedication needed to be serious about a leisure activity (any sustained, long-term leisure activity, that is).

The obvious way in which the Net is serious leisure is the ubiquity and use of email (Orlikowski, 2007). In the middle of the twentieth century it was possible to be contacted by one's boss or bank by phone or by telegram. However, email has become so mundane that the line between work emails and personal emails has been lost completely. People use their work email systems for personal communications. This means that many people do their leisure during office hours in their workplaces. But it also means workers respond to work emails during evenings and weekends. Managing an electronic in-box is the premier serious leisure activity of our age. Everywhere, at all times, and in every place where there are devices allowing access to the Net, there are victims of the post-industrial, neo-liberal global order checking in to their workplaces, deleting spam, deleting messages from corporate centres, responding frantically to line managers, reading jokes sent by colleagues, checking spreadsheets sent at four o'clock in the morning, writing messages to mothers and fathers and daughters and sons and lovers (Elliott and Urry, 2011; Orlikowski, 2007). Every email, even those that are deleted, needs to be assessed for its importance and ranked in order of priority. Every response brings more responses, especially those that are part of group exchanges.

People dedicate their free time to making the Net work efficiently. Some of this effort is for their own personal gain – designing one's own website promoting some kind of business or service – but a significant element of such activity is for the benefit of others who use the web. There are people involved in designing and sharing freeware (Arora, 2014). There are people who upload gaming programmes, who share files, who maintain databases filled with all kinds of things. There are those who contribute to Wikipedia and other user-generated content, developing expertise in editorial and fact-checking, as well as supplying specialist knowledge of the subjects of the content. There are those who engage in revealing hacks and spreading malware, spending hours of their leisure time toiling away to break codes and find short cuts into secure systems. There are people volunteering to develop websites for community associations, sports clubs and other communities of interest. Moderating is a significant form of serious leisure, as already mentioned. While some moderating work is undertaken by paid employees (for instance, where the moderation is taking place on some commercial social media platform), the moderators in chat rooms are essentially people willing to act as referees and censors, balancing the commitment to allow people to take part and have a voice with the imperative to ensure discussions are polite and within the remit of the Net's communal ethics. For these people the work can be very stressful, but the ones who maintain the roles do so because they believe strongly in the *voluntaristic* ethic. They believe in giving something back to the community of interest – their time and their effort – as it makes other people's lives better, though there may be more selfish reasons (self-promotion, power and control) underpinning their decisions to become moderators.

Digital leisure as serious leisure is found in the way individuals use social media sites such as Facebook and Twitter. Keeping up with these sites is not a trivial matter. Users feel the need to check in frequently and regularly, to make sure they are not missing out on updates, messages and photographs posted by others (Fuchs and Dyer-Witheford, 2013). Even where technological developments allow automatic updates to come through to users, they still need to follow the link through to be able to engage. But once users are on social media, they find hundreds of updates and discussions. The result is that social media becomes a leisure space that demands significant time and energy to work through. Users need to keep track of what their closest friends and family are doing, while making sure they do not give too much of their own private selves away to those who do not need to know such things. Social media gives users multiple stages and multiple public and semi-public roles to perform (Goffman, 1971). Knowing what to post, who to allow the post to be seen by and what replies and comments are necessary demands a great deal of self-control and careful analysis of the rapidly shifting social media space. We work hard at maintaining our virtual presence and our status. This is all the work of serious leisure, so much so that for some people using social media becomes a traumatic chore to be avoided.

The Net is inconsequential leisure

If the serious leisure of the Net has evolved from its communicative roots to become a product of the instrumentality of modern neo-liberal economies, this shift has also changed the way in which we might think of digital leisure as inconsequential leisure. Ken Roberts (2011, p. 8) defines inconsequential leisure as follows:

> Leisure scholars have been close to unanimous...that leisure behaviour is at least relatively freely chosen...this is possible because the particular ways in which people choose to spend their leisure time and money are relatively inconsequential, often for the individuals themselves and even more so for their wider societies (beyond the actors' personal social networks). The 'relatively' in freely choosing is in contrast to how most people's behaviour is controlled while they are at work, and relatively inconsequential is in comparison with decisions such as whether to take or to resign from a job, to quit or to continue in education, to marry or to divorce, and whether or not to become a parent...Modern leisure is typically separated from the rest of our lives by some combination of place, time or activity.

Individuals do the things they do in their free time because they have a 'relatively' free choice, and choose the things that give them pleasure, satisfaction, community, friendship and other forms of self-actualization. There are a whole host of caveats in the word 'relatively' – there are the usual constraints that limit that free choice due to social structures, orders and hegemonies. But Roberts is right to recognize this basic human impulse. Everybody wants to do things that have no or little significance in their free time, everybody wants to relax and enjoy the gentle thrill of not doing something very important. Inconsequential leisure, then, can be seen as something that is operating through Habermas' communicative rationality (Habermas, 1984). The Net might be defined as an inconsequential leisure playground. Here users can be Huizinga's *homo ludens*, finding pleasure in play away from the stresses of family, community, work and society (Huizinga, 2003; Sicart, 2014; Spracklen, 2011a). The Net provides spaces where one can read idle gossip, watch videos and television programmes, catch up with old friends and unwind through engaging in ludic activities.

In the early years of the Net, such inconsequential leisure was typified by the growth of gaming. From basic chess simulators to multi-user dungeons, the early ludic activities on the Net served as inconsequential respite for workers in the IT industries and in academic laboratories. Chat rooms became ways of meeting new people without having to go through the hard work of going out to bars or restaurants. As the Net expanded and more people became users, the metaphor of surfing became an apt one to denote the inconsequential nature of the activity. Once people could access the Net, where did they go? First of all they followed the advice of friends and journalists writing features about the Net, and typed in the names of the websites that had enticed them to sign up. Then they followed the hyperlinks from those websites to other sites, exploring for themselves the seemingly incredible, seemingly infinite extent of virtuality. The early users of the World Wide Web truly surfed the hyperlinks, following references and finding whole new websites with a whole new set of references and hyperlinks. This inconsequential browsing was fun for some users, but others struggled to find their way around the Net – so search engines such as Alta Vista and Yahoo ultimately emerged to organize the Net and allow people to find things they wanted to look at without having to guess the URL or flick through a dozen hyperlinks. These search engines did not reduce the inconsequential nature of browsing, but they eliminated the directionless nature of surfing. Search engines allowed people to find sites more swiftly, to satiate their search for some pleasure, some knowledge or some other inconsequential diversion.

As the Net has become more commercialized and colonized by instrumentality, it has remained a space for inconsequential leisure – but the kind of inconsequential leisure on offer has become more marketized. Browsing idly through social media might seem communicative in nature, but the systems are designed to trick us into conspicuous consumption or to fool us into being dupes for corporations selling advertising space (Langford, 200; Lupton, 2014). When we click to like or follow something we are giving those corporations important information about our tastes and habits. When we browse a page, that action is noted and retained in databases that allow corporations and governments to track us. For the corporations that have marketized the Net, our inconsequential leisure habits are easy to identify and easy to transform into instrumental leisure. Users who might say they like a particular craft beer might find themselves inundated with adverts and emails for other beers, for beer festivals and other forms of beer tourism. Users who read a news report about baseball will be forever deluged in suggestions for gambling sites, ticketing sites and auction houses that deal in baseball memorabilia. The entertainment industry has managed to colonize the Net to such an extent that people who post videos online of bands playing gigs can easily find themselves facing threatening messages from corporations telling the posters they are going to be sued for breach of copyright (Muir, 2013). Users who write fan-fiction about popular Hollywood movies, or who run fan-sites about those movies, are quite often confronted by the same threatening messages (Schwabach, 2011). And websites are becoming increasingly more all-encompassing, keeping users on them and reducing the number of links to other sites that might be owned by rival corporations or by non-commercial organizations – so the notion of a network of interconnected hyperlinks is being lost. That does not mean that the Net has stopped being a playground, a space for fun and diversion. The spread of new technologies makes this aspect of the Net more prevalent, and more widespread around the world. More and more people have the money and the resources to access the Net for inconsequential pleasure and leisure. But this just means more people are paying subscriptions, and more corporations are trying to make profits. Inconsequential it might still be, but digital leisure is more instrumental than communicative.

Conclusion

The Net is just another leisure space

Throughout history there has been a tension between people who want to relax and have communicative pleasure and leisure, and those who would seek to limit or stop those leisure activities. In Classical Rome, the Emperor Marcus Aurelius despaired of the depravity and lack of moderation in his senatorial elite, and others in the elite such as Seneca were dismissive of the leisure lives of the people of Rome. It was feared that the anarchy of communicative leisure would lead to insurrection, so successive consuls and emperors put on carefully managed entertainment to distract the people (Spracklen, 2011a). In Christendom and in the various empires of Islam, ruling elites ensured that the leisure lives of their subjects were controlled through religious edicts and diversions (Cameron, 1976; Hourani, 2005). In medieval England, kings concerned themselves with banning football and other communicative pastimes and encouraged young men to learn archery so they could be soldiers (Holt, 1989). In the Reformation in Europe, various protestant churches became so fearful of the leisure lives of the masses that they banned sports, drinking, fairs and festivals where people had a chance to have fun and engage in free, communicative discourse with one another (Borsay, 2005). Leisure spaces have always been contested between two Habermasian rationalities (Spracklen, 2011a). In the age of modernity that started somewhere in the nineteenth century and in which we still live, this contestation has continued, with instrumental rationality gaining the upper hand as wider society becomes completely rationalized, with leisure remaining one of the few areas of life where the onslaught of instrumentality can still be resisted.

Some theorists (as I have shown earlier in this book) have argued that the Net is somehow unique, either a space where all the evils of modernity are magnified, or a space that will bring about a utopia of freedom of speech, freedom of thought and freedom from control. There is no doubt that the technology of the Net has speeded up the ways in which people make connections, find things out and find pleasure. There is no doubt people are more aware of what is happening in the world, and feel less bounded by national cultures and traditional media, because of the rise of the Net. There is no doubt that the Net has given nation states and corporations more power and control over citizens. But these real effects of the Net should not lead us to suspend our critical judgement about its normality as a leisure space and its use as a leisure activity. The Net is no better or worse than other forms of leisure. It is interesting now because it is a leisure space that is being used by millions of people around the world, and academics, politicians and journalists are making all kinds of claims about its impact on humans and society. It is perceivable that the Net will continue to be as important in people's leisure lives over the next thousand years, in the same way that drinking beer has remained a popular leisure activity in Europe over a similar time in the past. It is also possible to perceive a future where the Net is something that no one does in their leisure life, a future where looking back the Net looks barbaric, or stupid, or petty, as gladiatorial games look to us.

The Net is nothing special or unique; it is just another leisure space where people try to do things communicatively, under the constraints and increasing pressure of instrumentality. Compare the Net with something like modern sports. At their most communicative, sports are forms of physical activity that people do freely, without any form of compulsion, and with few if any rules: people choose to run, or swim, alone or with others. This activity is clearly valuable for those who choose to do it. But, since the nineteenth century, sports have become codified, governed by institutions and rule books. They have become professional, and turned into a global industry. People do not play sport – they pay to watch other people play sport. This is an instrumental turn that has change the way people think about sport, and made sport more about nationalism and control and profit than anything communicative (Spracklen, 2015). The Net has not been around as long as sports, but it has seen the same trends changing the way it is used as leisure space. It was claimed in the early years of the Net that it would be a utopian, life-transforming, communicative leisure space, and many people found such strong forms of communicative identity and community online. There are still ways in which the Net can be used as a space for a whole range of communicative actions. But that communicative potential, the potential for the Net to be a true public sphere, a secure place for the construction of the lifeworld, is severely limited by the rapid instrumentalization of the Net.

6
Identity-Making and Social Media

Leisure spaces are key sites for the production of belonging and identity. As just another leisure space, the Net is obviously a significant site for such leisure work in contemporary society. Digital leisure, like other forms of leisure, provides both a communicatively rational way of interacting, and a space for the instrumentalization of such interactions. At the moment, I have taken to reading blogs analysing polling data ahead of the next General Election in the United Kingdom. I am interested in the way these blogs make slightly different forecasts based on their models, and the way in which members and supporters of different political parties choose to argue for or against certain results. One of the blogs, politicalbetting.com, is interesting for leisure studies because the blogger is helping people make sense of the elections odds on the gambling market. The blogger wants people to see the strength or weakness of particular polls so they can make sense of the chances of political leaders and parties gaining success, so the readers of the blog can then make the right (most successful) bets. I do not intend to bet, but I am curious about the service provided by the blogger and the rational debates that take place below the line (contrary to the expected stereotype).

This chapter explores the emergence and importance of social media and online social networks in everyday leisure time and leisure practices. I will look at the ways in which social networks are used to build a sense of community and belonging, and the ways in which social networks serve as Goffmanesque public spaces in which people perform acceptable social identities (Goffman, 1971). I will trace how the Net has become a social network and communicative leisure space in more general terms away from the branded and commodified sites such as Facebook. I will show that fans of sports, music and other forms of popular culture can use the Net to discuss their private obsessions with other fans. But I will show that the Net can also be a place where social activism can be supported, where politics can move from the online to the offline to build effective protests and campaigns. While this development is a boon to radical activists on the left, it is also something that can be and is utilized by activists on the far right. Hence, the communicative freedom of the Net, as I will show, is prone to producing climate-change deniers as much as anti-fascists.

Continuities of belonging and identity

People have always found a sense of community and belonging through social networks. Historically, social networks were organized around families, localities, tribes, workplaces, faith groups and, in modernity, the nation state. All of these forms of community and belonging are imagined and imaginary: that is, they are organized around a past that is imagined or constructed from myths of belonging and exclusion; and the symbolic boundaries that define the community are the result of social psychological processes that are imaginary. Cohen (1985) suggests that the imaginary community may be contingent with particular localities, but whose membership is bound only by symbolic boundaries, tacit knowledge and shared meanings. People make sense of what they observe from their own point of view, hence any interaction between people involves an exchange of symbols to enable one set of interpretations to be understood by the other members of the interaction. Thus, the imaginary community becomes a place for the transaction of meaning, and access is achieved through an understanding of these meanings. One can see that the concept of the imaginary community describes a multilayered member group, with symbolic boundaries closing off inner levels. A suitable analogy would be an onion, with each onion skin being a symbolic boundary, allowing membership of the imaginary community at a number of levels. However, because the boundaries are created by the users, one can also have tension as meaning and symbols are contested and defined: thus, the imaginary community gives us a dynamic picture of agency and structure.

The invented tradition theory of Hobsbawm and Ranger (1983) treats history as a narrative created in the present which looks backwards. In looking backwards, a story is told that justifies ideologies in the present, which does not necessarily relate to actual events and experiences of the past. One can see that Anderson's (1983) concept of the imagined community of the nation shares this idea of the use of the past in creating and justifying the present, though instead of ideology or personal identity, the imagined community defines a nation. This idea of inventing or imagining the past has understandably come under criticism from a number of directions. Following the work of Wilson and Ashplant (1988), this selection process can be seen to be biased by the interests of the present ideology. And following Baudrillard (1988) it can be argued that the pre-existing experiences and the invented experiences become conflated and impossible to distinguish from one another, that 'history [has become] instantaneous media memory without a past' (Baudrillard, 1988, p. 22): so the real experiences, while they may have happened, are indistinguishable from the invented tradition. We need to be concerned with the historical discourses in the present, and how they are used to create boundaries and cultural icons.

A more trenchant critique of Hobsbawm has come from Anthony Smith (1993), who argues that traditions and their role in defining nationhood cannot be described as inventions, and fabrication and manipulation are not the primary means through which the (re)construction of tradition takes place. As he suggests, 'traditions, myths, history and symbols must all grow out of the existing, living memories and beliefs of [people] ... their popular resonance will be greater the more continuous with the living past they are shown to be' (Smith, 1993, p. 16). This dismissal of the imagining and its role in defining community is also expressed in criticisms of Anderson. In particular, there is concern that nations and nationalisms are more than just a psychological invention. In response, I would argue that although the discourse uses terms such as 'invention', 'imagined' and 'imaginary', this does not imply that the external is dismissed in place of a community or historical story that someone just made up in their head while sitting in front of a fire. What Hobsbawm, Anderson and Cohen are saying is that discourse, symbols, perceived realities, shared understandings and hegemonic ideologies are far more persuasive in both defining history and identity – what actually happened and who we actually are become meaningless questions because we cannot answer them without recourse to these imaginings. Secondly, by speaking of imagination, we are not saying these ideas and perceptions are wrong or false. Rather, for the people doing the imagining, it is the reality they use to shape their everyday life (Cohen, 1985).

In these social networks, leisure has played a key role in shaping the imaginary and imaginary community. Leisure is one of the ways in which social networks become performative spaces. For Goffman (1971) and the symbolic-interactionists, all human meaning and action has to be interpreted to be understood. These interpretations include the meaning given to symbols as well as our motives. Goffman describes a world where our interactions with others are not necessarily authentic; in other words, we 'role play' situations conforming to societal roles expected of us. A shared social reality therefore exists, and the social construction of reality and identity could be said to take place. Which sports we like and play, which foods we eat, what we drink, the books and films and music we like, all of these leisure forms provide uniforms for our performance of certain identity-making roles. If one is to be seen as belonging in a social network, one must dress the part and act the part, and do the correct leisure.

This notion of performativity in social networks is similar to the notion of 'webs of significance' theorized by Geertz (1973). These webs are spun by human actors searching for meaning and belonging. These webs create social identity, and are predicated on interactions with others. These webs of significance are public spaces, where our performance of the right sort of identity allows us to join the imaginary community. Social networks are spaces that allow this Goffmanesque identity work to take place. Everybody in a given social network will be performing the role they think gives them the correct social identity, the right form of belonging. To be seen as an authentic member of the Western middle classes, for example, one might promulgate in the social network of the workplace an interest in fine wine and classical music; one might show one's colleagues that one drives a car that has the right status, and one might engage them in conversation about a typically middle-class sport such as rugby union (Spracklen, 2013a). At every stage of the performance of middle-class identity, one looks at the others in the social networks to gauge how much they accept the performance. In social networks, there is always interaction between people in the network. Sometimes the arbiters of belonging have control of many layers of symbolic boundaries, and they allow people to have partial access to the community (who belongs in an extreme music scene, where belonging is only achieved by those who can demonstrate they have undertaken a long pilgrimage – see Lucas, Deeks and Spracklen, 2011); at other times, belonging is easily achieved through the right ritual and uniform (watching a soccer match in the pub). Where this interaction is not communicative, the webs of significance appear like the histories mentioned by Marx (1963): we make our own destinies, but our histories are not of our choosing. So we have to perform the right roles to be accepted into the imagined, imaginary community, but sometimes it is impossible for us to do so because we are ostracized by our gender or class or some other social structure. This identity work has always taken place in social networks, and leisure has always played a key role as a prop in the performance. As we have entered late modernity, the Net is just another leisure space where social networking and performativity operate.

The Net, social media and the example of Facebook

The Net has become dominated by social media in the 2000s and the 2010s. The first social media website that became globally prominent in the 2000s, MySpace, allows individual users to build their own pages and connect with friends. When it was first set up it allowed bands to create pages that shared music and videos, and it allowed fans to follow their favourite bands (Tripp and Herr-Stephenson, 2009; Wilkinson and Thelwall, 2010). MySpace grew so big that it was bought by the transnational company News Corp, which expected to make a huge profit on the investment. This commercialization of MySpace meant that it became dominated by adverts, and the simplicity of its design was hampered. At the same time, scare stories in the mainstream media about pornography and paedophiles made parents wary of allowing their children to use the site (Tripp and Herr-Stephenson, 2009). However, young people had already switched from MySpace to Facebook and Bebo, and other social media sites, seeing MySpace as just a site for listening to music rather than a social network.

With the launch of Twitter in 2006, Facebook has become less fashionable (Arceneaux and Weiss, 2010; Murthy, 2011; Panek, Nardis and Konrath, 2013; Van Dijck, 2011). By the time you read this, both may have followed MySpace and bulletin boards into unfashionable obscurity. Twitter is designed for the smartphone users, where technological limitations of screens and keyboards mean it is difficult to write or read anything beyond 140 characters. With Twitter, it is easy to make a quick comment about something and to read other people's comments without having to scroll down a screen. The function of hashtagging makes it easy to share tweets with others who have decided to read anything with particular hashtags. The limitations of the characters and the use of hashtags have led to a new form of language emerging on the site, which shares features with early Netiquette but which has taken the hashtag along with the demotic of text-messaging (Van Dijck, 2011). Twitter allows people to follow celebrities and gain their insight. It allows celebrities, politicians and corporations to control their image and message. It allows urban hipsters to connect with one another to discuss craft beer and artisan pizza; it has also become a place where people can engage in verbal abuse and trolling. The anonymity of Twitter (the fact that it allows fake accounts to be constructed, the lack of any real form of moderation other than a fairly passive complaints procedure) makes it easy for users to engage in bullying and sexist, racist and homophobic abuse (Bishop, 2014).

In my own social network, everyone is on Facebook. There are two exceptions. The first is an anarchist who has turned his back on it as a product of governmentality and State surveillance, even though he uses the Net and has a smartphone. The second is a graduate student of mine, who seems to be similarly concerned about the issue of giving her personal data to corporations. Everyone else uses it to a greater or lesser extent. I have friends and colleagues who have out-of-date personal pages on Facebook, who use it only to connect with things important to them, but mostly people seem to be on Facebook updating their pages with photos, posts and videos, as well as commenting on other people's posts. People seem quite happy engaging in the etiquette of liking each other's posts, giving the 'thumb up' equally to posts that are highly political, deeply personal or perfectly mundane. There are moments of political disagreement, but mostly the comments tend to fortify the original post's opinions. The only place where there is disagreement is where people post their liking of a particular band, and others mock them for their poor taste. Interactions on Facebook reinforce the sense that everybody thinks the same, though of course we choose who to friend and who to follow, allowing ourselves to be surrounded by people like us. This creates not a Habermasian public sphere – rather, an exclusive private space that is at the same time publicly viewable by anyone and everyone.

This is the one fact that will date this book very precisely. All the 12 people I spoke to for this research are on Facebook. This is the way people connect to distant relatives, colleagues in other countries; it is how some people do business, how people do the work of serious leisure involved in organizing dance classes and nights out. It has become the social media of the first years of the twenty-first century. But it seems already to be on the turn: as older people like my own father connect to it to like pictures and posts, younger people and hipsters have switched to other social media (Schiermer, 2014). Facebook is not fashionable, and even its users complain about its transformation into a mass market website. As one person in this research explained to me: 'they should call it Familybook... all I see these days is boring photos of other people's children'. Others object to the way in which Facebook has become dominated by adverts and sponsored links, sometimes carefully disguised as personal posts. One person told me that he 'hated the way Facebook thinks it knows what I like', while another complained about the way in which Facebook had made it look like he liked a transnational corporation to his friends. Despite these concerns and complaints, all of the people I spoke to used Facebook on at least a daily basis. The availability of smartphones and laptops and the ubiquity of workplace PCs make accessing the Net a part of every middle-aged, middle-class British person's day – and despite the popularity of Twitter (which was used by nine of my respondents), Facebook remains a key social media site that people feel the need to check into. Even if they do not update their own pages, people are on Facebook reading the posts of their friends, liking photos and liking pages put together by corporations, groups or organizations. On Facebook, the rule is that no one is allowed to have fake identities – everyone is a real person with real personal data, real friends and real likes. Where people set up fake or pseudonymous accounts, Facebook reserves the right to shut them down. This reduces the scope for trolling, scamming and predatory paedophiles to operate, but people do circumvent these rules: for example, young people use false dates of birth to set up accounts (Panek, Nardis and Konrad, 2013).

I am on Facebook, and have been since December 2007, when two friends from university separately sent me notifications to become their friend. I was suspicious of what data might be collected by Facebook, but decided on the face of it that it would be a good thing (and an easy way) to get in touch with old friends. Initially, I set myself a number of rules about what I would do on Facebook. I would keep my private life off it, I wouldn't post updates about my life, and I wouldn't sink to the seemingly desperate act of making friend requests. The first rule ensured a measure of privacy and confidentiality. I did not see why Facebook needed to know which schools I went to, for example, or other important personal details. The second rule was my 'student' rule. As a lecturer I do not think it is appropriate to put anything on the Net that could put me in a difficult position with students. In that sense, it was an extension of the second rule. For that reason, I also decided never to accept a friend request from a student until they had left university. The third rule was a way of trying to stop me becoming addicted to increasing the number of my friends, and a way to make me manage the potential size of Facebook. Initially, I ruthlessly patrolled the 'no post' rule and 'no making friend requests' rules. But as I used Facebook more and more, I started to break both rules. There were key moments in my academic career (writing a book, becoming a professor, for example) that I wanted to celebrate with my circle of friends, especially since a large proportion of my Facebook friends were academics in leisure studies and metal music studies. So when a book was published, I told my friends about it. I have also reacted to things in the news that are related to one of the subjects of my research. The other rule ended up being broken through the desire to contact and speak to people for academic research and networking – and I confess I sent a friend request to William Shatner, the actor who played Captain Kirk in *Star Trek*, because I do on occasion get foolishly fan-boy about things (he is the only person I have connected to in this way). Facebook, then, has become my way of maintaining social networks around my work, though I still use it for the leisure activity of personal interactions.

Facebook is a great way to maintain contacts and social networks. The software allows members to personalize what they read and who they interact with, and gives them the opportunity to work and take part in inconsequential leisure. However, the work of performativity is challenging. It takes time to read everything posted, even the things posted only by your closest friends and family. As well as making sure you politely engage these important connections, you have to work out the best way of responding to others. That is all before you decide what things to post that will gain you the right kind of cultural capital (Bourdieu, 1986), which will allow you to pass the symbolic boundaries you want to get past (Cohen, 1985). Facebook is a babble (and indeed a *babel*) of competing performances, all demanding attention and demanding the imprimatur of an authentic performance: the 'like' by a key taste-maker, the comments that justify the performance. To borrow another Biblical metaphor, the imagined and imaginary communities mediatized through Facebook are built on shifting sand, and what people post today as the marker of a particular social identity may look completely unfashionable tomorrow. The performativity is always taking place and the social identity is always provisional, subject to the changing mood of the people in the social network. As I write in 2014, people are proving their cultural capital and their worth in the imaginary community by making jokes that reference the television programme *A Game of Thrones*. But in six months' time, it will be another television programme that has captured the attention of this fickle general public. There is also a psychologically distressing form of performativity at work on Facebook that resembles the LinkedIn social network's inflation of employment successes (Harris and Rae, 2011; Van Dijck, 2013). People use Facebook to perform confident, fun, outgoing roles – the person out every night with a dozen friends, or the successful mother working as a city lawyer taking her daughter to violin class (Van Dijk, 2013). This is a form of boasting and bending the truth of our messy lives into picture-perfect moments of social confidence and success. At best this competitive performativity turns Facebook into a parade of narcissism; at worst, it actually threatens people with psychological trauma (Rosen, Whaling, Rab, Carrier and Cheever, 2013).

Despite the importance and popularity of Facebook (or perhaps because of it), it is a highly problematic website. Facebook wants to know who we connect with and what we like so it can sell advertising space to corporations looking to sell things to us. Facebook is a corporation with a vested interest in protecting its profits and its place in the market. At the moment it is free to register and use Facebook because they need the billions of users to generate the data for their advertisers. But the corporation may change its business model if the instrumental rationality of its financial plans dictates such a move. And it is difficult to disconnect from Facebook – it isn't just hard to make that disconnection on the website, it is difficult to make because the design of the site is so visible and ever-present. It has successfully integrated itself into people's lives, becoming the first place we go when we want to tell people things about our successes. Not only does the organization pay to get its products built into new smartphones and laptops, the system is designed to be attractive – the updates from other people demand our attention, persuade us to get involved, and once we are chatting with others we can keep chatting for ever. Facebook suggests pages we should like, and friends we might know. It is designed to keep us locked in and using the system, and we do so only half-conscious that everything we post to Facebook becomes the property of Facebook. We allow Facebook to track us, to identify us in pictures and to make decisions about what we are allowed to post. Facebook reserves the right to play with our data and to experiment with our news feeds (see Brandimarte, Acquisti and Loewenstein, 2013). Finally, Facebook seems to construct a record of our thoughts and our likes that would be very useful for a totalitarian or paranoid government to have – it is an open book of our desires that any security agency can use to protect the hegemonic interests of nation states.

Social networks and communities of interest

A, one of my respondents, has a daily ritual of checking her favourite websites. She does this if she is on her smartphone at the weekend, or in her office during the week. She checks her Facebook and Twitter accounts first, replying to messages and comments, then reads 'important' things on other websites she browses (the *New Statesman* magazine, Channel 4 News) before reading the spoof website *The Daily Mash*. If she has time she might log on as a user on an alternative music forum and make a few comments about things with her friends who post there, but this social networking is less important for her than the networking done on the corporate websites. Another respondent, B, is more engaged with social networking. Not only does he tweet regularly, throughout the working day, he spends a large part of his evening chatting on a soccer fans forum. A third respondent, C, uses Facebook to advertise his work as an artist, while making comments about things happening in the news media. He spends money on eBay on old comics and discusses comics and science fiction in a number of chat rooms, though he is not a regular user of these websites. My own ritual when I access the Net in the morning is to look at the local news, three rugby league websites and their chat forums, and a heavy metal chat forum where gigs are announced. I do sometimes post to the heavy metal forum, but so far I have never reached the point where I post on the rugby league forums. My social networks are constructed on Facebook, where I am closely involved in the International Society for Metal Music Studies page, and where I spend ten minutes every day (usually at lunchtime) catching up with old and distant friends. If I have more leisure time and access to the Net I will go to a small number of other music sites, the *Times Higher Educational Supplement* (news and features about higher education) and the Secret Leeds forum, which involves discussions about hidden places and histories of Leeds (my home city in the United Kingdom). While the Net might be huge, the sites we visit are actually small in number – and the social networks we make are equally small (Lupton, 2014).

Every individual using the Net has certain rituals and behaviours. The Net has key uses for each of us. We use the Net as a space for entertainment – we seek pleasure and satisfaction through watching or reading or listening to or interacting with something. We use the Net for gathering information – news, weather forecasts, the times of flights and trains. We use the Net to buy things. And we use the Net to form social networks through communities of interest. When we access the Net it is not always easy to delineate our motivations and intended uses. But whatever we do on the Net, we are seeking social identity and belonging, and using the Net to create a sense of community through identifying with communities of interest. That can be seen when we are consciously seeking to join in conversations on a chat room discussing the merits of DC Comics. We want to share our love of those comics, and our knowledge of them with others who have similar interests (it is possible for people who hate comics to join a forum discussing comics just to wind people up, but these trolls are usually found out by moderators and expelled – see Bishop, 2014). Belonging to a particular professional soccer team's unofficial fan forum creates a sense of community belonging as strongly as wearing the club's colours on the train to work.

But other uses of the Net create such social networks, too. When people choose to read the news on a conservative news website instead of a liberal news website they are behaving *as if* they were making those choices in public. The owners of the website and the other readers of it will not know that we have made a choice to read it, but we have made the choice to identify with the politics of the site and the public reputation the site carries as if we had bought a newspaper and read it on the train. Respondent A mentions the Channel 4 News and the *New Statesman*. She does not interact with these sites, but she does read their news. She gets a sense of belonging to a thick social network (Geertz, 1973), one associated with the middle-class radical-left cosmopolitanism of each. This gives her meaning and identity that is as strong as that found on a soccer fans forum.

Similarly, when we choose to construct our Facebook pages or our avatar identities in chat rooms, we are presenting to an imagined public an identity that they will think is both acceptable and proof that we are close enough to them in our tastes for us to be seen as part of their public. In posting about heavy metal, I have to prove to the others in the community of interest that I know who the good bands are and which ones are jokes, and I have to prove I know something about the history of heavy metal and which of its genres are legitimate in the particular forum. People who post in chat rooms use pictures and references in their signature lines to prove they know something about the subject of interest: *Star Trek* fans use pictures of Klingons for avatars, and reference dialogue from important episodes (Booth, 2013; Scholz, 2013). Whisky drinkers will test each other's knowledge of single-malt distilleries and the taste of particular expressions and make clear which they prefer, while showing off their visits to distilleries on Islay (Spracklen, 2011b). All interaction and connection with the Net is a game of identity-making and community-making, where we choose to show off our position within certain established, acceptable social networks. And even where people are being iconoclastic they do so with the intention of being seen as part of an iconoclastic culture – such as the comments under YouTube videos, where trolling, being snarky or bored or unimpressed is the norm (McCosker, 2014).

Social activism – radical left

In my first full-time job following my PhD, I was a policy and research officer for the Liberal Democrat councillors on a city council. It was a politically restricted post (that is, I was employed by the council and could not engage in certain political activities), but I was expected to network with other people working for the Liberal Democrat politicians. This meant accessing via a dial-up modem a Liberal Democrat conferencing system hosted by an ISP called CIX. The Liberal Democrats were ahead of the other main political parties in the United Kingdom when it came to using the Net to share information, discuss ideas and make decisions. I saw the value that CIX gave to the politicians seeking to find ways to win elections, but there was value as well in the way it allowed the party's officers and researchers to feel part of a wider social movement. At the time, the Liberal Democrat party had a strong radical-left caucus; as the people using CIX were younger researchers and politicians, this side of the party was usually dominant in discussions online. CIX gave the radical-left caucus of the party (what others might call social liberals, those who believe in the importance of the welfare state and the role of the State in promoting social inclusion, in contrast to the economic liberals who prefer smaller states and free markets) a feeling of purpose and legitimacy: they could come to agreement about how egregious the New Labour Government was acting, while taking their own MPs to task if they failed to say the right things. The Liberal Democrats made significant gains in elections and the popular vote over this period, applying grassroots and community campaigning to every street, and the CIX conferencing system probably played a key role in that advance (former leader Paddy Ashdown used the system frequently).

The Net continues to play a key role in supporting the rise of new social movements and radical politics more generally. As discussed earlier in this book, Castells (2012) has identified the way new social movements and the radical left have been able to mobilise, communicate, campaign and outwit their rivals. A new generation of anti-capitalism activists situate the serious leisure of their campaigning and activism online (Bennett, 2003; Chatterton, 2008; Hammett, 2014). There is still the need to get activists to march on streets and to assemble outside banks and other sources of radical anger, but this high-profile, media-friendly action is planned and publicised on the Net. The new generation of radical activists all use the Net as a primary source of organizing and information-gathering because this is how they have always used the Net – they are the world's first Net-citizens

(Arora, 2014; Castells, 2012). Anti-capitalism activists have attempted to turn the nihilist-hactervism of sites such as 4-Chan into morally good actions – breaking into websites and systems owned by transnational corporations and governments, disrupting service, stealing information that reveals the corrupt nature of global capitalism, or just leaving a rude message (Fitri, 2011). Others use the Net to create informal social networks of petition-signers and lobbyists, making mass emailing and million-number petitions easy to organise. While some critics think this means political activism on the Net is something less real (it is easy to click and sign a petition, but how many of these people try to make change in the real world?), the lobbying campaigns and virus market-ing of radical social movements does raise the profile of issues and does influence the decision-making in the public sphere (Arora, 2014; Castells, 2012; Hammett, 2014). The work of volunteers raising money for charities is also made easier by the Net, whether it is specific websites that handle financial transactions (with the questionable share of the proceeds that some take), or just mass emails and posts that say someone is about to climb a mountain for Greenpeace. Local campaigns against unwanted development succeed through the use of the Net as serious leisure space; for example, as I write this, there are well-organised cam-paigns against fracking (getting oil from rocks underground by blasting the rocks with hot water) in the United Kingdom that are using the Net to lobby, publicise and effect change (see frack-off.org.uk).

More mainstream radical activism – campaigning and organizing political parties on the left, the work of trade unions and national and transnational NGOs and charities campaigning for social justice and the environment – continues on the Net alongside the activism in the real world. Half of my respondents expressed membership or support of a radical-left organization, and they either read the relevant website or subscribed to mailing lists. This did not make any of my respondents identify themselves as politically active. None of them had stood for election, or worked as an agent or officer of some organization or party, and only one had delivered leaflets on behalf of a party. Their member-ship or support through donations, or just the support in kind offered by the Facebook 'like', is enough for them. They support the aims of radical-left politics and want their friends and colleagues to know they are keen to challenge the inequities of capitalism, neo-liberalism and globalization. They found a strong sense of community in expressing their politics, and performed it publicly to gain the approval of their peers. While this aspect of their communicative digital leisure might seem morally empty, it is recognition that their ability to seriously change the world is limited by their work and family circumstances – by funding the work of others, they at least change the world vicariously (Castells, 2012). The social networks of radical-left activism have also given them ways to discuss policies and politics globally, while acting locally in their homes and on their streets. This can be seen in the way some of my respondents are involved in growing their own food on allotments, in volunteering to clean up local parks, and in supporting local businesses instead of chain-stores owned by transnational corporations. All this activism in the real world is researched and reported online in their leisure time, in posts on their own Facebook pages or on the pages of community or green groups.

Social activism – radical right

None of the people I spoke to use the Net to be active in rightist politics. All the respondents to my small-scale research projects are people I know fairly well, so it is no real surprise that none of them expressed an interest in right-wing politics. But the right is heavily involved in organizing and campaigning on the Net. I do have some friends who are part of the mainstream right, such as supporters of the Conservative party in the United Kingdom, and they use Facebook to post stories from right-wing sources and pass comments on these. Their semi-private sphere includes me because I am their friend on Facebook and in the real world, but there is evidence that people use social media to reinforce their political ideologies through isolating themselves from those who have different political views (Gustafsson, 2012). The tools of social media make it easy to choose to unfollow or un-friend those people who belong to the other side, and so our feeds become mutually reinforcing and selective, reducing our interactions with the others and limiting the value of the Net as a site for dialogue. It is not good for communicative rationality and the public sphere to limit our conversations to those with whom we agree.

Mainstream right-wing parties and politicians in the West have been effective at using social media to bolster support and engage in positive and negative campaigning (Åström and Karlsson, 2013; Bos, Van der Brug and De Vreese, 2011). Their control of the media in many nation states has allowed them to extend their hegemony into the virtual leisure space, using the tools of spin and persuasion to make their views on neo-liberalism and nationalism become the norm. They have used the Net to pursue the demonization of the poor, women, migrants and minority ethnic groups (Bos, Van der Brug and De Vreese, 2011). They have used the Net to convince people that anyone can be successful in life as long as they work hard, the American dream that is at the heart of the myth of neo-liberal choice (Hillygus and Shields, 2014). But the real strength of the Net's social networks has been exploited by the radical right, or the far right, from the *poujadistes* of the Tea Party and the UK Independence Party (UKIP), to the Islamists and the neo-Nazis and fascists of the Aryan fringes (King and Leonard, 2014; Mammone, Godin and Jenkins, 2013; Spracklen, 2013a).

The Tea Party and UKIP are both far right fringe factions that have shifted the mainstream of centre-right politics to the extremes (Hillygus and Shields, 2014). The Tea Party has been a lobbying group connected to the Republicans, which started out as an extreme libertarian, patriotic movement giving voice to the disaffected white working class of America, the part of society most troubled by globalization, post-industrialization and the recession. That it is funded by rich donors with interests in pursuing global capitalism does not matter much to those who think the Tea Party speaks for them. The Tea Party has tapped into a wider vein of popular radical rightism in white America, which distrusts federal government and bureaucracies, thinks multiculturalism and feminism are bad for the country and which believes America has been betrayed by those trying to impose pacifist, socialist world-government on it. This radical rightism draws on fascist and neo-Nazi theories about the decline of the country, and Christian fundamentalist theories about the rightful role of America in world politics (ibid.). The Net allows the Tea Party to draw upon an entire set of ideas, policies and communities that come from this radical-right milieu and to mix and match videos and news reports that fit their narrative of decline and betrayal. UKIP has drawn on this same social network of angry people and communities, using the Net along with other media to entice voters to their pro-British, anti-foreigner message. This narrative of bad migrants has of course been at the heart of mainstream British political discourse anyway, so UKIP are the happy recipients of the racist stories put out and publicized by the Conservatives and their friends in the tabloid newspapers (Lynch and Whitaker, 2013).

Elsewhere, I have shown how the far right has used music subcultures on the Net to propagate their politics and normalize elitist notions of whiteness, purity and nation (Spracklen, 2013b). For fascists and neo-Nazis, the Net provides a communicative space where in their defence they can invoke Netopian commitments to free speech and allow everyone to have their point of view heard (King and Leonard, 2014). Varg Vikernes, the metal musician from Norway who is known for his band Burzum and for his extreme radical-right views, can use his website to write long books and articles propagating his views alongside details of his music. The nihilistic music of Burzum serves to bring music fans closer to his beliefs about racial purity, heritage and pride. The Net is also used as an internal organizing device for radical-right groups intending on bringing disruption to the streets. Just as social movements on the left find value in the communicative leisure space of the Net, where the private and the public can be carefully delineated, new radical movements on the far right find resources, support and organization. This can be seen in the success of the far right in the United Kingdom, where groups such as the English Defence League and Britain First take part in various marches, invasions and stunts (Allen, 2011). Perhaps the biggest success story of the far right is the Islamo-fascist movement associated with Isis in Syria and Iraq. This movement is involved in armed insurrection, terrorism and struggle as it tries to impose an extreme right-wing, neo-fascist version of Islam in the nation states of the old Islamic Caliphate (Klausen, 2014; Storey, 2012). Like other similar Islamo-fascist groups, Isis is comfortable with appropriating digital technology for propaganda and recruitment purposes. Official Facebook page and Twitter feeds show grim videos and photos of the latest massacres, and call on Muslims to join in the jihad. Individual soldiers are encouraged to post their own updates on social media from the front line, encouraging other young Muslim men in their countries of origin such as the United Kingdom to 'do the right thing'. For young men brought up on video games and used to using the Net to inquire about the nature of their faith, this is a powerful and attractive discourse.

Conspiracy world

Part of the radical-right milieu that feeds into the discourse of the Tea Party and UKIP (and others on the extreme right fringe) is the assumption that the truth about the world has been hidden from the people-at-large by the people who run the Establishment. This assumption draws ironically on similar debates on the left, which draw on ideas about mediatization and hegemony that run through much Marxist theory. There is clear evidence that elites use the media and education and popular culture to keep the masses docile, so that the elites get to keep their status and power. There are conspiracies to make us buy things, there are diplomatic understandings beyond formal agreements, and there are cover-ups by governments seeking to maintain their reputations (Gramsci, 1971). The radical right takes these facts as evidence of deeper, active conspiracies designed to eliminate their freedom and reduce America and the West to socialist servitude. The real problem of climate change caused by modern industry, something that most rational scientists who are experts in the field agree is actually happening, becomes a conspiracy by socialists, politicians and diabolical others to place restrictions on the economy (Antonio and Brulle, 2011; McCright and Dunlap, 2011; Norgaard, 2011; Washington, 2013). Being sceptical about climate change becomes a marker of status and belonging among the radical right (McCright and Dunlap, 2011). They draw upon real scares about bad science, the limits of science and unethical practice by scientists to say that climate-change science is weak, or full of holes, or funded by vested interest (again, there is an irony in the fact that most of the sceptical resources and campaigners rely on funding from industry groups with a vested interest in denying the fact of climate change – see Brulle, 2014).

The Net fuels the growth of climate-change denial, as it has other conspiracy theories. For the climate-change deniers there are pseudo-scientific blogs and websites that make extravagant claims that have not been tested through the mechanics of scientific peer review. There are news magazines and channels that repeat climate-change denial as if it has been proven that the climate-change science is a scam. The growth of the climate-change denial movement is supported by the radical right and normalized by groups such as the Tea Party and UKIP. As it receives huge amounts of funding and support it is able to dominate discussions online. It has become something that 'normal', 'right-thinking' people think is true – governments lied to the people about all sorts of things, scientists are in it for themselves, so why should anyone believe them? Even reputable news organizations such as the BBC feel bound by some misplaced ethic of balance when it comes to climate change, as if the deniers have any basis for their claims against the tens of thousands of research papers that prove it is happening.

The Net has made such belief in the untrue much easier to sustain. In the early years of the Net, conspiracy theories were already part of the popular discourse. In the 1990s, the world of Ufology, the people and organizations seeking to establish the truth about sightings of alien spaceships took a turn towards radical-right conspiracies (Bell and Bennion-Nixon, 2000; Dean, 1998; Knight, 2002). Stories about the United States Government suppressing news and information about UFO sightings and crashes led to speculation about what it was the government was hiding. The consensus was that crashes at infamous sites such as Roswell had led to the United States Government keeping aliens (alive or dead) and alien technology (including back-engineered spaceships) at Area 51. These ideas were popularized by shows such as *The X-Files*, and became dominant memes in online culture: the government was lying, manipulating people and even killing them to hide the truth about its interaction with aliens. These conspiracy theories soon gathered in other conspiracies – it was claimed that the moon landings never happened, it was claimed that there were secret societies secretly controlling everything and everyone, it was claimed that fluoridation of water supplies was a trick of some kind. The pompous lie dressed up as truth through pseudo-scientific language and analysis became part of the conspiracy theory's mode of persuasion – alongside more folky appeals to people to judge for themselves. Net-citizens were exhorted to be suspicious of what they had been taught to be true, and to find things out for themselves. This was part of the Net's utopian ethics (Aupers, 2012; Lewis and Kahn, 2005). But in the hands of people plugging conspiracy theories it became a way of convincing people that up was down. Like climate-change denial, believing that the American Government has aliens in a bunker somewhere, right next to the film set where the moon landing was made (down the corridor from the room where Elvis eats his breakfast) is exciting because it is iconoclastic, a way of proving one is smarter than the gullible folks who watch the mainstream news. These conspiracy theories still have enormous power and popularity on the Net. While the alien conspiracies have become less ubiquitous in everyday popular culture, they are still discussed and analysed online, along with more recent conspiracy theories.

Hovering around the conspiracy theories on the right were the old lies about the Jews: Jews as secret haters of Christians and Muslims, Jews as pullers of strings and manipulators. These lies have existed in Christian and Muslim public spheres for many years, but the Net legitimizes them. When Islamist terrorists attacked America with such devastation in September 2001, it was a matter of minutes before the far-right conspiracy theorists were at work online, making claims about the truth not being told. An entire industry of 9/11 truthers emerged to point out how unlikely the accepted narrative of the attack was, and how likely that it was actually someone else playing some kind of evil trick (Jones, 2012). Both American far-right conspiracy theorists and Muslim conspiracy theorists found a common scapegoat: the Jews must have been behind it to try to get America to fight in the Middle East; the Jews had been told to stay at home on the day of the strikes on the World Trade Center (Durham, 2003; Jones, 2012). These are dangerous and pernicious lies, because they feed into legitimate protests about the actions of the United States and Israel. On the Net the real questions about the invasions of Afghanistan and Iraq, the limits of neo-liberal interventionism and the rise of an American Empire get submerged in the noise about 'bankers', Zionists and the Jewish lobby.

Conclusion

The Net is positive space for constructing and maintaining social networks, identity and belonging. There is real communicative action at work in the formation of what is clearly communicative leisure. But the Net's instrumental nature makes it fail as a truly communicative space. People can find communities of interest and like-minded people to share politics with, but the Net is actually weak as a form of public sphere. Earlier in the book I cited Habermas' belief that the Net was a failure as a public sphere because it only creates exclusive communities of interest, and in this chapter I have shown there is little evidence that social media and the Net more generally create the bridging capital needed to build such a public sphere (Putnam, 2000). The Net encourages people to find community only with those we want to find, and the rise of conspiracies and far-right political spaces shows that the Net allows people to only read and engage with information that supports their prejudices and ideologies.

Furthermore, social media and the Net's wider social networks might make it easier to connect with one another, but the technology and the normalization of its use raise huge ethical concerns around surveillance and control. Are we comfortable in sharing so much data about ourselves with software developers, telecommunications companies and the governments that work with them? Rather than being a positive, communicative space allowing communicative leisure to take place, social media seems to be by design made to make the surveillance work of nation states and corporations easier. People who are worried about terrorists and paedophiles might argue that this is a fair loss of privacy and a fair amount of control, but such surveillance and governmentality has already limited the leisure of people online: in the fight to control illegal downloading, as I will show in the next chapter.

7
File-Sharing and Net Ethics

Ownership is problematic politically and ethically. Anarchists would say that all property is theft and everything should be shared in common between us. Liberals would say that private property and rights to that property are fundamental freedoms, as well as starting points for a democratic, more equal society. Which is right? And how can we apply any ethics of private property or commons to the digital leisure space? This chapter examines the practice of downloading music and film files. I will begin with an overview of the sociology and anthropology of file-sharing, and its pre-internet equivalents. I will explore the prevailing practices and the commercialization of YouTube. I will explore the ways in which corporations and governments have reacted to illegal downloading through the construction of commercial downloading sites and transnational agreements and legislation on illegal downloading. I will explore Net users' attitudes to downloading through an analysis of blogs, forum sites and in interviews. I will look at the ethical arguments for and against illegal downloading and copyright violation, and will suggest that users of the Net have lost their ability to make moral judgements, notwithstanding the anti-capitalist urge to steal from transnational corporations.

The sociology and anthropology of file-sharing

For the purposes of this analysis and discussion, I will use the modern concept of file-sharing in a new way. File-sharing comes from modern technological culture to refer to two related acts: the posting of data in a digital repository of some kind; and the accessing or downloading of that data by some other person (Mahoney and Haigh, 2011). File-sharing is at the heart of discussions about the impact of 'illegal'

113

downloading. I want to use the concept of file-sharing in a broader way to describe similar interactions and practices that took place before the emergence of the Net. When I was growing up in the 1980s there was panic from the entertainment industries about pirating of their copyrighted products. Industries and corporations have always concerned themselves with their products being pirated or counterfeited, but this was a new development caused by the spread of a new technology. This was the era of the home-video recorder, which allowed people to make copies of films from television or – if they had two recorders connected together – from videos rented from shops (so long as they fiddled with the anti-piracy catch on the side of the video). The movie and television industry wanted to make money from the home-video technology, which is why they licensed their products to be rented from specialist home-video stores, but they were not keen on people using the technology to produce unlicensed copies of industry products (Hilderbrand, 2009). The industry put pressure on politicians and journalists to start a moral panic about the people making and selling pirated copies – they were portrayed as criminal gangs, linked to drug-dealing, and the concept of the modern-day 'pirate' was imprinted on people's minds as an unscrupulous rogue (Benson-Allott, 2013). Pirated copies of videos were mocked as being of poor quality – a warning that continues to this day about films and television programmes (Hilderbrand, 2009). This was an example of file-sharing, the creation of data (analogue copies of films) and the consumption of that data (buying a pirated video from a stall at the back of a market). The problem of pirated videos lasted as long as the analogue technology existed alongside the structures of the industry, and as the creative industries switched to digital, it was inevitable that the problem would transform into that which the industry and legislators grapple with today.

The case of the pop music industry is similar, but with a key difference. As with movies and television programmes, the pop music industry in the 1980s was faced with a 'problem' of file-sharing, which was caused by the widespread adoption of new technology. In this case, it was the spread of cassette recorders and home stereo-systems with twin-deck cassette recorders (Drew, 2014). The pop music industry relied on people buying records in shops after hearing songs on the radio, or after getting a recommendation from a magazine or a friend. There were organizations making pirated versions of singles and albums, but these operated mainly in developing countries – in the West, the production and pressing of vinyl records was carefully controlled by the industry and by governments, and the only unlicensed vinyl were bootlegs of live gigs sold in specialist shops out of the gaze of record labels and managers (Daschuk and Popham, 2013; Eschenfelder, Desai and Downey, 2011). Cassette technology allowed music fans and consumers to easily make copies of records or radio shows. On one level, much of this was for personal use, transferring a vinyl album to cassette to be able to play it in the car or in a Walkman, or making a mix-tape of selected tracks for one's intimate friends (Drew, 2014). But cassettes allowed other forms of file-sharing to emerge. It became possible for new artists to copy demos and send them out directly to labels and journalists. It also became possible for people to trade tapes between each other through the post. Music magazines specializing in certain pop genres would carry adverts for pen pals and fanzines. Cassette copies of demos and albums were passed around extensively by the extreme metal music scene, often with the consent of the artists themselves, people not signed to any label – or signed to a tiny independent. For the artists, the tape-trading network allowed them access to a dedicated fan base who would listen to their music and buy the album if and when it appeared in the record shops (Harris, 2000).

Another file-sharing example from history is from further back in time, but we need to look at it because the issue of copyright and intellectual ownership (what is now called 'property rights') stems from the spread of the technology. The printing press was a Chinese invention from the eleventh century CE. In Europe, the technology was first used in the fifteenth century. The printing press developed in Europe used fully movable type to create entire pages of text, alongside woodcuts for illustrations. The printing press arrived in Europe at a time of intellectual and cultural growth, with demand for books sustaining an industry of people copying text by hand from one manuscript to another. The printing press made copying much faster and much cheaper, allowing the publishing houses to create vast profits and feeding the intellectual progression of the Renaissance (Eisenstein, 1983; Elias, 1978, 1982). Printers published whatever they could sell, printing books by dead authors as well as living ones, with permissions and without permissions. On the one hand, then, there were people involved in this early file-sharing: the printers creating data, the consumers purchasing data. On the other hand, there were authors who did not receive money for the publishing of their work. Some authors did get fees for their work, especially as printers realized they were in competition with one another to secure the work of well-known authors with a public audience. Then the printers themselves became worried – what if a printer printed copies of another printer's book? This led at first to publishers agreeing rules about copyrights, who could and could not copy a published work (Bettig, 1992). Publishing houses then pressured governments to protect their rights, though the subject and writ of copyright was uncertain for many years. Later, it led to recognition that the author of a work was owed the right of recognition that they were the author, which (much later) led to the author receiving the protection of copyright in many countries (Deazley, 2006). Finally, international trade agreements established the copyright rules that exist today, with the rights of the author and the publisher protected and upheld by signatories to the agreements (ibid.).

Establishing intellectual property rights is a marker of a nation state or a number of nation states operating in modernity. They are part of a broader system of instrumentality and rationality that govern the relationship between nation states and citizens, and the relationship between nation states (Habermas, 1984, 1987, 1990). This system makes individual citizens limit their freedoms for the good of the nation state – the freedom to walk where one likes, for instance, becomes restricted because nation states want cars to be able to drive on roads to boost the economy, and nation states want to use land for military training or power projects. In a modern society, says Habermas (1984, 1987), the instrumentality of the State limits our communicative actions. Individuals generally do not make the laws in the countries in which they are born, they grow up enculturated into accepting those laws – and the power to change them (the public sphere) is limited, even in liberal democracies. The rights of copyright protect the creator of the work, but are primarily designed to protect the industry that has published the work (Bettig, 1992). They are also designed to control the relations between countries and to maintain existing power relationships. The idea of copyright is a form of instrumental intervention on the free market. It is a form of protectionism designed to stop investors and industries being undercut by others. The idea of copyright protects capital investment from the decimations of the unregulated free market. Industries say they build film sets, printing presses and train engineers and producers, and all this would be threatened if the products of their investment were allowed to be copied without payment or permission. Nation states measuring their success through the instrumentality of GDP and the economy argue that is in their interests to secure copyright to defend their creative industries from competitors abroad who do not respect copyright. The laws of copyright are imposed by hegemonic nation states on others during international trade discussions, and become part of the rules of engagement through which regulated global capitalism operates (Robinson and Gibson, 2011). Alongside commitments to protect copyright, nation states agree on procedures for policing copyright's transgression – copyright breaches become matters of police investigation. Copyright exists because it suits the hegemonic powers of nation states and corporations that it exists. The creative industries argue that they would not survive in the globalized and virtual market if copyright was allowed to be broken.

This argument seems to hold weight when one considers the recent history of the pop music industry. Before the rise of the Net in the 1990s, the music industry was dominated by transnational corporations. These transnational corporations made billions of dollars in profits and had enormous political and cultural power over an industry and a form of popular culture that had only really existed across the Western world since the 1950s. The pop music industry had grown from economic practices of the early twentieth century, which was dominated by the thinking that profits were made from selling and publishing sheet music. The rise of the single and the pop charts, and pop music on radio led the industry to make huge sums of money from their share of the profits on physical recordings. By the 1980s, the pop music industry had its own production lines for artists: huge sums of money were spent developing mainstream acts, hiring song-writers, engineers and producers and session musicians, and sending artists on tour. At the same time, huge sums of money were spent on marketing and gifts for DJs and journalists (Fairchild, 2012). Getting airtime on radio or television was crucial to selling records and making it big, so it was essential to get the decision-makers and critics onside. A record could sell by word-of-mouth, but most records sold because journalists in magazines or DJs on the radio were telling people a particular artist's new record was great. Most of the money made by artists was channelled back to the industry, either through labels or managers, but a handful of successful artists made huge sums of money (Cloonan, 2013). Pop music was sold through record shops or stores that sold a variety of goods (such as the chain store Woolworth's), with albums being marketed to 'serious' genre fans, and singles to younger consumers. Outside the mainstream was a thriving independent and underground scene – localized and limited to genres (Bennett, 2001; Hodkinson, 2002; Kahn-Harris, 2007). These scenes thrived by claiming to be more authentic and less commercial than the mainstream, though of course they adopted the marketing techniques and discourse of that mainstream, and celebrated when one of their bands crossed over to the charts. Along with these scenes, a number of pop music subcultures thrived in countries and across borders, some alternative and radical in political focus (Spracklen, 2014), some grounded in the burgeoning dance music scene and some associated with the globalizing heavy metal scene (Bennett, 2001; Harris, 2000; Kahn-Harris, 2007).

Now, in the second decade of the twenty-first century, in the age of the Net, the pop music industry has changed. It is still dominated by multinational corporations but their profits and share of the market has dropped. The old business model of investing heavily in new acts has been replaced by a reliance on existing acts and brands crossing over from Reality TV (Cloonan, 2013; Nunn, 2013). The major labels still have their pop stars but the gross number has diminished, with labels concentrating on those acts that are already deemed to be global celebrities, or those that have the potential to be transformed into celebrities due to their particular audience, or appearance or market-share. Many of the artists who do continue as artists beyond the handful of major-label celebrity pop stars, the travelling bands and musicians, do not make enough money to be full-time professionals. They are struggling to make a living from record deals and royalties because the labels are cautious about signing acts. To survive as musicians they are having to diversify, to run their own labels or merchandising, or increasingly to have another job that pays their bills. Music fans increasingly choose not to buy music, instead surfing the Net, downloading and streaming. Virtual sales are increasing for the major labels, but not enough to off-set the global decline in physical records. At the same time, illegal downloads/file-sharing are increasing (Dilmperi, King and Dennis, 2011; Sterne, 2012). For some artists, this is a good thing: the DIY route is thriving, and while many big indie labels have vanished, some smaller ones survive to promote alternative music (Hesmondhalgh, 2013).

In the early years of the Net, users advocated a free exchange of ideas and a suspicion of commerce. This was part of the Net's utopian ethics, drawing on Western and American notions of individual liberty, alongside counter-cultural suspicion of nation states and corporations. As part of this utopian ideal, file-sharing was commonly used to share and develop software, such as the open-software system known as Linux (Benkler, 2002). It was argued that the sharing of knowledge was the best way to progress humanity: to spread knowledge about human rights, equality and diversity, and science (Arora, 2014). As we have seen earlier in this book, the Net was envisaged as a libertarian community (a Netopia) where freedom and open-ness were privileged (Castells, 1996; Long, 2012; West, 2013). Users of the Net revelled in personal privacy and anonymity, while sharing and using data uploaded by others. The Net was viewed as a common ground, where everyone had a stake in the use of the space but where nobody ultimately owned it. Decisions about what happened on the common ground were communal and consensual, based on liberal individualism but working against the hegemonies of private property and profit. No one had the power to claim ownership of any data on the Net – at its extreme limit, this ideology led to people claiming everything on the Net was free and everything was accessible so long as one was able to be connected to it (Rojek, 2005a). The Netopian insistence that property rights and copyright were outmoded meant that users were encouraged to copy and paste files as a statement of their rejection of copyright law.

The first file-sharers believed that they were liberating the Net from market ideology and introducing an ideal of true, public, open commons (Arora, 2014; Lupton 2014; Rojek, 2005a). They were also just sharing content they thought was cool, such as information about cheats on games and pictures of cats and porn stars. At first, the limited capacity of the Net stopped music and moving images from being shared, but technological changes meant these things soon dominated the bandwidth of Net users (Aspray and Ceruzzi, 2010). In addition, the entertainment industry itself had largely converted its products from analogue to digital: from VHS and vinyl to CD and DVD (Anderson, 2013; Bennett, 2001; Rojek, 2005a). Files (at first only music, then with new versions of the Net, films and television shows) could be uploaded easily by people in the industry (from journalists with review copies to accountants searching their own company's database), but also by consumers who bought the copyrighted product. Digital technology allows consumers to copy and paste files from the products to their computers. It allows them to upload such files to websites. Like tape-traders, file-sharers have evolved a system of sharing the burden of buying and uploading files, so now most things produced by the entertainment industry – albums, games, television shows, movies – can be found online for nothing (Dilmperi, King and Dennis, 2011).

That the ideal of the free Net did not match the reality of ownership on the Net did not matter to the advocate of the ideal – if capitalists and nation states were encroaching on the common ground of the Net, it was incumbent on the citizens of the Net to step back further out of sight, or publicly resist this invasion of the commons (Arora, 2014; Fuchs, 2010; Lupton, 2014). As we have seen, corporations and nation states have tried to colonize the Net – and have had much success (see Chapter 8 later in this book). But they have come up against the utopian ideals that try to maintain the Net as a communicative space for communicative politics and communicative leisure. This can

be seen in struggles to gain (free) open access to scientific papers published behind paywalls, for example (Leonelli, 2013). It can be seen in
the rise of systems that maintain anonymity such as the Diaspora social
network and Tor (Martin, 2014). In practice, though, the impact of the
utopian ideal is seen in the way it has meant users of the Net have consistently avoided paying for subscriptions for data on the Net, believing
that data here should be free beyond connection charges. That means
file-sharing of data that is free and in the public domain, as well as the
sharing of data that has been copied from some copyrighted sources.

That is, it means that 'illegal' downloading – the sharing of digital files
of movies, television shows, books and music without permission from
the creator or copyright owner of that file – has become normalized in
the everyday culture of the Net. There are counter trends to this: musicians who give away their music for free; musicians who sell their music
online in digital formats; companies that sell music; advert-funded services such as Spotify where artists/labels pay for music to be streamed;
and similar entrepreneurial work in other creative industries. There are
examples where artists and others in the creative industries have used
the Net to sell traditional works of art that become art because they are
not digital – for example, there is a counter trend in pop music for vinyl,
and entire genres of rock and heavy metal where music is recorded on
analogue systems (Schiermer, 2014; Sterne, 2012). For the rest of this
chapter, I want to focus on the 'illegal' form of file-sharing or downloading. The notion of 'illegal' supposes that the rights of ownership
and copyright in nation states and in international agreements can be
extended to the virtual space. Downloading is not always downloading –
as I will show, songs, movies and videos might be posted on YouTube or
an equivalent hosting site.

Attitudes to downloading

File-sharing and breaches of copyright hit the headlines in 2000 when
the heavy metal band Metallica filed a lawsuit against the company
Napster (Marshall, 2002; Woodworth, 2004). The band claimed the
website was allowing its songs to be shared in breach of their intellectual property rights. In the same year, a number of American music
labels and companies took Napster to court making similar allegations –
essentially, that Napster was allowing copyright to be breached by its
users who shared copyrighted MP3 music files. Napster had been established in 1999 and the industry association had started its legal case
almost immediately (Alderman, 2008). Like other file-sharing systems,

Napster allowed people to create anonymous accounts and share files with everyone else who had an account. The technology and capacity of the site made it easy to share MP3 files, which had been cumbersome to upload and download on other sites. Even before Napster hit the headlines, its website had millions of users, especially in America and in higher education establishments where students could access the Net through powerful servers. Napster was not the first file-sharing website to become a site for uploading and downloading music (Sterne, 2012), but it epitomized the moral ambiguity of the time. File-sharing operated through a peer-to-peer system. That is, the creators and owners of such sites allowed users to connect with other users and share what they liked. The owners of the sites did not want to know what their users were sharing. This is why they allowed users to be anonymous, why they chose not to monitor what was being shared. They claimed they were providing private and secure exchange systems, and did not hold themselves morally responsible for the content. It was suggested that individual users would not countenance a breach of their own privacy and rights, that individual users demanded the right to share files freely and anonymously because this was a core ethic of the Net (Marshall, 2002).

While the courts ultimately decided Napster had to take more punitive measures to control breaches of copyright, including identifying individual users who were breaching copyright (which Napster could not do, which led to the company shutting itself down in 2001), members of the public were not persuaded that they were doing anything wrong (Alderman, 2008; Woodworth, 2004). Other websites appeared that mirrored the systems and services of Napster, and file-sharing continued on globally infamous sites such as Kazaa.com and The Pirate Bay, where new technologies allowed for quicker speeds and bigger file sizes, leading to the file-sharing of entire movies. Alongside these big sites, smaller sites and file-sharing on forums and discussion boards continued to take place (Dilmperi, King and Dennis, 2011).

Fans of heavy metal mocked the multi-millionaires of Metallica threatening to sue poor college students who had downloaded their songs – heavy metal bands were supposed to embody rebellion and anti-mainstream counter-culturalism, and here was a band whose members collected expensive wine and arts trying to make a moral case that they were losing money (Woodworth, 2004). Other artists who were complaining about the breaches of copyright included multi-millionaires such as the hip-hop star Dr Dre and the pop star Madonna (Alderman, 2008). Music fans in general who had fast, broadband or workplace access to the Net, started to upload their digital music for others to share, while downloading music other people had posted. Despite campaigns by the music and movies industries warning about the dangers of copyright theft and piracy and linking such activity to criminal gangs and hackers, millions of users of the Net around the world see no real danger or crime in 'illegal' downloading (Dilmperi, King and Dennis, 2011; Sterne, 2012). They are aware that they are breaching copyright laws but do not think this is morally different from getting a tape of an album from a friend, or uploading their CD to an MP3 player (Giesler, 2006; Huang, 2003; Sterne, 2012). 'Illegal' downloading seems to be viewed like speeding on a British motorway – everybody knows it is against the law, but so many people think it is okay to be ten or even 20 miles over the speed limit that it feels like cars driving at the speed limit are driving too slowly.

This may sound like ingenuous pleading on my part, but I have never downloaded anything that is in potential breach of copyright. I have downloaded some tracks that have been given away free by bands, but I still like the feel of a finished album in my hands. I do use YouTube to occasionally listen to music to get a feel for a band's work, however, and I have never been concerned whether the original poster has cleared it with the copyright holder. In my small research sample, two of the 12 participants admitted they had downloaded music from file-sharing sites. Five people were music fans who used the Net to download music legally, either free samples from bands or from an established retail store such as Amazon or iTunes. I suspect that some of the others may have been involved in downloading copyrighted material, but such file-sharing is not something these individuals felt comfortable discussing. This shows the moral uncertainty felt by Net users who engage in activities that might be perceived as being forms of dark leisure. The two respondents who did admit to being involved in file-sharing both told me they no longer do it. One of them was involved as a teenager in the early 2000s, listening to dance music tracks shared between his online and offline friends. This was not done through a formal account on a website, just through exchanges of emails and messages. The second respondent said they had been active in file-sharing because everyone did it, and because it allowed him as a student to listen to a wide range of music that he could not afford to buy. He suggested that the music industry 'deserve the kicking they got because they, the cost of the albums, it was way too much, it was a rip-off really'. For him, the inequity of the capitalist instrumentality at the heart of the music industry sowed the seeds of its own destruction – instead of reducing prices to keep customers going into record shops and buying albums and singles, the music industry responded to the rise of 'illegal' downloading by increasing its prices. As someone who still buys physical copies of albums, I feel anger at the way in which the industry has failed its consumers by hiking up prices, failing to invest properly in genres that have big fan bases and abandoning traditional music media. The industry is still fundamentally concerned with making short-term profits rather than creating and sustaining long-term music fans as consumers (Arditi, 2012).

YouTube is one of the spaces online where the industry has used its copyright-holding power to limit the involvement of music fans. The website was established in 2005 at the height of the rise of the so-called 'Web 2.0', when technological increases in capacity and speeds combined with the rise of mobile phone use to allow personal users the possibility of filming events and watching video clips online (Burgess and Green, 2013; Kim, 2012). It allows individual users to post video clips of anything and everything, though the clips and the comments about them are subject to moderation and deletion. The website became a space where people shared videos of individuals doing stunts and falling down holes, and cats playing the piano – things that had been shared via email or on discussion boards, the most popular videos that showed the banality and bathos of our everyday lives (Burgess and Green, 2013). Other users, however, were interested in posting videos of old television programmes and movies, live concerts and gigs, and music videos. The spread of mobile phones gave fans at gigs the ability to post footage of their favourite bands, often to the encouragement of other fans and even the bands (Edmond, 2014). Some music fans crated unofficial videos for their favourite songs, especially for acts that had never released official music videos: these videos were the subject of artistic appreciation and competition among users (Burgess and Green, 2013). More simply, music fans would post entire albums online as videos, often with the album cover as a still image, or a collage of photographs of the band. In alternative and underground music subcultures, this became the easiest way to listen to music from an album that was no longer available to buy. Entire communities of users emerged to share obscure music through the website, sometimes with the active involvement of artists, but more often than not without any official backing. My own interests in black metal have been met through being able to listen to demos from the 1990s not available for sale on YouTube, but also through sampling albums by bands I am intending to see live or simply sharing the best songs with others via email and Facebook.

YouTube was such a success that it was swiftly bought by Google, which has ensured the website remains bundled into smartphone apps and the new generation of tablets (Kim, 2012). Its ownership by Google has protected it from some of the most rigorous defenders of intellectual property rights. However, Google is part of the transnational network of corporations that control the Net, so it is inevitable that YouTube has become more commercialized and regulated. From its inception the site warned users that it was illegal to post videos that were copyrighted to someone else without permission (Burgess and Green, 2013; Edmond, 2014). But the site's paid moderators were not strict in enforcing such rules, not least since they were charged with tracking down pornography and videos supporting terrorism, and copyrighted material formed a large part of the content (Kim, 2012). Copyright-holders in the entertainment industry have responded to this in two ways. First, major companies now have their own YouTube accounts, which post official content and raise revenue through showing adverts. Second, they have persuaded Google to employ more time and resources to shut down videos and posters who are in potential breaches of their copyright. This means it is now difficult to find content by a transnational corporation's entertainment products posted without prior permission. If material is posted, it is quickly removed. The only content that seems to remain posted is critical commentaries, spoofs and recordings of live gigs, which is presumably left alone to show the world that the corporations and their lawyers aren't so bad – even George Lucas can laugh at himself and the people who joke around with Star Wars (after all, they are fans and their jokes keep the brand in full view – Elovaara, 2013).

Content from small labels and companies, from little-known artists and those that were obscure even when they were working can still be found on the website, as there are no company lawyers sending threatening emails to Google. There is still a surfeit of amateur videos that include copyrighted music as part of the soundtracks to the action they present: ska-punk for skateboarding accidents, 80s house for monster trucks. Much of this would probably be removed if the artists and labels were able to find the time to track it down and notify Google. Some bands and artists actively encourage people to post content without seeking permission (Edmond, 2014). There is a view that it is impossible to pursue every breach of copyright, and the music industry has changed so much that it is impossible to make money from records. The best way to survive as an artist is to develop audiences that buy tickets for gigs and that buy merchandise sold by the artist (Ogden, Ogden and Long, 2011). For these people, every video viewed on YouTube, whether it is officially posted or not, is one potential new fan. This can be seen by the way many bands encourage fans to post footage from live gigs. One can also find on YouTube a range of television documentaries that remain viewable, even though comedies, dramas and soap operas are subject to being taken down – it is as if the corporate workers and lawyers are concerned more with limiting mass cultural entertainment rather than elite cultural education and edification. As the systems used by Google get more sophisticated, copyrighted content is being identified and removed quicker. This allows the entertainment industry to make more profit from advertising revenue. And it reduces the communicative space in which digital leisure occurs.

The ethics of downloading: the case for the defence

In the previous section of this chapter, I introduced some arguments that try to justify 'illegal' downloading. These arguments are familiar to anyone who has read blogs on the Net, or articles in offline media about the 'problem' of file-sharing. They are raised by those who actively engage in the practice as well as those who might have done it at some point in the past. There are others that I have not yet mentioned but which will also be familiar. Nonetheless, it is necessary I think to stop and critically reflect on the morality, politics and ethics at the heart of each of these arguments. I will run through the main arguments in this section, critiquing those that are weak before summarising what I take the strong arguments for 'illegal' downloading to be. I will then provide a critique of the strong arguments in the next section. This critique draws on the work of others (see Dilmperi, King and Dennis, 2011; Huang, 2003; Langford, 2000; Rojek, 2005a; Rosenthal, 2014; Sterne, 2012) but is ultimately my own attempt to understand why people download 'illegally', and why they think it is okay to do so. In the next section I will again draw on other people's work but make my own critique of the main arguments.

The first thing people might say to justify the practice of downloading is: 'everybody does it'. This of course is a weak defence of any action, though it does suggest there is a communicative norm that individuals think they are following. First of all, it is not clear that everybody is doing it. There are millions of people actively involved in downloading files 'illegally', but millions of people who do not. Some of the people who do not download don't have access to the Net, but there are millions of Net users who feel uncomfortable ethically with the practice, or who just do not see it as a priority in the leisure choices they make. Second, just because lots of people do something that has become almost a social norm or seemingly part of everyday leisure does not make it morally right or even acceptable under some constrained circumstances. This justification can quite easily be ignored as it is not a proper justification, merely an observation.

A more considered justification is: 'it doesn't hurt'. True, downloading copyrighted material only damages the profits of corporations and their intellectual property rights, along with those of the artists. People who engage in file-sharing of copyrighted material are not building bombs, or sharing information on how to build bombs. They are not sharing child pornography. But is it true to say it does not hurt? We might not have any sympathy with transnational corporations making losses. We might even rejoice in the fact that a corporate executive has been fired or lost a bonus, or the fact that a shareholder might not make a dividend. But there are musicians who have not been able to maintain successful professional careers because people are not buying records. Some of these musicians have had to end their careers early and find other work, which is not easy when all you know how to do is set up a microphone and sing. This has had an impact on their families and their personal health. Younger musicians starting out are finding it almost impossible to become full-time professionals, and many are making the decision to abandon or curtail their careers (Arditi, 2012; Ramirez, 2013). Again, this directly harms their life course, their relationships and their personal health – it is not just a loss of possible income. If musicians stop making music the next people harmed are the fans who have no new music to listen to, and though this harm might be considered trivial it has a strong consequence: music becomes limited to material in the mainstream and material from the past, and subcultural belonging and identity are lost to commodification and instrumentality (Spracklen, 2014).

A third justification is that of the discerning consumer: 'I like to try before I buy'. This suggests that we are not dupes of marketing or commerce, and we are acting as communicative agents, rationally sampling the world around us before making our purchases. Anything that appears to fight back against capitalism and the ruthless imposition of instrumentality is a good thing – and there is some merit in this. We all like to know what we are getting, we all need to read reviews before we buy anything or go anywhere. No one would buy a holiday without reading about the destination and the airline and the tour company first. Many bands and labels recognize this argument and now offer free samples or videos – I have written this chapter while listening to a live stream of the new Opeth album posted by their label on a music magazine's website, which I will buy as soon as it comes out. The streamed content on YouTube (whether official or unofficial) also allows people to sample music without downloading it permanently into their ownership, so in one sense people can treat YouTube like an uncurated and free travel exhibition. But if this justification were coherent, the millions of people downloading would have spent enough money for physical record sales to avoid the tumultuous decline. This has not happened. People are not trying before they buy. They are trying without buying. The analogy is not between 'illegal' downloading and choosing a holiday – it is between 'illegal' downloading and taking cakes and muffins from a coffee shop home to try out which one you might eat the next time you go there.

A justification related to the previous one is: 'It broadens my musical tastes – I wouldn't have heard Tuvan throat-singing without file-sharing'. This is saying you like to sample before you buy, but the focus is on the development of your taste and your ability to resist the marketing pressure to find some authentic music not known by the mainstream. By being able to explore a broader range of music you get a deeper sense and experience of diversity, a richer taste for the authentic and the non-commercial. This is a seductive argument. But it is false for two reasons. First of all, it is quite possible to find out about Tuvan throat-singing (or the equivalent) without 'illegal' downloading. The Net gives people a chance to find out about new forms of music and culture from other people or from reading other people's reviews and blogs. The Net also continues to provide valid space for the work of cultural critics seeking to nurture an interest in things beyond the commercial mainstream. And it is still possible to read books and magazines and talk to people in the real world about what they like. Second, the justification presupposes that it is possible to have a pure connection to a form of music or a form of cultural taste. Actually, all taste is mediated through cultural capital, so we never experience any form of culture without coming to it through our habitus and the things we read and the things we have been told about (Bourdieu, 1986).

A more nuanced justification goes something like: 'I bought the CD so why can't I copy it for my friends?' This is actually a convincing argument for fair use of the copyright. In buying a product legally from a shop, for example, there is an assumption that one has bought the right to use that product. When I buy a coffee, I get to drink that coffee, or I get to pass it on or throw it away. I might even decide to re-sell my coffee to a friend who is thirsty. Now copyright laws limit our use of the things we buy that have copyright attached to them, such as books and records. There are legal clauses that allow us to share such things privately and for our own pleasure, but which threaten us with breach of copyright if we start to make numerous copies without permission. When we buy things we do not necessarily own them outright – we buy them and use them on the caveat that we must not offend someone else's property rights. This might lead to someone arguing that copyright laws are unrealistic and favour the corporations that pay lawyers to police them.

This takes us to the heart of matter. There is in the file-sharing movement a political philosophy that starts with the ethical claim that information should be free (Sterne, 2012). In history, there are countless examples of the restriction of information and knowledge, the collection of information in the hands of those who are privileged enough to able to afford it. Drawing analogies from the common land that was divided up and bought by elite landlords in Western Europe, philosophers have argued that hegemonic power has taken control of knowledge that used to be shared freely in more communicative cultures and communities (Foucault, 1973, 2006). In the Scientific Revolution and the Enlightenment, the discourse about how the world operated and how best to live was suppressed by the social and cultural elites: religious leaders, landlords, aristocracies and capitalists (Gramsci, 1971). In practical terms, millions of people lived through the last two centuries in poverty and ignorance, legally free and equal but practically in bondage (Hobsbawm, 1987; Spracklen, 2011a). The purpose of the Net, according to many of its first users and advocates, was to free people from ignorance and share true knowledge about the world and human rights. As such, the Net is argued to be something that should be free. If it is not free it cannot work to counter discrimination and ignorance, and promote equality and human rights. The Net's early generation relied on the free work and discourse of its users, and this freedom should be preserved: it is argued that the Net operates as a form of virtual commons, where files are shared between others and everyone takes responsibility for the betterment of the community, against the logic of capitalism (Arora, 2014).

Women and minority-ethnic groups are still held in control by many cultures and communities because of the control leaders have over access to information: racial myths, gender orders and religious rules all draw their power from the commodification and privatization of information. Copyright laws are ways in which information – knowledge about the inequities of the world – is privatized and controlled (Rojek,

2005a). Copyright laws also turn information into commodities, profit-making products that restrict the rights of others to make use of that copyrighted information. For example, in the United Kingdom, it has become typical for academic publishers to make sure authors have paid for copyright clearance on things such as song lyrics. The result is academics choose not to use song lyrics in their research, which is *de facto* a limit on freedom of speech and freedom of academic inquiry. The critical independence of musicology and music studies is threatened by academics silently turning away from an analysis that will cost them money they do not have.

Copyright then, is morally wrong. It gives too much power to the copyright owners and reduces the autonomy and freedom of others who might wish to use information that is subject to property rights. This is not about respecting private property, a matter that vexed philosophers such as Kant (Oliver, 2014). This is about corporations extending their rights beyond what might be ethically justifiable. It is arguable that all forms of private property are morally wrong: when property is owned by private individuals, societies become unequal, riven between owners and the others. The moral injunction against private property is shared by many religions, which see such individualism as a form of sin or a form of wrong thinking that stops individuals attaining some spiritual escape. It was also shared by many Marxist and Anarchist political theorists, including Marx himself, through the nineteenth century. For these thinkers, private product is a convenient myth constructed by elites to maintain their power and limit the power of others (Löwy, 2014). From such perspectives we can see that copyright laws are just new ways for capitalism to control the masses. Intellectual property rights become an absurdity that has no place in an ideally communicative lifeworld (Habermas, 1984).

But we do not live in such a lifeworld, and the ideal is not really lived by most of us. We live in a society where we keep on buying things, from apples to houses. Most of us are grossly offended if something we own is stolen, because we live in a society constructed on the logic of capitalism. We live in a capitalist society, but the law does not support the free trade of ideas and information. Rather, the law protects established corporations and restricts the rights of new entrants into that market. Copyright acts like a form of censorship on people who cannot afford to pay for copyright clearance, which limits freedoms of speech and freedoms of expression. In the United States, the constitutional rights of citizens to freedom of speech are enshrined in liberal publishing laws. There is strong recognition of the fact that citizens need to be free to share ideas and information in a progressive, communicative public sphere – this is good for democracy and for the State. When ideas and interactions are censored it is morally wrong – and copyright forces people without wealth to censor their interactions. Copyright is morally wrong because it is immoral to give money to corporations. Capitalists have exploited the labour of others to earn their capital for hundreds of years, and now they expect us to continue giving them money. By refusing to pay for music files downloaded online, one destroys the power of the music industry, which, it is supposed, is only a good thing.

Contra downloading

Given the final claims about the immoral nature of private property and copyright, and the immoral nature of global capitalism, it seems peculiar that I want to make the case against 'illegal' downloading and file-sharing. You might think I only want to make money from the royalties I get from my books, and that I am pleading the case of the publishers too conveniently, since I clearly have some sort of vested interest in them. To make my own position clear: I do not own any shares in any corporation (I own one share in a community sports co-operative), and my royalties from my books have never amounted to anything above a few hundred pounds each year. I do not want people to buy or loan this book to make me money; all I want to do is share my knowledge and ideas with those who might be interested in them. I have chosen a publisher that I trust, one that can do the work of editing and marketing that I cannot do alone. If you are reading this book then the publisher has done their job of persuading you or your library to buy it. For all I know, you might be reading a pirated version of this book, hastily photocopied in the library or transferred into some e-reading device. If you are, please do the right thing and buy this book. Because this is the product of my own labours and you are violating my personal rights and stealing my creative works.

Why is such file-sharing morally wrong? Let us begin with a religious commandment. Many religions make it clear that stealing is a sin, or something that is immoral. If one takes one's neighbour's oxen one takes away their chances of good health and a happy life. If we lived in a utopia where power was distributed equitably we might be able to find things in common and construct a world where property is shared, but in reality the world is grossly inequitable. Every day people are robbed, assaulted, raped and killed. Each of these acts is an attack of some kind, and each creates deep psychological trauma. This is why most religions abhor such acts. They make humans baser and less pure spiritually and mentally – both the offender and the victim suffers. Where there are exceptions and controversies over these tenets, there is no doubt that religions have tried to capture the essential moral compass of how we have to live with one another. It is not enough to be lawless and wild, because that way lays untrammelled savagery.

The stereotype of anarchism is a product of conservative imaginations, but history shows that the communicative ideal of the lifeworld can often be disrupted by violence – communicative rationality leads inevitably to agreements about rules, about how we treat one another. Hobbes, for example, argues that humans need the framework of government and law to survive and progress (see discussion in Raphael, 2013). Paradoxically, this allows a public sphere to emerge in early modern society that is communicative in nature, which shows itself to be a crucial space in establishing the rule of law and the principles of Kantian liberal democracy (Oliver, 2014). Kant himself has shown that humans are given a moral imperative to obey the law, because laws are written by rational beings who are subject to the scrutiny of other rational beings (O'Neill, 2013). In every set of laws known to us in the written record, there are concerns about theft and violence, with rules against such things and punishments. Much of this is designed in practice to support the power and wealth of the hegemons, of course, with common thieves being brutally executed while aristocrats who steal land with impunity get another title for their villainy. But just because the laws are biased, it is still possible to argue that the laws are grounded upon universal moral imperatives or calculations. It is a rule in most law codes, both ancient and modern, to condemn theft because no one is happy when their possessions are stolen: thieves and anarchists complain when their own material is stolen. It is a rule that individuals will be held responsible for their own actions. It is also a rule in most law codes to undertake a form of utilitarian calculus to try to make as many people as possible happy with their lives under the laws. Here we might turn to the work of John Rawls, who suggested that fairness in a society might be understood as ensuring both a redistribution of wealth (a levelling of inequality that does not eliminate inequality) and the construction of laws that ensure everyone has the same basic freedoms, including the freedom to personal property (Rawls, 1971). His theory of justice shows that societies work best when these two principles act together and balance out their opposing tendencies – the pull of complete individualism, which reduces equality, and the pull of the levelling of inequality, which reduces the freedom of individualism.

Some acts of theft may be permissible under such a Rawlsian frame-work (taking radical action against factories damaging the environment?), but it is difficult to see how copyright theft might be one of them. It might feel right to take money from an evil corporation, and the music industry is a particularly egregious one, but there are harmful consequences. First of all, as we have seen, the music industry is suffering real harm, along with other creative industries, from this wide-scale theft. The individuals who run these industries may not garner our sympathy but they are fellow human beings. The second consequence is the collapse of these industries and forms of artistic endeavour. Musicians and novelists and others need to make a living from their work – now they can't, and they struggle on trying to keep their artistic careers as a form of serious leisure (Stebbins, 1982). How long they continue is debatable. But if these people give up, the fans that are downloading content illegally have destroyed the very form of culture they like.

Conclusion

There are people who create new works of art through playing around with intellectual property online, and there are people who set out to destroy or at least upset the capitalist world order. While I have complete sympathy with both human acts, and both acts display a form of communicative rationality and leisure, I cannot ultimately come out in favour of such acts. While we live in the neo-liberal society of late modernity, such acts undermine the cultural and leisure habits that give people meaning and purpose in their lives. That is, the artists who make work that gives people such fulfilment need some protection against copyright theft, otherwise they will stop creating the work that people care about. Some of that work might be commodified rubbish, of course, but some of it has lasting aesthetic and moral value (Adorno, 1991). As I will show in the next chapter, there is so little left online that is not commodified that we need to protect the non-commercialized material as much as possible – and that is why we need copyright.

8
Digital Leisure and Commodification

On 11 November 2014, the BBC News reported on a record day of sales for the Chinese retail website Alibaba ('Alibaba's Singles' Day sales exceed predictions at $9.3bn', http://www.bbc.co.uk/news/business -29999289, accessed 30 November 2014). The BBC reported that Alibaba had popularized and promoted the idea of Singles' Day, a special day for those who were not in a relationship to feel good about themselves. For Alibaba, this means persuading its customers to spend huge amounts of money on presents for themselves. The company might argue that Singles' day is just a bit of fun, and they are only responding to the needs of their customers, who are old enough and responsible enough to spend wisely – but the hype around the website and Singles' Day makes it almost impossible for users to resist being swept along in the torrent of spending.

Crazy consumption is not just associated with insecure middle-class Chinese office workers, and I could have easily opened with a news story about Black Friday, the day before the holiday season in America, or the post-Christmas sales in the United Kingdom. This chapter explores commodification through gambling, shopping, sports and gaming on the Net. In the first section, I concentrate on gambling sites and the increasing professionalization of the corporations that run them. In the second section, I focus on shopping, comparing big corporations such as Amazon with niche retailers. The third section of the chapter explores the availability of sports content on the Net, and the increasing use of the Net by professional sport and sports-media corporations to sell content. The fourth section will examine online role-playing games and other games. I will show that all these forms of leisure space and leisure activity on the Net are increasingly being taken over by large corporations who try to hide their ruthless commodification through the adoption of idealistic, individualized Net-speak.

Gambling as communicative and instrumental leisure

In the Roman Empire, gambling was a commonplace leisure activity. There is archaeological evidence of dice found in taverns, staging posts and military camps. There is literary evidence that gambling on the throw of the dice was a popular and addictive part of Roman leisure lives. Julius Caesar thought nothing of using the casting of die ('alea iacta est...') as a metaphor for his re-telling of his own break with tradition and law when he crossed the river Rubicon to take control of Rome (Billows, 2004). We hear of the Emperor Augustus, for example, being so obsessed by gambling on dice-throwing that he would spend hours in the company of other gamblers, even though publicly he enacted laws that made gambling illegal (Southern, 2014). While Augustus thought gambling to be immoral and contrary to the pious nature of Roman masculinity, others in Roman society thought nothing of placing bets on dice, on gladiatorial contests and on chariot-racing (Balsdon, 2004; Toner, 1999). In the latter, spectators could elect to pick one of four colours, representing the colours of the chariot-racers: blue, green, white and red (Cameron, 1976; Spracklen, 2011a). Bookmakers would offer odds just as they offer odds today, ensuring that colours that were favourites had the lowest returns on a bet, and the colours least likely to win had enormous returns (Balsdon, 2004). As with gambling today, managing the laying-on of bets and the calculation of odds was a careful science that encouraged gambling while ensuring safe profits for the bookmakers. There was no shortage of people willing to place extravagant bets, whether in the stadia of Rome or the forts of the Roman frontier – and there are cases throughout the written record of people ruined by their gambling debts (Toner, 1999). Later on, the colours had become a combination of professional teams, exclusive guilds and hooligan gangs: the Blues and the Greens (Cameron, 1976). In this period, the bookmakers developed close relationships with the Blues and the Greens, and it is quite probable that match-fixing was as common then as it is now in professional sport (for match-fixing now see Caruso, 2009).

The growth of Christianity and the arrival of Christian emperors with Christian laws led to a moral campaign against gambling and the sports and games that fed it (McGrath, 2012). From Constantine onward, Christian emperors tried to control the leisure choices of their citizens as part of an instrumental morality – banning leisure activities that went against the teachings of the Church (such as the killing of gladiators) while limiting other activities. Early Christian theologians and writers argued that gambling was wrong because it was based on greed and avarice – it encouraged people to dream of becoming wealthy while making them bankrupt, and distracted them from work and family. At the same time, it brought ruin on so many of its participants, both poverty in the real world and hell in the afterlife (Brenner, 1990). Many Christian theologians retained this stance on gambling. There is still in some Christian denominations an injunction on the act and a warning that gambling leads to spiritual dangers (Robbins, 2004). In Islam, the rule on gambling is much clearer. Gambling is one of the activities that is restricted or forbidden by an unambiguous text in the Qu'ran, Sura 5: 90–91, which warns the believers that gambling is the part of the work of Satan, an activity designed to sow discord among the faithful (Kunhibava, 2011).

Despite the efforts of religious moralists, gambling has been and still remains an everyday leisure activity in modern societies (Brenner, 1990). In leisure studies, there is some debate about the legitimacy of gambling. Is gambling something that leisure scholars should study as a communicative or inconsequential fork of leisure? Some structuralists and feminists in leisure studies have argued that gambling remains highly problematic (Wood and Tirone, 2013). It is argued that gambling is a commercial activity that takes money from the poor; it is said that gambling is a con-trick, an industry that serves no benefit to the well-being of society (Cotte, 1997). When politicians are faced with decisions on whether to allow casinos or bookmakers to open in their communities there is an inevitable moral panic about people being 'fooled' into spending money they do not have, chasing a dream that will not come true (Critcher, 2008). When national lotteries are created there is a debate about whether this is the first step towards a nation of gambling addicts, bankrupted and destitute. The same arguments against gambling reappear: stupid people are being conned by evil industries, and this is causing them social and spiritual harm. Some leisure theorists talk of gambling as being somehow deviant or dark (Franklin-Reible, 2006; Stebbins, 1997).

There is no doubt that gambling is addictive, and dangerously so for those who become addicted to the thrills of winning. But gambling has provided an opportunity for many people to engage in worthwhile, communicative leisure experiences. Carolyn Downs has shown how bingo clubs serve as spaces for working-class women to escape the inequities of the gender order and domesticity (Downs, 2010). The pleasure of gambling is just one part of the communicative leisure such bingo-players find in each other's company. Horse-racing events are other spaces where people gamble as part of a wider communicative leisure experience, and understanding the form of the horses is a long-standing serious leisure pursuit (McManus and Graham, 2014). Where gambling is legal according to a nation's law code, it is part of the wider leisure industry. As Ken Roberts has suggested, the gambling industry is one part of the global leisure industry, meeting a need and supplying services, giving satisfaction and pleasure to its customers (Roberts, 2004). It is, he implies, wrong for us to make moral judgements over things that have been made legal and which are part of a long-standing leisure practice.

Online, such activities have spread massively. In the years before the arrival of the Net, when politicians in Great Britain were discussing the legalization of betting shops, there was a dominant view that making betting shops legal would help regulate and tax gambling (Brenner, 1990). Regulation allowed the State to limit the size of bets, the number of bets and the things that could form a legitimate bet. Regulation allowed the State to raise revenue. Regulation allowed the State to force the industry to run programmes aimed at ameliorating gambling addiction, and allowed the State to control the advertising of gambling products and services. The Net challenges this by allowing gambling corporations to operate in tax havens or other unregulated spaces. There is still an industry of traditional companies involved in gambling that have online operations alongside their real-world betting shops. But these traditional companies have been joined by new corporations that take full advantage of their virtual, global nature to maximize their profits and reduce their risks.

None of the respondents in my small research sample had used gambling sites online (or rather, none of them admitted to using them). My own experience of gambling sites comes from being a personal tutor to students in my university. Gambling is something that many of my students seem to do routinely on the Net. For some, gambling takes the form of various spread-betting on professional soccer. Gambling on the outcome of big matches, or on the scorers in matches (or when goals might take place), seems to allow these students a way of sharing the visceral experience of watching sports and talking about sports with their friends. Gambling on professional sports is as old as the chariot-racing of the Roman Empire. The rise of modern professional sports and sports fandom makes gambling a key part of modern sports culture. Before the Net in the United Kingdom there were football pools organized nationally, where fans could predict the scores of every professional soccer game (Forrest, 1999; Jones, 1984). Online, this form of gambling is multiplied exponentially, with every variant in every minute of almost every elite game around the world open for a bet – and increasingly, bets are available for leagues and sports below those elite levels (d'Astous and Gaspero, 2013). Gambling on soccer enables my students to show off their knowledge to other students – the sums seem immaterial. But every year there seems to be one student who tries to make money from some form of online gambling, whether it is betting on horses, bingo or poker. The temptation to move from a social form of gambling, a communicative leisure activity, to a more instrumental profit-seeking enterprise is not surprisingly very high for students having to pay off large loans. The allure and addictive nature of the technology makes it very easy to click through one site to another, and click to make another bet or gambit.

The technology of the Net has made it much easier for unregulated and illegal gambling to occur. Anonymous protocols and the 'dark web' make it possible for criminal gangs to control gambling syndicates around the world, moving money from account to account, moving headquarters from country to country ahead of Interpol (Martin, 2014). Such global, virtual, invisible gambling networks have created an industry of match-fixing and horse-doping, where gamblers or bookmakers interfere with athletes and others who might be able to act or not act at the crucial moment of action (Caruso, 2009). The legal gambling industry is concerned that such activities undermine their own profits, so they are at the forefront of investigations into suspicious bets and transactions (ibid.). But the brutal and direct bribery and violence that surrounds illegal match-fixing is only an extension of the conversations undertaken with various informants by the bookmakers about things that are going on that might have an impact on an outcome, and the computer models they run to accurately predict outcomes (Banks, 2014). The rise in illegal gambling leads to moves to regulate and legalize gambling in new markets, which favours the corporations that make a show of being social and morally responsible (ibid.).

Gambling sites and associated 'risk' gaming sites for things such as poker and bingo are big business on the Net (Lee and Byun, 2014; Wood and Griffiths, 2008; Wood and Williams, 2007). Smartphones and tablets allow apps to be used that reduce the time and thought over whether one has the resources to play another game or make another bet. Gambling sites use advertising to entice new users, with claims offering people free money to make bets. Like other parts of the commodified leisure industry, gambling corporations have taken advantage of the successful rise in targeted advertising. In the 1990s and 2000s, Net users reacted against the spread of pop-up ads selling everything from porn to plumbing, and ISPs and software designers worked on new systems that blocked the ads. The communicative power of the Net to resist the over-commercialization of virtual space disappeared by the 2010s. New browsers and website software seem to be designed to allow the owners of such things to make money from selling advertising space and data on users to advertisers. The result is that it has become commonplace at the time of writing to struggle to find the text one is looking for among the adverts inserted in and around it. Gambling companies have used this technology to both legitimize their practice and activity and ruthlessly compete with one another for punters (Lee and Byun, 2014).

Finally, Orford, Wardle and Griffiths (2013) show how online gamblers have complex motivations and behaviours (see also their work with colleagues: Wardle, Moody, Griffiths, Orford and Volberg, 2011). For some, gambling online seems to be an extension of their offline gambling habits. For others, they only gamble online, though such activity is part of a wider social network in the real world. Their work suggests that there are a small number of online gamblers who seem to be investing an unhealthy amount of time and effort into their gambling. These, they suggest, are probably well known to gambling companies or at least tracked on the online systems, so it might be possible for companies to invest effort to target these individuals with support for addiction. Of course, it is questionable whether such companies would engage in this kind of intervention. In other work, Wardle and her colleagues have noted the way in which the online habits and practices of gaming are becoming more like gambling, with games with gambling mechanisms built into them risking virtual currencies (Parke, Wardle, Rigbye and Parke, 2013). These are available as apps or on social media, and are advertised and described as harmless fun – but they act to create a normalization of gambling and may be a way of making young gamers into adult gamblers (Gainsbury, Hing, Delfabbro and King, 2014).

Shopping

The first purpose of the Net was to share information about the nature of any nuclear strike on the United States. The second purpose of the Net was to allow scientists and engineers to share work-in-progress, undertake experiments and discuss research protocols. The third purpose of the Net was to allow individuals to make friends, learn new things and argue over marginalized aspects of popular culture. Now it seems the fourth and possibly the final purpose of the Net is to provide a site for immediate gratification through shopping (Fuchs, 2014; Leiss, 2013; Lupton, 2014; Ritzer and Jurgenson, 2010). The transnational corporations such as Amazon and eBay that exist alongside independent and specialist retailers allow consumers to follow every passing whim and interest with a purpose. When email was in the process of replacing the hand-written or typed letter, experts and journalists predicted the end of postal delivery services (Jolly, 2011; Milne, 2012). What would the poor deliverers of mail do if there are no letters to deliver? The digital age has brought a steady stream of parcels and new delivery services, predicated on enormous warehouses, economies of scale and cheap labour, which makes the forecasters of postal doom seem strangely naïve. It is now possible to live anywhere in the world and consume anything that can be shipped in a parcel to your doorstep, or to the nearest pick-up point. Just last night my wife ordered earthworms for our horned frog, and today I ordered a copy of a journal. I have been buying books online since 2000, when I was told about the ease with which you could order academic texts with Amazon and Books On-Line (BOL). Amazon and Google are experimenting with robots and drones that might do the delivery work, but for now the consumption habits of digital leisure are maintaining the jobs of the entire postal industry.

Of course, you also need access to the Net and access to cash. The Net may be a quick and convenient way for some people to shop, but the technology and the costs limit the opportunities of others. Many people do not have credit or debit cards because they are deemed to be high-risk (low value?) customers. I choose not to have a credit card for ethical reasons, and that limits the amount of places online that I can buy things. Many people do not have access to the Net, or do want to access the Net because they are uncomfortable with handing over personal information. Others are simply unused to using the Net. For these people the Net is not a consumerist paragon, it is a monster that devours high streets. Record stores and bookshops have closed around the world in their thousands, with entire national chains and independents losing their business to the parvenus of the Net (Arditi, 2012). My home town has lost two bookshops in the last eight years, and now has none. Online shopping companies are now becoming dominant in other markets, threatening their high-street equivalents in electrical goods, furniture, clothing and even groceries (Laing and Royle, 2013; Stephens, 2013). Our shopping choices in the real world have become limited as a result of the baneful influence of the transnational corporations.

Shopping is an old leisure activity that emerged with the specialization of labour and the development of monetary economies, when people realized they could make money selling their products or services, and others realized they could save time and effort by buying those products and services (Davis, 2013). It is the basis of the ideal capitalist free market, free from interference or control by hegemonic interests. Monarchs and aristocracies were only interested in mercantile activities as a means of raising taxes for warfare, and it was left to the urban middle classes to fully develop capitalism in the early modern cultures of the world. Shops became spaces where the new bourgeois social order could be constructed and defended, and where new arrivals in towns and cities could learn to become active consumers (Habermas, 1989).

In the West, with the advent of industrialization and high modernity, shops became symbols of civic pride, with city councils striving to build new high streets, which were suitably attractive for shop-owners to invest in (Davis, 2013). The rise of nation states allowed local businesses to become national chains, building ever-bigger shops (superstores) in competition with one another. The urban elites had enormous wealth, which they spent on conspicuous consumption of un-needed goods, showing off to one another and to everyone else about their taste (Veblen, 1970). For the middle classes, an industry of shops and products emerged to help them buy cheaper versions of the same things, along with a credit industry that offered huge loans for goods the middle classes would otherwise not be able to afford to buy (Davis, 2013). For the working classes, retail and shopping were constructed as good uses of their leisure and their surplus cash: shopping was a way of becoming civilized, becoming bourgeois (Veblen, 1970); it was also a way of keeping the working classes in their place (Davis, 2013). Shopping became a way of celebrating the rise of America, the defeat of Communism and the supposed steady progression of the neo-liberal world order (Zukin, 2004). By the end of the twentieth century the normalization of shopping had led to huge shopping malls, transnational corporations and the decline of independent shops (well before the rise of the Net) against the power of national chains (Bauman, 2000; Davis, 2013; Žižek, 2010). But the spread of shopping and the normalization of shopping as a leisure activity presupposes that people have the money and the freedom to shop.

It is one of the ironies of modern Net culture and ethics that the process of commercialization and commodification that has turned it into a virtual retail park has been less of an issue for users than breaches in security and State surveillance. Amazon started out as a hip retailer of books and records, and struggled to make real profits in its early years, leading some commentators at the time to predict it would never turn a profit – that it would go bust like other early dot-coms that disappeared after the collapse of the financial bubble (Brandt, 2011). Its initial customers were people trying to purchase obscure books and things from the back catalogue of music labels, products that were not readily available in a high-street shop (ibid.). Amazon quickly extended its market share by doing deals to sell best-selling books and records at prices lower than those found in the real world. It launched e-books and kindles, and followed others in selling music as downloadable MP3 files (Warr and Goode, 2011). As it has set up business around the world it has looked to reduce tax payments by setting up head offices in tax havens (Palan, Murphy and Chavagneux, 2010). It has constructed warehouses all over the world and fought publishers and suppliers over the terms of its contracts (Brandt, 2011). It has introduced targeted recommendations that try to persuade each user to purchase other things (Pariser, 2011). And more importantly, it has expanded the range of products it sells. When I looked at the amazon.co.uk website today (11 September 2014) I found it had 17 'departments' in its 'store' (the quaint phrases that remind us of the multi-department stores that used to exist on every high street): Instant Video (for live-streaming); Digital Music; Appstore for Android (applications for smartphones); Kindle e-readers and Books (e-books, not physical books); Kindle Fire Tablets (the Amazon range of tablets); Amazon Fire TV; Amazon Fire Phone; Books (eventually, some real books, though this will also take you to Kindle and e-books); Movies, TV, Music, Games (physical music recordings are a small subsection of this department); Electronics and Computers; Home, Garden, Pets and DIY (that is pet supplies, not actual pets, I think); Toys, Children and Baby (again, no actual babies for sale); Clothes, Shoes and Jewellery; Sports and Outdoors; and Car and Motorbike (supplies and related equipment). Amazon has become the online retailer for almost everything, so it is no surprise that people using the site end up walking away with impulse purchases of golf clubs and satnavs alongside their DVD box-sets.

Everybody in my small research sample used the Net for buying things: plane tickets, holidays, wine, books, movies, shoes, tickets for live events, records, phones, organic vegetables, magazine subscriptions, sunglasses, egg-timers. While everybody agreed with the sentiment that Amazon is a bad influence on high-street shopping, and everybody seemed to be aware that Amazon had what we might call unethical practices in management and accounting, everybody still used Amazon for purchases. Buying things online has been made easy by the technological evolution of the hardware and software supporting the Net. First, designers developed secure transaction services such as PayPal or the multitude of other systems that reassure consumers that their personal data is safe. Second, the proliferation of secure and reliable browsers in the workplace has happened at a moment when work patterns have changed: it is now possible for many workers to purchase goods in their lunch breaks, or (where they do not have ruthless management) during working hours when they have a free five minutes. It has become common in modern offices to see people printing out tickets and hotel reservation details. The rise of eBay is linked to the ability of working people to keep track of auctions in real time during their office hours, for example (Lampe and Ploeckl, 2014). Third, shopping online has been boosted by the global spread of smartphones, tablets and app technologies. It is now possible to hear music on a video clip and make one click to buy the album online at Amazon or iTunes.

The dominance of transnational corporations on the commodified Net and the way in which they can ensnare users through ads, apps and links make it difficult for smaller businesses to survive. Small businesses cannot compete against the power of the global corporations with their marketing divisions employing hundreds of digital analysts to manipulate social media – the setting up of fake accounts that plug products, the harvesting and purchase of personal data, and the recruitment of celebrities to make endorsements on their Twitter feeds (Jin and Phua, 2014). When I started to buy extreme heavy metal music online there were two web-shops based in the United Kingdom where I could usually purchase an album I had read about in a magazine. I also had an independent shop in the centre of Leeds that sold heavy metal records. All three of these shops, online and offline, have closed due to a combination of illegal downloading (as discussed in the previous chapter) and Amazon offering albums at lower costs to potential buyers. But the elimination of independent retailers has allowed independent record labels to build their own online presence. I would much rather buy a record directly from an independent label or a band itself than going to Amazon. Similarly, I try where possible to buy books direct from publishers.

How much difference this makes to the commodification of the Net is difficult to tell. It could be argued that buying goods from independent websites is still about consumption and commerce. As users of the Net we are complicit in turning it into an unconstrained marketplace where buyers and sellers haggle with each other and abuse one another in the pursuit of bargains and sales. This is not communicative leisure. This is instrumental leisure at its worst, transforming human relationships into commercial transactions, and changing the way we talk to each other and present ourselves online. On social media, for example, we are busy hawking our opinions and our tastes, feeling good when we have made a profit on likes and re-tweets. On dating sites we pay our money and literally sell ourselves to strangers, who spend their money to either get a date or a laugh at our expense. It is better for us that independent retailers get our business online, and if they are local businesses we can feel good that we are being sustainable and community-focused. But all this buying and selling is a distraction from the fact that shopping on the Net has had a negative impact on real-world villages, towns and cities. Not only are shops closing, but as humans we are becoming alienated and isolated from one another as we stop going out to our local shops. We have abandoned feelings of well-being, attachment and sociality for individuation, global capitalism and stuff in brown parcels.

Sports

The Net has made it relatively easy to watch sports content. Three of my respondents watched professional sports events online. One of them used YouTube to watch clips of rugby league matches. As he explained to me:

> There is so much on YouTube these days, especially stuff from Australia. You can get NRL matches on there now, there is an official page. I watch a lot of that when I can. Not so much the Super League stuff...I like to watch matches from the eighties, the biff in the State of Origin back then. Some people have edited these highlights together...then there are the classic matches from the Challenge Cup, like the 1985 final...it's like every Micron video from the time has been uploaded.

The other two respondents used official live-streaming and video feeds to follow their favourite Premier League soccer teams and the big games on the professional soccer calendar. Watching footage of professional sports has been one of the drivers of the evolution of broadband, smartphones and Wi-Fi (the other being pornography – see Chapter 10). Sports fans have been trying to share video clips with each other since well before the emergence of the Net. In sports newspapers and magazines (especially fanzines) from the 1970s onwards it was possible to find adverts offering film reels (then VHS videos) of big matches. Some of this filmed content was sold officially through licensed companies giving a share of the royalties to the clubs and governing bodies (Jhally, 1984). My respondent mentions Micron video – this was a company in Wigan that produced VHS recordings of dozens of key matches in rugby league's history. But the home-video and video-camera technological revolution of the 1980s offered fans a chance to buy or borrow poor-quality videos filmed at sports events, or recorded from television broadcasts. Recording matches and events directly from one's own television set allowed people to re-watch their favourite sporting moments, and it allowed people to build up collections: all the matches from the 1986 World Cup; every year of the Super Bowl between 1983 and 1993. The availability of these collections, and the trade in copied or pirated videos meant that sports fans before the arrival of the Net had already become aware of the globalized reach of sport (Horne, 2006; Wenner, 1989). When I was a youngster in this period I was already familiar with Australian rugby league, just like my respondent: I was so familiar with the Winfield Cup (the premier competition of the New South Wales Rugby League, which became the premier competition of the Australian Rugby League) that I had a favourite team: the Parramatta Eels, and a favourite player: Peter Sterling. And as a fan of Hunslet in England I had watched the 1965 Challenge Cup final on a VHS tape that had turned the players into blurry ghosts, as it had been copied from a copy of a copy of a copy.

The commercialization of professional sport in the 1980s and 1990s means that while there is more sport broadcast on television, much of it is on subscription-based channels. Transnational media corporations such as News Corp and Disney realized that sports attract large numbers of loyal followers, and so they bought the exclusive rights to show sports on their subscription channels. The sports governing bodies got more money to spend, the clubs in the elite leagues got more money to spend – so they were happy to lose the wider audiences of free-to-air television (Horne, 2006). Some sports fans rejected the notion that they would pay to watch their sports, but most either paid for personal subscriptions or developed a new habit of watching the sports events in a bar that had pay-TV (Messner and De Oca, 2005). With the increase in subscriptions, these transnational media corporations guaranteed the economic survival of their pay-TV ventures. They could then spend money buying other sports and other leagues, as well as selling on the rights to the sports to other broadcasters (Spracklen, 2013a). With captive audiences of loyal fans watching their favourite sports, it was easy for the corporations to make even more money by increasing charges for adverts, sponsorships and endorsements, so long as the clubs and the governing bodies got their share. The Net was from the beginning an extension of this marketization of elite sport. The sports-media complex allowed corporations to cross-sell to sports fans, to share personal data and target campaigns (Horne, 2006).

The Net has created an industry of illegal downloading and live streams of sports events (Billings, 2012; Hutchins and Rowe, 2012). Some people with legitimate access to television broadcasts or official live streams allow others to access them on the Net, just like file-sharers of other television programmes and movies. Digital files and streams appear from inside the sports-media complex, posted by disaffected workers. Hackers break into broadcast feeds and share them. And fans create their own coverage of key matches and events, using their own phones and cameras. Some of the content watched by my three respondents is unofficial and unlicensed. The edited highlights mentioned by the first respondent are made from material owned by television companies from the 1980s and 1990s, spliced together so that the viewer sees the tackles and the tries. Other material is transferred directly from a video made by a company (such as Micron). I have watched on YouTube an entire documentary about the rugby league club Doncaster made in 1980 by Yorkshire Television. It could be argued that this is fair and creative use of copyright – certainly no lawyers have persuaded YouTube to take this footage down – but this is the limit of acceptability. The people in charge of copyright and brands at the NRL in Australia probably enjoy watching these clips, and probably think it is good for their profits if rugby league fans can watch the raw 'biff' action from the early State of Origin matches (when Queensland played New South Wales in the first years of the series there was inevitably a lot of action, from one-on-one fistfights to all-in brawls). But they ruthlessly patrol for clips from more recent matches – I cannot find any other than those posted by the official NRL feed, which suggests that they are taking action and sending in the lawyers as soon as they find anything that breaches their copyright.

Professional sports organizations have been quick to exploit their copyrights and trademarks online (Billings, 2012; Hutchins and Rowe, 2012). The top sports clubs around the world – the NFL and the NBA in the United States, the top teams in the English soccer Premier League and a few other soccer teams in other countries – have invested billions of dollars in selling their products to existing fans. It is possible to purchase merchandise online or in an official club shop – but websites give clubs and leagues the ability to sell access to exclusive digital content, such as videos of matches, histories and interviews with players. Manchester United, for example, has its own digital television channel, available on subscription through the website. Clips from the digital channel are also free to view on the website, as tasters designed to entice the fans to sign up to it. Such digital content is important for fans of a club such as English soccer's Manchester United because there are millions of them around the world (Roberts, 2004). Fans in Taiwan or Timbuktu can watch the free clips and pay for other exclusive content in order to feel as connected to the club as someone in Manchester reading the evening newspaper. There is a symbiosis between the clubs, the leagues, the sponsors and the broadcasters. It is not clear what parts of the websites are paid-for adverts, and which are editorial content – in fact, everything on the websites is an advert, for the sport, for the sports-media complex, or for their 'partners'. Such content is designed to make existing fans buy the brands associated with the partners. To be a proper fan one must support the club and its sponsors. So a Manchester United Fan is (as of 12 September 2014) encouraged to gamble at bwin.com with a 'free' £30 bonus, to fly with Aeroflot, send parcels with DHL, drive a Chevrolet and wear Nike clothes and sneakers; at the same time, the fan is encouraged to buy match-day hospitality, to bid for a signed portrait of a previous manager, to book a tour of the ground and its museum, and to download any number of apps to his or her smartphone.

Digital technology is now making it possible for broadcasters to sell viewing rights for individual events, as well as seasons of matches. The original ideology behind subscription television was to convince the fan of two things: they would be able to see all the action, and they would miss out if they did not buy the package. The latter proved more persuasive than the former – people complained about having to pay, but they did pay because they worried they would miss out in conversation about the sports action. Fans are now tempted to buy a range of digital products – not just one-off events, but analysis programmes, insider interviews and elite VIP packages with added clips. When video was replaced by DVD, consumers were persuaded to buy the films they already owned by the promise of additional extras. These extras, with a few notable exceptions, were and are generally rubbish: deleted takes, promo interviews and the inevitable documentaries showing us how the film was made. But consumers have bought into the notion that is worth paying for something exclusive, and now they will pay for every possible gradation of exclusivity possible in their sports viewing. Fans are driven to financial ruin trying to keep up with the payments while others look down on the average sports fan for not being able to afford the VIP extras. All this demonstrates the appalling consequences of the commercialization of professional sport and the commercialization of the Net – sports fandom has become a commodity traded between transnational corporations with every new contract (Horne, 2006).

Gaming

Playing games is one of the oldest known leisure activities evidenced in the archaeological record (Spracklen, 2011a). As Huizinga argued, humans became truly human when they became playful, pleasure-seeking creatures: what Huizinga refers to as *homo ludens* (Huizinga, 2003). The need for play is seen in children and adults around the world, it is a universal need in the human condition (Sicart, 2014). Many academics have explored the problematic nature of finding satisfaction in play in our modern, post-industrial society. Play seems to be a way of escaping the instrumentality of modernity and connecting to intrinsic motivations, a way of finding company or a way of finding release (Debord, 1995; Sutton-Smith, 2009). It has been suggested that the right to play is a universal human right that needs to be protected and nurtured (Caillois, 2001; Huizinga, 2003; Sicart, 2014; Sutton-Smith, 2009). In my book *Constructing Leisure* (Spracklen, 2011a), I argued that the need for play and the need for pleasure are linked to our need for communicative leisure. What makes us human is our ability to explore our self-identity and our place in the world, focusing our attention on our play and interacting with others. Play enables us to be a part of our communicative lifeworld (Habermas, 1984).

Gaming is an organized form of play that is still recognizably playful (Crawford, 2005, 2011). Where play is instinctive and fluid, gaming is about following rules that set limits on how to play the game. When people play chess they have to know the restrictions on the moves allowed for each piece, and the purpose of the game (to checkmate one's opponent). Games can be invented by anyone, and players of games can sometimes choose collectively to decide which rules count, but by agreeing to play a particular game one usually agrees to abide by the rules (Wittgenstein, 1968). This may seem restrictive and instrumental in its rationality, but actually following the rules of a game still allows one to get enjoyment and satisfaction from playing it. People who play games historically have used games to find deep pleasure and – when playing a game with others – a communicative space where identity and belonging are constructed and shared (Parlett, 1999). When I solve a cryptic crossword I feel so happy I find myself smiling at the world.

When I meet a friend who is trying to solve the same crosswords, we bond over telling each other our favourite clues and setters.

Online gaming is an extension of the video gaming culture of the final three decades of the previous century (Donovan, 2010). Games that first appeared on standalone gaming platforms are now available with connections to the Net, so that multi-player games can take place with gamers from anywhere in the world (Crawford, 2011). There are games that can only be played online, or through special software down-loaded onto computers, tablets and phones. Some of these games are puzzle-solving or educational in nature. Concerned parents want to help their children become smarter and more successful in later life, so they give their children educational games. These games allow children the chance to be playful and engage communicatively with computer-generated characters and other players. They teach children the value of talking to each other politely, while giving parents reassurances that their children are not subject to unsuitable pressures and ideologies (Buckingham and Willett, 2013). Game-designers in return have created entire range of games for children to play online that are fun, playful and appropriate, from simple solo games where a child has to gather fun objects to entire online worlds where children can interact in carefully moderated environments (Linderoth, 2012). At the same time, adults of a certain age who are nervous about their own competencies and intelli-gence and perhaps fearful of dementia play puzzle-solving games based on things such as Sudoku.

Multi-player online gaming is descended from role-playing games from the 1970s and 1980s. The most famous role-playing game of this period, one that still exists in the real world and in an online form, is *Dungeons and Dragons* (Ewalt, 2013). In this game, one person acts as the master of the game (a dungeon master or games master) and is in charge of making sure the rules are applied while being responsible for explain-ing the scenario and how the action unfolds. The other players have characters with special skills and weapons. These act together to explore the world of the game, reacting to the situations presented to them by the master. This game was incredibly popular when it was first launched because it allowed young people, mainly young men, to imagine them-selves to be in a fantasy world where they could hit goblins and steal treasure. But role-playing games could be ways in which people found communicative leisure, playful satisfaction and human development. The games taught players the value of communication, co-operation and puzzle-solving – players who rushed into fight monsters soon found their characters dead. And although *Dungeons and Dragons* was limited in the scenarios and campaigns it offered, other role-playing games allowed people to take part in more communicatively rational activities: exploring galaxies in spaceships, or running guilds in fantasy towns (Fine, 2002).

The popularity of such interactive games led to gamers joining multiplayer games organized through the mail, then, when the technology allowed it, multi-player environments on bulletin boards and newsgroups (Ewalt, 2013). Role-playing games were readily adapted to the Net, becoming spaces in which computer programmes could replace the games master, and which allowed players to interact easily and move through adventures quickly (Crawford, 2011; Donovan, 2010; Fine, 2002). Science-fiction fans created online games based around *Star Trek* and *Star Wars*, allowing players to create new parts of their favourite universes and to interact with famous characters and spaces (Hark, 2008). With each generation of technology, online multi-player games have become more complex and more popular. *World of Warcraft*, mentioned in the first chapter, exemplifies the communicative potential of such vast gaming spaces (Corneliussen and Rettberg, 2008; Ducheneaut, Yee, Nickell and Moore, 2006). In the game it is necessary to make alliances with other players. Players who are working together might be from anywhere in the world, and be any age or any gender. Players working together have to solve puzzles and defeat enemies; they can also explore places, drink, eat, have sex, have fun and learn about the fantasy world through which they are moving. Players can talk to each other in the game but also message each other out of the game – this discourse can create strong bonds of identity and friendship, challenging players' prejudices and perceptions of the others (Crawford, 2011; Linderoth, 2012). In other online games/worlds, such as *Second Life* and *Minecraft*, which are not about killing monsters, but about exploring aesthetics, society, belonging, transformation, culture and design, the communicative rationality at work is even more prominent (Boellstorff, 2008). Players in these games create identities, worlds, buildings, rituals and spaces that provide satisfaction, deep play and communicative leisure away from the mundanity of the real world.

However, online gaming is part of the instrumental turn of the Net, and our relationships with it. *World of Warcraft* and similar fantasy role-playing games perpetuate the gender order and racial stereotypes. Rather than being spaces of communicative interaction they become sites of misogynistic, homophobic and racist abuse (Daniels, 2013; Peck, Ketchum and Embrick, 2011). Female gamers have been attacked for complaining about the rampant sexism among the gaming community and the wide gaming industry (Thacker and Griffiths, 2012). It is all too clear that online gaming panders to a base, heterosexual male fantasy: tough warriors battle it out with each other, and female characters are hyper-sexualized (Peck, Ketchum and Embrick, 2011; Salter and Blodgett, 2012). The gaming industry is culpable in ignoring female gamers and producing products that cater to the sexual thrills of teenage boys (Crawford, 2011). Elsewhere (Spracklen, 2013a) I have shown how online games such as *World of Warcraft* normalize racial thinking and racialized hierarchies – in these games, every race has its essential characteristics, and every culture (human or non-human) is judged by how much is portrayed as exotic in relation to the default norms of whiteness. The fantasy genre more broadly is predicated on white, European medieval societies, landscapes and cultures, around which the Other revolves.

Misogyny and homophobia are best characterized as a form of sexual violence, a symbolic violence that nonetheless leaves its victims traumatized, marginalized and alienated. This violent symbolism is related to the wider normalization of actual violence (Kirsh, 2011). Games have always had an element of competition and *defeat* in them (chess is a symbolic representation of a real battlefield, for example). Video games and online games, however, have made violence central to the success of their players. To succeed in many of these games one must kill either other players or the thousands upon thousands of computer-generated characters: zombies, cops, Nazis, aliens or whoever else is standing in the way of victory. Young players of these games learn to forget the horror of the violent imagery and action in which they become immersed – they become desensitized and see the death and the blood as just cool stuff to talk about with their friends. Violence becomes something that is simultaneously unreal and hyper-real. It is unreal because the games are like cartoons, signifying nothing apart from titillation and childish fun. It is hyper-real because the power of the graphics programmes gives the images a vivid and believable quality. The result is that violence has become part of the rules of interaction online, creating a digital culture that thinks women are whores, Arabs are terrorists and guns are cool (Salter and Blodgett, 2012). This culture treats other humans as targets or 'buddies', de-humanizing and commodifying everyone in it – not least the players themselves.

Games such as *World of Warcraft* are also highly problematic in the way they normalize the logic of capitalism. Within these games, there is a trading system that players can join providing they go out and steal some treasure from somewhere. The purpose of the games becomes the accumulation of wealth and the consumption of products. That is, to progress in the games one needs to steal or purchase artefacts of some kind that are crucial to solving some crisis moment in the game. Currencies and markets within these games teach players how to be good neo-liberals. They then reach out beyond the game-worlds into real life. So it has become possible to buy and sell virtual currencies and virtual products in the real world, as can be seen with the online markets for *World of Warcraft*. The end point is that the rich can buy their way to success by using their real-world wealth to accumulate virtual resources, or, as mentioned in the first chapter, using their money to pay poor people to do some of the character-building work online for them (Harambam, Auters and Houstman, 2011). Users of *Second Life* might well say their world-creating activities are about exploring human nature and collaboration, yet their worlds are built with virtual currency, which has its own exchange rates in the real world (Boellstorff, 2008). To get ahead in *Second Life* it helps if one has the right economic and cultural capital, and the virtual spaces inside it have become reproductions of the real world, spaces with banks, businesses and places of worship. Rather than reject the instrumentality of the modern world, this is affirming that instrumentality through mimicry.

Another form of the commodification of interactions on the Net through online gaming is evidenced in the way in which gaming is a form of compulsive, addictive behaviour. Online games are often designed so that one needs to spend money in the real world to keep on playing beyond the first free hours or levels (Donovan, 2010). These games are deliberately addictive, to keep the players hooked on the visceral pleasures of killing and completing tasks. Like rats in a laboratory maze taking the pain of an electric shock for the price of a nice treat, gamers keep on paying and playing to get the stage-managed thrills of the computer programme. This means online gaming is a profitable business, one that now sees adverts for games shown on television and cinema screens, as well as corporations paying for product placement and adverts within games (Crawford and Gosling, 2009). This commodification of the gaming leisure experience has reached the level of modern, professional sports. There are millions of games fans around the world who are willing to pay to watch professional gamers compete against each in competitions for big prizes. Professional gamers are adored by fans, and their exploits and videos are followed avidly. Big tournaments bring in professionals from around the world and are sold out in minutes, and sponsors and advertisers fight to win contracts (Faust, Meyer and Griffiths, 2013).

Conclusion

The corporations that have colonized the Net make a big play of being our friends. They adopt the communicative values of the Net to try to fool us into thinking they are interested in anything other than our custom and our money. But our digital leisure habitus is primarily shaped by commercial transactions and consumption of some kind – whether it is shopping, consuming games or sports or being engaged in gambling activities. We create accounts and fill in our card details, and allow ourselves to be persuaded that consumption makes us feel good. The free exchange of ideas and information envisaged by the prophets of the Net has been replaced by Singles' Day and Amazon Recommendations. In this over-commodified space of instrumental leisure, how can users hope to keep their communicative rationality? In the next chapter, I will explore the extent of communicative action in the digital leisure spaces of subcultures.

9
Digital Leisure and Communicative Leisure

It is easy to turn to the Net to find out what it means to be alternative, to be a goth or a punk or a metaller. One can find Wikipedia and other forms of wiki pages discussing the history, the music and the fashions, along with hundreds, if not thousands, of pages set up by people to try to define this alternative subculture *as they understand it*. There is no official definition of alternative subcultures, of course. There is no International Guild of Goths, which sets out the parameters of gothness in some fine-detailed treaty. There is no rule book on how to be a punk, with specially trained punk police monitoring public spaces and arresting people who break the rules.

This chapter will look at the Net and alternative subcultures. The first section of the chapter is a definition of what alternativism is, which draws on my previously published work (Spracklen, 2014; Spracklen, Richter and Spracklen, 2013). The rest of the chapter explores the ways in which online networks have become safe spaces for alternative subcultures such as goths, punks, extreme metal fans and musicians, with a slight digression to those interested in alternative philosophies. I will show how alternative scenes can shape their own identities and communities in the safety of the Net, away from commercial interests and the rejection and prejudice of mainstream society – especially where alternative subcultures exist in countries that have histories of political, social, religious or cultural repression. In exploring each subculture separately, I will explore how the Net is used by these alternative subcultures as a repository of their histories and their music and their fashions, but how such attempts to provide authentic accounts of their subculture are challenged by people within the community (who pose questions about authenticity and elitism) and by commercial interests looking to co-opt the subcultures.

Alternativism

This chapter draws on debates about subcultures, counter-cultures and alternativism that have been the focus of attention in sociology and urban and youth studies (Bennett, 2000, 2002, 2006; Hebdige, 1979). From the Chicago School onwards, academics have tried to explain and understand the ways in which individuals and groups form or impose identities that are connected to, but different from, the mainstream popular culture of societies (Bennett, 2001, 2002; Blackshaw, 2010, 2014; Hall, 1993; Hebdige, 1979; Hodkinson, 2002, 2005, 2011, 2013; Holland, 2004; Maffesoli, 1996; Pavlidis, 2012; Kahn-Harris, 2007; Rojek, 2000b, 2010). Some of this debate has focused on the hegemonic status of elite, high culture and the ways in which power is used to impose popular cultural identity on other forms of culture and practice (Adorno, 1991; Gramsci, 1971; Hebdige, 1979). Others in the debate have argued that the age of late modernity or postmodernity are responsible for the construction of subcultural identities, whether the people in them are constrained by being identified as subcultural, or free to pick and choose neo-tribal identities across a range of subcultures (Maffesoli, 1996; Rojek, 2000b). Subcultures have been defined as deviances from the mainstream, though increasingly researchers have shown how subcultural belonging forms subaltern and marginal identities (Brah, 1996; Holland, 2004; Skeggs, 2013). Hebdige describes the rise and fall of subcultures in popular music as a Gramscian trick of appropriation – young people create new subcultures around music genre, the subculture becomes acceptable in the mainstream and commodified, and the subculture fades away. Some subcultures are sometimes identified as counter-cultures, movements that challenge the mainstream of society and the power of hegemony, unlike other subcultures that offer only limited ways of resistance (Storey, 2012). In other work, I have explored the ways in which alternativeness has become a way of defining the subcultural in leisure spaces as something that is truly counter-cultural (Spracklen, 2014, pp. 2–3):

> Alternative leisure has been the subject of much research in leisure studies and the wider subject fields of sociology and cultural studies (Bennett 2006; Dilley and Scraton 2010; Fendt and Wilson 2012; Griggs 2012; Pavlidis 2012; Stebbins 2011). For some researchers, alternative leisure is about lifestyle and the neo-tribe, picking and choosing identities in the face of liquidity, postmodernity or globalization (Griggs 2012; Pavlidis 2012). In these analyses,

alternative leisure becomes just another piece of positionality and performativity, much like dark leisure or deviant leisure (Rojek 2000b). Clearly, the notion of alternative as neo-tribe is part of the neo-liberal individualism of contemporary leisure (Bennett 2000; Blackshaw 2010; Maffesoli 1996; Rojek 1995, 2000b, 2010). But another way of thinking about alternative leisure is to understand the political underpinnings of alternativism, the oppositionality that was and is associated with alternative culture. This way, alternative leisure becomes a radical politics of young people, the working classes and others bereft of power, jobs and status, who find in the collective resistance of alternative leisure solace and communicative satisfaction.

(Debord 1995; Lefebvre 1991)

Following Hebdige (1979), one can see at this moment in time a series of subcultures that remain leisure spaces for counter-cultural alternativism: music scenes, community and street arts, environmental activism, neo-paganism and alternative spiritualities, walking and other non-competitive forms of physical activity, and so on. These are all forms of communicative leisure by definition – they are all things that people do, or spaces people go to, where there is an attempt to reduce or resist capitalism and other forms of Habermasian instrumental rationality (Habermas, 1987). Alternativism has to be oppositional in its nature to capitalism, and for the construction of communicative rationality and the lifeworld, because we live at the moment in late modernity when capitalism is global and all-powerful (Spracklen, 2009). There are many forms of alternativeness that are not communicative, and therefore they are not authentically alternative or oppositional. Much of the New Age movement, for example, is a replication of the dogmatic beliefs of mainstream religions, mapped onto the sales and marketing techniques of modern capitalism (Hanegraaff, 1999; Zaidman, 2003). That is, much of what counts as New Age is structured by its historical roots in the counter-cultural moment of the 1960s but its claims to be an alternative to the mainstream are weak. Rejecting the mainstream does not mean retreating into obscurity – it means fighting back against the commercialized and commodified world. This form of oppositionality was explored by Spracklen, Richter and Spracklen (2013, 168), who argue:

Oppositionality is the way in which individuals, subcultures, counter-cultures and other counter-hegemonic movements reject the restrictions of instrumentality and express their refusal to conform as passive consumers...While it is clear that some people, pace Bourdieu, have the right cultural, social and economic capital to be successful oppositionalists (cf. Rojek 2010), the liberty to be able to act and to oppose is constrained by the enormous cultural, political and social powers of the instrumental structures ranged against freedom of expression and movement.

At the current time, there are some subcultures that exhibit the ability to be counter-cultural and oppositional, especially ones that are associated with alternative forms of popular music: heavy metal, punk and goth. As we have seen earlier in this book, all three of these subcultures flourished online in the early years of the public Net, in the age of bulletin boards, newsgroups and message boards. The .alt newsgroup in particular solidified links between the musical scenes and other forms of alternative lifestyles. For example, in the first two decades of this century, the stereotype of the alternative person is someone who wears a lot of black, maybe a black band tee shirt, and someone who has tattoos and piercings – and while there are countless exceptions to this stereotype, it is usually safe to assume that someone with a black band tee shirt is a fan of metal or alternative music, and safe to assume (probably a safe bet in some countries and age groups) that someone with such a shirt may well have a tattoo or a piercing (Baulch, 2003; Spracklen, 2006). Yet the connections between the music subcultures and black clothes, tattoos and piercings have only come about through a process of fashion changes, evolutions in tastes and the normalization of a set of statements about what constitutes identity on .alt newsgroups and online generally. In the 1980s, heavy metal's fashions were more colourful, with the only dominant style being perhaps blue denim (Kahn-Harris, 2007; Walser, 1993). Likewise, goth fans in the 1980s wore a range of punk and post-punk fashions, only some of which were black and purple (Harriman and Bontje, 2014; Weaver, 2013). Tattoos and piercings were relatively rare in the 1980s, with tattoos associated with bikers and piercings limited to noses and ears (Kuwahara, 2005). The Net brought interests in tattoos and piercings from fetish communities into the alternative music subcultures. In the rest of this chapter, I will discuss metal, goth and punk online in more detail, along with some related online subcultures. This work will draw heavily on my own knowledge of all three, my own positionality as a fan-researcher and my own research on metal and goth.

Metal

Heavy metal has emerged from the hard rock scene of the 1960s and 1970s as a separate genre of its own, with sub-genres and subcultures developing around the world (Kahn-Harris, 2007; Weinstein, 2000). In the 1980s and 1990s, these sub-genres became established musical forms with associated subcultural identities: thrash, death and black, for example. Before the Net, heavy metal spread into different countries through the proliferation of fanzines and mainstream magazines (Kahn-Harris, 2007; Spracklen, 2006). For extreme metal such as death metal and black metal, the fanzine and tape-trading community provided bands with a chance to find fans, and vice versa (Harris, 2000). Death metal started out as a global scene, with bands, labels and studios situated in a few disparate countries: the United States (of course), as well as Sweden, Brazil and a handful of others. The first generation of black metal was equally global. These scenes, however, were marginal and truly underground – the bands and the fans were few in number and surrounded by a mainstream heavy-metal community that was dominated by the big thrash bands, hair metal and sleaze rock. With the arrival of the Net, heavy metal and its extreme metal sub-genres have been made more easily accessible to music fans who have had the technological and cultural capital to be able to explore online (Spracklen, 2006, 2009, 2013, 2014). There are websites dedicated to all the key genres and sub-genres of metal, sites that aim to provide accurate information about every band that has released something, and others that provide richer discussions about key bands and musicians. There are foreign-language websites about global heavy metal bands and genres, or metal in particular countries where that language is used. On Wikipedia fans contribute to providing information about the history and evolution of heavy metal and its key genres, with some superficial success, though the analyses are limited by the ways in which writers on Wikipedia only reference sources that are just other fan-sites (Spracklen, 2014).

The globalization of black metal came just before widespread adoption of the Net, and the absence of mundane information about the bands in the Norwegian second wave probably made the bands, their music and their infamy more notorious within and outside the heavy metal community – word spread about black metal on the basis of rumours about the key musicians (were they Satanists?) and the crimes they committed (Spracklen, 2006, 2013b, 2014). Information about bands and albums and genres online has given fans and bands spaces to find each other, whether it is illegal file-sharing sites, MySpace, YouTube, Spotify or Bandcamp. It is now possible to listen to every obscure black-metal demo from the infamous Norwegian bands by doing a simple Google search, whereas before the Net one had to know someone who had a copy that they were willing to tape. The Net has also made it easier for fans to find bands without the mediation of critics in the music press or managers at labels – this has led to a global expansion of metal but at the same time a difficulty in exploring metal beyond the bands that do get into the mainstream media, because new people to metal lack knowledge of the wider scenes and scene histories.

Metal's musical centre of gravity has shifted from North America and Europe to the global South, where metal has become part of everyday popular culture in countries such as Indonesia and Malaysia, reflecting the establishment of a young, urban class (Ferrarese, 2014; Wallach and Clinton, 2013). In countries in the Middle East with strict laws about blasphemy and morality, heavy metal is listened to as a way of creating a space to resist autocracy and theological rule, and governments try to ban or regulate the music (LeVine, 2008). But heavy metal is also used as a way of promoting nationalism and religious identity as well as a way of resisting it – so there are Israeli bands that promote tolerance and peace with their Palestinian neighbours, while there are Israeli bands that support Zionism (Kahn-Harris, 2007; LeVine, 2008). Heavy metal has become a globalized form of pop music that creates a particular form of secular belonging: being metal is being an individual and a rebel against the mainstream, and a member of a global community identified through shared history, clothing and musical appreciation (Weinstein, 2000). Online, heavy-metal fans can argue with each other the merits of particular sub-genres and bands, and in doing so they find common cause (Spracklen, 2014).

Heavy metal is seen by its fans and performers as representing something that is more authentic, more alternative than the pop music mainstream, because it has values about honesty and truth built into it. It is seen by its fans as something that provides shared identity and fellowship, both in the performativity of its *communitas* (Turner, 1969) and its anti-establishmentarianism (Kahn-Harris, 2007; Spracklen, 2006; Weinstein, 2000). All fans have to do is find a forum or social media page online where they can prove their metalness and they become accepted into the metal global community – and metalness is easily proved through following the rules of the look, the ideologies and the knowledge (of the key bands, sub-genres and what is currently cool). Metal is such a large and contradictory subculture that it is easy to find a place where one belongs, and its simple declarations of faith make it reasonably open to newcomers. Anyone can go online and become a metal fan, though there are sub-genres such as black metal that are deeply problematic and less welcoming of others (though that does not stop black metal fans listening to and liking online bands from Indonesia, Brazil and China). In countries around the world, then, heavy metal is a subcultural form that is both deeply transgressive yet safe. Heavy-metal fans may occasionally be rounded up by police who perceive them to be threats to morality in Egypt or Malaysia (Ferrarese, 2014); however, the real transgressive choices are made when people use the Net or public spaces in oppressive countries to declare their homosexuality or atheism.

The articles of faith of extreme metal are defended by websites run by authoritative fans, freelance journalists, musicians and others who claim long-term involvement in the sub-genre scenes (Spracklen, 2006, 2013). The website deathmetal.org comes up on the first page of a Google search for 'death metal', and it establishes its credentials by pointing out that some of the content on it dates back to 1988 – that is, it has inherited reviews, articles and information about bands from the fanzine movement. Its writers are well known on the extreme metal scene, and though younger fans do write for the website it is dominated by a hardcore of older fans and journalists who have been writing for the website, other sites and fanzines for many years. These are 'authentic' extreme metals fans who have the ability to influence opinions and ideas about what is proper metal. Most of the material on the site is based on album reviews, but there are some opinion pieces (hidden away beyond the main page) that have been published over the years from 1997. These try to answer questions about what metal is, what extreme metal is, and whether there are limits to what metal can be. One recent post by Cory Van der Pol deserves to be read in full as a warning about metal becoming accepted by the mainstream, and some fans' desire for metal to be accepted.

> It was once common for metalheads to complain about being misunderstood, and their music not being understood and accepted. Now it is accepted, and it has rendered it harmless. What did that rendering was all the metal bands ripping each other off, churning the original ideas into a mush of imitation. In fact, the problem is that metal when understood is in fact misunderstood, and keeping it not-understood is what is required for people to go back to method instead of just trusting its conclusions as gospel and repeating them in recombined form. Metal is in fact like a snake consuming

itself. As soon as orthodoxy is established, it is destroyed and its destroyer rises only to be in turn consumed itself. Parallels can be drawn to ocean waves cresting and then self-destructing, the need for forest fires, how predation ensures that prey animals get smarter, or other natural metaphors. What it fears is the calcification and a related process known as social acceptance. When a group of people encounters a new idea, it mocks it, then tries to destroy it, and finally accepts it. But once the idea is accepted, the process of calcification happens as society assimilates the idea as conclusion and throws out the methods, but even worse, the nature of having the idea accepted means a process of compromise which shaves off the parts of that idea that offend various segments of society (think of a PTA meeting: can't move the parking spaces, or you upset either the church ladies, the teachers' union, or the parking authority). Social acceptance destroys ideas through imitation and compromise. This process goes back to metal's birth. The members of Black Sabbath couldn't get on board with the happy hippie world around them, so they made their own music which destroyed that illusion with powerful sound. They were reacting to the acceptance of conclusions from the past period, the 1950s, in which people were fed on Dale Carnegie style salesmanship as a means to success. As a result, society stopped being truth-oriented and started being feelings-oriented. Happy feelings meant a sale. Ten years later, happy feelings meant social success. Salespeople knew that acceptance and inclusiveness made sales, so they made their advertising as innocuous as possible. The hippie movement imitated this but used politics instead of profit (at first) as their guide. The problem was that the hippie portion was just as fake as the 1950s salesmanship portion. Similarly, the current imitation of the 1990s black metal scene or worse, the 1980s emo and shoegaze scene, is completely fake. The fifteenth Blasphemy clone is as burnt out as the fifteenth Beatles clone or fifteenth Dale Carnegie graduate. All of it is emulation of the past through its surface, which fundamentally disturbs the metal outlook. For underground metal, all that is left is to seek total nihilism or negation of values, or to pick values that cannot be compromised and thus cannot be assimilated by society. If you want to know why metal has been drifting toward extremes lately, this might explain it. All of this is a rather long path to saying what every teenage music fan does not want to face: it's time to stop talking about how you are misunderstood. You don't want to be understood. Even more, being understood would destroy your chance for growth and turn you into an identical suit-wearing conformist droid marching off to do the same stuff the last generation did, and we can see them drinking themselves to sleep every night. When people obviously don't get what you're about, thank them. They're helping you grow, just like they're helping metal grow every time they run into a WTF moment and toss it out in the dustbin.

(Van der Pol, C., 2014, 'Why metal will never be understood, and never wants to be', 3 April 2014, http://www.deathmetal .org/article/why-metal-will-never-be-understood-and-never -wants-to-be/, accessed 13 August 2014)

The Net has made it possible for fans to make these strong arguments about the communicative rationality at the heart of the extreme metal subculture. Yet it is the Net that has made extreme metal and metal more generally accessible and popular globally. The complaint that young people are making a mistake by demanding metal's acceptance is correct. Metal's fundamental ideology is about individualism. Having heavy-metal bands winning the Eurovision song contest, or getting to speak at various parliaments around the world about the benefits of the metal industry to national economies is not something to be celebrated. As more and more people think heavy metal is as equally valid as any other form of popular music, it becomes just one other commodified lifestyle choice in an instrumental rationality of playlists and profit margins. This is the central point made by the deathmetal.org writer when he mentions the bands that are created to tap into things that have come into fashion. Most heavy-metal bands are in it for the money, and play the sub-genres they play because they think this might be the time to make money. There are thousands of similar bands playing sub-standard metalcore and other meaningless derivatives. For deathmetal.org this dilutes the essence of metal – metal is not about following trends and trying to make it, but rejecting everything about the mainstream.

Goths

Go online and it is easy to find out anything you ever wanted to know about goths. In my paper about the 'heat death' of subcultures I say (Spracklen, 2014, pp. 5–6) 'in this century, goth has become an accepted form of subculture, both for young people choosing an 'alternative' identity and for older people continuing to express a feeling of subcultural identity through declaring themselves (still) to be goths' (see also the discussions about authenticity in Brill, 2008; Hodkinson 2011, 2013; Spracklen and Spracklen 2012, 2014). I suggest in Spracklen (2014) that in the mainstream of popular culture, goths are mixed up with emos and metallers to become one alternative fashion statement. That is, being goth has become a confused teenage rebellion and a confused makeover, a byword for every shade of alternative subculture in the public gaze, in the minds of self-styled goths and even in the law (Garland, 2010). This confusion is replicated online in websites designed by goths for goths, and websites that identify aspects of goth culture for worried parents or possible would-be goths. Searching for 'goth' on Google brings up an enormous range of self-referencing and unreferenced information provided by Wikipedia and other popular fan-sites. Online one can be told how to be a goth by wikiHow or FAQs on other goth sites (Spracklen, 2014).

As I argue in my paper on the 'heat death' of subcultures (ibid.), the transformation of goth from a radical music subculture to a fashion choice shows that goth has become disconnected from its historical roots in goth music and post-punk radical politics (Harriman and Bontje, 2014; Weaver, 2013). Once upon a time, to be a goth was to be part of a communicative leisure space and form, struggling against the baneful influences of capitalism and commercialization on popular music. Of course, all pop music is commercial, and all bands and labels are caught in the trap of selling identities to pay their bills – but this post-punk radical goth subculture attempted to resist the most egregious aspects of instrumentality in the music industry. Fans made their outfits instead of buying expensive clothes from chain-stores, bands ran their own labels and people in the scene publicly espoused support for various radical causes such as environmentalism, vegetarianism and veganism, and anti-racism (Eckart, 2005; Spracklen, Richter and Spracklen, 2013). Now on the Net, goth is defined by a meaningless 'darkness', a blackening of mood and space that shades over the radical oppositionality that once created goth. Wikipedia says that 'the Goth subculture has survived much longer than others of the same era, and has continued to diversify. Its imagery and cultural proclivities indicate influences from the nineteenth-century Gothic literature along with horror films' (http://en.wikipedia.org/wiki/Goth_subculture). The survival and diversification of goth is obviously true. More debatable is the confusion between the goth music scene and Gothic literature and Gothic horror (see the critique in Spracklen and Spracklen, 2012, 2014). They are influences now because people have confused goth with Gothic, but in its original post-punk communicative leisure state, such connections were never explicitly intended. People have deliberately obfuscated goths, the Goth and even the original Goths (see below).

To become a modern-day goth all one needs to do is read the rules and specialist knowledge on the Net. Listening to music is recommended but the important thing seems to be to the 'staple goth look'. On one of the FAQ pages, there is a long account of the history of goths that attempts to show the authentic development and evolution of the subculture, which begins and ends – almost certainly intentionally amusingly – with the original Goths that plagued the later Roman Empire and its successor states:

2. What is the gothic subculture?

The original Goths were an ancient Germanic tribe which split into the separate Ostrogoth and Visigoth tribes in the third century. The Visigoths secured their place in history in the year 268, when they invaded the Roman Empire and swarmed over the Balkan peninsula. Post-Roman invasion, the word 'Gothic' became used to describe the uncivilised, ignorant or barbarous. The Renaissance humanists of Italy used this negative sense to describe a style of architecture prevalent in Western Europe, which they detested. This resulted in the term becoming synonymous with the dark and ominous, like the architecture itself. Its use expanded to cover the macabre in the 19th century, when it was used to describe writings such as Mary Shelly's Frankenstein. The term 'gothic' became increasing used throughout the 1980s to describe both a style of music and a movement growing out of the ashes of punk rock. By the late 1980s goth had become mainstream, with bands such as All About Eve, The Sisters of Mercy, The Mission and Fields of the Nephilim – all labelled as gothic rock by the music press – finding commercial success. A distinctive and arresting fashion had developed too, with long crimped hair (dyed black), voluminous velvet dresses (black), tight jeans (black) and leather jackets (also black) all forming part of the staple goth look. As the music media lost interest in goth in the early 1990s, it started to shrink from view. However, united by a common love of dark music, a network of fanzines and friendships held the scene together. Goth nights sprung up around the country to play the music more general alternative nights would not. Goth re-established itself as a bona fide underground scene, rapidly finding new fans and exploring different directions in both look and sound. Bands from the 1990s such as Rosetta Stone and Children on Stun explored electronic music to a great degree, whilst still maintaining a distinctive guitar-driven gothic feel. Many goth nights were also havens for industrial rock, which resulted in a certain amount of crossover between the scenes. Bands popular in today's scene include The Birthday Massacre, The Crüxshadows, Inkubus Sukkubus, The Last Dance, Manuskript and Partly Faithful (ex-Screaming Banshee Aircrew). Electro-industrial and EBM (Electronic Body Music) projects such as Combichrist, Front Line Assembly and VNV Nation are also popular with many, especially the contingent known as 'cybergoths'. Many cybergoths also enthuse about rhythmic noise; sometimes known as power noise, its sound is typified by projects such as Converter and early Noisex. The scene is alive and active, supported by its own infrastructure of promoters, designers, manufacturers and musicians. Furthermore, goth shows no sign of going away; it has an irrepressible persistence, much its namesake, the ancient Goths.

(http://gfaq.ogive.org/, no date of posting, accessed 15 August 2014)

Interestingly, the account of the ancient Goths is superficial and partially inaccurate, just as the account of modern gothic music and gothic subculture is superficial and partially inaccurate. The division between Ostrogoths and Visigoths occurred later, and their place in history has more to do with their defeat of the Emperor Valens and his army in 378, or the sacking of Rome in 410 by Alaric, than the raids they made in the third century (and if one was to mention those raids in the third century, surely the most infamous and spectacular was the one that led to the death of the Emperor Decius in battle with them in 251?). On the history of the modern goths, the connection is made again with the Gothic literature of the nineteenth century and the music of movement, as if they shared a dark ideology – gothic was just a term invented by bands and journalists to describe the sounds of the bands, a throwaway term that did not demonstrate a continuity between the Gothic movement of the nineteenth century and the goths of the late twentieth. The real post-punk scene and the gradual evolution from it of some bands and clubs and fans that used gothic to describe themselves are absent in this narrative: at the time, goth could have come to be known to posterity as post-punk, new wave or any other tag. The accident of a few bands becoming successful at selling records loosely associated with goth (even though most of the bands had different musical signatures and styles) led to the boom in goth rock the narrative identifies. The narrative becomes more accurate when it gets to the slump of the 1990s, and the survival of the goth scene as an underground network of clubs, fanzines and friends. By this stage in its history it had become a subculture that was identifying primarily with rules of darkness and alternativism appearing on the .alt newsgroups – that is, goth was becoming a lifestyle identifying with the idea of vampires, darkness and magic while losing its focus on politics and even music itself (Spracklen and Spracklen, 2012).

The narrative is optimistic about the future of goth. Judging by the bands listed as current, the narrative can be dated to the first few years of this century. Since then, goth has grown worldwide as a globalized cultural phenomenon, with young people dressing in black in shopping malls in every major city, as spoofed by the cartoon *South Park* (Crosby, 2014). But the centrality of the music and the depth of the underground scene have been affected by the rise of goth as a commodified choice in the neo-liberal marketplace of identities (Bauman, 2000; Rojek, 2010). Goth has become just another lifestyle choice for Westernized, globalized teenagers, a fashion associated loosely with the earlier form of goth (Spracklen, 2014). For the contemporary goth, the important aspects of being goth are distilled down to wearing black, feeling dark and buying gothic outfits in the specialized shops online and offline. Goth has become as spooky and alternative as a Halloween costume, something that parents and grandparents can understand and accept as part of a healthy neo-liberal mainstream identity. The counter-culture has become the mass culture, as Hebdige (1979) shows. Goth is no longer about deviancy and challenging the mainstream, or a rejection of mainstream politics and prejudices in favour of radical, communicative forms of leisure spaces (Habermas, 1984, 1987; Spracklen, 2009, 2011a, 2013a). Goth now is acceptable, and its adherents follow the rules on the Net about how to be a goth on wikiHow and other sites, and laugh at the notion that goth might have anything to do with a music scene or a radical political community (Spracklen, 2014).

A number of older goths have taken to trying to establish their authenticity through rejecting aspects of more recent aspects of goth culture. For example, a United Kingdom-based DJ who calls himself Old Goth is clear about what he takes to be 'proper' goth:

> Spins: goth, post punk, deathrock, dark indie/alternative, and a little bit of 'billy
> Definitely doesn't spin: EBM/Futurepop, industrial or metal, even if people do insist on thinking that it belongs in goth clubs. They're wrong.
> Likes: Captain Morgan rum (dark or spiced), Kraken, Absolut vodka, a good brandy, a nice cup of tea, cinnamon coffee, laughing, sleaze and scandal, lost causes, pirates, conspiracies, gothtart and her

corset collection, chilli, cheese, sausages, things with skulls on, random silliness. Oh, and DJing.

Hates: Glowsticks. People with no ambition. The thought that Marilyn Manson, VNV Nation, Nightwish or Cradle of Filth and their ilk are considered gothic. Ignorant people. Tomatoes. Rhubarb.

(http://www.martinoldgoth.co.uk/, no date of posting, accessed 18 August 2014)

Some of this list is arbitrary, of course – there are no arguments over the status of rhubarb in the history of goth, or tomatoes in the commodified, commercialized modern goth scene. Old Goth is clear, though, that he plays (spins) only music that falls under some specific sub-genres. He prefers the music of the 1980s or that inspired by the 1980s (post-punk, dark indie, deathrock and psychobilly) and rejects the metal and dance (EBM: Electronic Beat Music – see Brill, 2008) turn of goth in the 1990s and 2000s. His rejection of metal and dance leads to him listing people who dance with glowsticks and metal bands in his list of hates. Marilyn Manson is the frontman of the band of the same name, who has become a shorthand point of reference for anyone in the mainstream who is asked to think about goths – he is the 'poster boy' of corporate goth. VNV Nation are an industrial band. Nightwish are a ridiculously over-the-top operatic metal band from Finland who are the leading band in the 'goth metal' scene. And Cradle of Filth are a black metal band turned dark metal band, with no relationship to goth but who have stolen some ideas from the goth scene (Spracklen, 2006).

One of the ways in which goths sustain the sense of oppositionality to the mainstream is through embracing alternative sexualities and alternative faiths (Goulding and Saren, 2009; Spracklen and Spracklen, 2012). The Net is a useful source of community and inspiration for goths who wish to celebrate sexual identities that are offensive to the mores of mainstream societies around the world (Eckart, 2005). The evolution of the 'alt' community online has allowed people around the world to find people with similar tastes and desires, and goth is by its nature inclusive of people who experiment with performing fluid gender roles (Brill, 2008; Holland, 2004). But the embrace of alternative sexualities is not just an embrace of dark leisure experiences, it is a recognition that goth accepts (albeit within the constraints of goth fashions) and nurtures alternative norms of feminine and masculine beauty (Spracklen, 2014; Spracklen and Spracklen, 2012). The communicative leisure space of the Net gives goths a chance to explore ways in which they can find positive comments from their friends about their make-up, their clothes and their bodies, even where those bodies might not conform to Western ideals.

Alternative, neo-pagan spiritualities also find a place in the online goth space. In the 1990s, goth took a neo-pagan as well as a Christian turn following its fading from mainstream (Hodkinson, 2002). The pagan turn was influenced by the turn to paganism in wider popular culture in western Europe at the time: the resurrection of the film *The Wicker Man*, the work of comic writers Pat Mills and Alan Moore and the music of New Model Army and Inkubus Sukkubus (Spracklen, 2014). Neo-paganism was and is a rejection of the worst aspects of modernity, the homogenization of identities, the globalization of capitalism and the destruction of the environment (Magliocco, 2011; Rountree, 2012). Neo-pagans respect the importance of locality and history, myth and continuity. Some forms of neo-pagans are explicitly metaphorical, though many neo-pagans insist that they actually believe in the spirits they call upon. Neo-paganism is a call to return to older ways, a respect of the earth and a respect of the female. As such, the neo-pagan turn was also influenced by the existing radial green politics of the goth scene, which meant many people involved in goth were animal rights activists and vegans – the line between celebrating the earth and worshipping it is a fine one. The Christian goth scene provided a similar radical political space for goths, but its strict religious views often sat at odds with the unformed and inclusive faith of neo-paganism (Hodkinson, 2002). With the arrival of vampire goths and *Buffy the Vampire-Slayer* on television in the 1990s, it became harder to be a Christian goth. The Christian goth scene continues to exist – and has a strong existence on the Net (see Possamai and Lee, 2011) – but it does not have much influence on contemporary goth culture.

The neo-pagan turn remains dominant in the goth scene, especially that part of it which maintains a claim to being the authentic inheritor of the 1980s and 1990s subculture. Neo-paganism has led to a number of other underground subcultures such as the neo-folk scene and people who choose to live lives away from the modern world altogether. The former is a music scene associated with elitist ideologies, and many of the bands in the scene have played with far-right politics (though the more famous ones such as Sol Invictus have distanced themselves from the far right – see Spracklen, 2013b). The latter is the movement associated with pagans who re-enact life in medieval villages – it is now possible to seek advice on the Net about how to create such a village life, either with friends or through paying to travel on holiday to such a village (Carnegie and McCabe, 2008).

Another twist in the modern underground neo-pagan goth subculture is the emergence of gothic tribal belly dance. Tribal belly dance is a reaction to the male-centric performances of traditional (cabaret) belly dance. Instead of tight, revealing costumes and erotic wiggling, tribal dancers perform wrapped in costumes drawing on Native American and Central Asian traditions. The dances celebrate strong femininity and belonging. Gothic variants of this add in goth music and fashion. In Spracklen and Spracklen (2012), we explore the beliefs and identities of dancers in a gothic tribal belly dance group. It allows the dancers to perform their neo-pagan beliefs, or play at being pagan even if they are atheists. In Spracklen and Spracklen (2012, p. 358), we discuss this potentiality of paganism in the goth scene:

> Paganism and other alternative spiritualities in the Goth scene are chosen by individuals as expressions of their faith, through a communicative choice...This communicative agency is expressed through a desire to be seen to be counter-cultural or individually distinctive in a liminal, transgressive sense. Individuals in the Goth scene deliberately seek out Goth as a place to express themselves through dark leisure: something out-of-the-ordinary, something that plays with mainstream fears of unbridled sexuality, the carnivalesque and the dark spiritualities of anti-Christian paganism and elitist Satanism...Leisure is a place where communal identity can be felt through communicative action: our respondents all expressed a view that they are part of a scene, the Goth scene, a community to which they belonged, and which allowed them space to explore and make visible their alternative spirituality. Dark leisure helps these individuals become something they desire: a goddess, an acolyte, a dancer through choosing.

The successful spread of the gothic fusion tribal belly dance scene is entirely due to the availability of videos on YouTube and elsewhere on the Net. These videos, performances of dancers or groups, or instruction videos, enable dance styles and fashion styles to be copied and developed. For some belly dancers this leisure form is a way of being alternatively feminine and feminist (Holland, 2004). For others there is a serious element of faith at work. Whatever the rationale for getting involved, the Net, in this case, is the space for communicative action. The events and activities that take place in the gothic fusion belly dance scene bring together people from around the world, and the only way these people can come together is through exploiting the power of the virtual world.

Punks

The most enjoyable thing though about doing the site has been the interviews with the bands and when I say bands, I mean the smaller bands; the ones the music journalists turned authors and the original bands all take the piss out of as just copyists of the Pistols and Clash and casually wipe from the history of Punk. In interviews, TV and books it's the same people who are defining punk on their terms airbrushing out important bands like The Stranglers and Damned and while their view is of course valid it's the only one getting any airing and its [sic] wrong. I hope this site challenges this myth. It was the small bands who were on the frontline playing to people like me, the 'dog soldiers' dressed in various bits of tat, across the country taking the flak releasing the one classic single then splitting and changing and sowing the seeds for later bands like Joy Division and a host of other people. Punk means different things to different people and every generation has its new punk. Who am I to slag it off.... enjoy it.. after '79 it's just not for me. What this site is still about though is the MUSIC and always will be. I don't give a shit about Record Dealers, Record Labels, books or the money making bonanza that punk has become in retrospect. This site makes no money, takes no advertising, is answerable to no-one and aims to share the 'Punk Experience' brothers and sisters. If I tread on toes so f***ing what. If I like something I'll say it. If I don't, don't expect praise.

(Marko, P., 2001, 'Welcome', http://www.punk77.co.uk/welcome topunk77.htm, 21 June 2001, accessed 25 August 2014)

Punk is one of the most over-mythologized subcultures to have come out of pop and rock music (Bennett, 2000, 2001, 2006; Duncombe and Tremblay, 2011; Hebdige, 1979; Herrmann, 2012; Sabin, 2002; Sanders, 2013; Savage, 2002). The movement coalesced in a very short period of time in the 1970s in both the United States and the Great Britain. A number of musicians and fans were trying to make rock music that rejected the ponderous overtones of stadium bands such as Led Zeppelin and Pink Floyd, while also rejecting the histrionics of the heavy metal scene (Savage, 2002). Punk music was fast, short and played with scorn for the generation of bands dominating the headlines of the music press. As with heavy metal and goth before it, punk did not start out recognizably distinct and uniform in its subcultural norms, and many punk musicians did not think of themselves as belonging to a subculture called punk. The punk scene created its own fanzines, and its own labels, with a radical politics of rejecting the mainstream infusing this communicative leisure (Hebdige, 1979; Sanders, 2013). But very quickly journalists in the mainstream press identified punk as a new thing, musicians and managers switched to punk bands, and major labels started to sign acts: the Sex Pistols encapsulate this corporate takeover of punk in its infancy.

As punk went mainstream and entered the charts, it followed the trajectory of co-option and commodification charted by Hebdige (1979), who drew on the work of Raymond Williams (1977, 1981) on cycles in cultural hegemony. Some punks rejected the corporate takeover and resorted to developing alternative forms of punk such as hardcore, psychobilly, crust and post-punk. The crust scene has retained its radical politics and its commitment to veganism and fighting capitalism (Dunn, 2011). The hardcore scene shared similar politics along with straight-edge (anti-alcohol) abstinence, though it has been continually adopted by bands and labels operating in the music mainstream (Haenfler, 2006; Liptrot, 2014). Punk itself has become one other genre in a crowded lifestyle marketplace. In the global North, punk can become a party music for sports jocks in colleges. In other areas, punk still carries a message of radical, communicative resistance, with outcasts identifying with it in places such as the Russian far north (Pilkington, 2010, 2014).

What punk means today is mediated through discussions and information on the Net. For those punks who were around in the moments of the subcultures creation, fan-sites such as the one highlighted at the beginning of this sub-section serve as spaces to sacralize memory and authenticity (Moore, 2004). Constructing and curating such memory sites is the work of serious or project-based leisure (Stebbins, 2009). As well as preserving accounts of what happened and which bands and labels were important in the 'pre-1979' punk scene, this particular website constructs a particular form of authenticity about being punk. While the creator is happy to acknowledge different forms of punk exist, temporally and spatially, by creating the website and discussing the bands who formed the underground, DIY scene, authenticity is constructed and affirmed: here, the website explains, is the source material for everything else that followed, and here is the moment of communicative truth before the invasion of capitalism and fashion. There is clearly a touch of nostalgia in this, a belief that the scene was somehow more authentic in one's own youth, but the facts are that the punk scene has become bigger and global, a key part of the pop music industry that provides catchy, shouty songs for drunken teenagers who think they are being rebellious by swearing (Sanders, 2013). Older punks then rightly cling on to their youthful identities as memories of a time when to be punk was genuinely dangerous and genuinely subversive (Bennett, 2006).

For others the Net is a way of finding out about punk bands and punk sub-genres, through using various music sites as well as reading official and unofficial sites. Much of this is inane conformity and commercial fashioning, such as occurs with goth. People write nonsense about scenes and clothing and individuals think this is what they need to be a punk. There are entire global scenes of people listening to the pop-punk of bands such as Green Day believing they are being punks (Dunn, 2008). But there are ways in which the Net can provide a space for real, useful information and genuine punk spaces. There is, for instance, information about psychobilly at the gloriously named fansite 'The Wrecking Pit'. On this site there is the usual mix of news about upcoming events and reviews of new releases. But alongside that there is a forum where new fans can find out about key bands and albums, and older fans can share their memories about them. There is also a concise Psychobilly FAQ that cites an academic book on the scene's emergence in the early 1980s around the band The Meteors. Reading this, a punk fan can understand how psychobilly was a reaction against the politicizing of the punk underground in the crust era, and a retreat to an invented 1950s America where zombies and vampires roamed the streets at night. Then they can follow the links to the key bands and the clothing stores, and build up their insider knowledge. This way it becomes possible to declare oneself as a psychobilly fan on the forum, while also perhaps going to a psychobilly gig, looking the part with the cartoon mixture of punk and rockabilly styles (Arsel and Thompson, 2011).

Conclusion

The Net can be a morally good leisure space for alternative subcultures. As I have shown in this chapter, there are times and spaces on the Net where authentic, alternative subcultures can find communicative action. The Net has made it easier for metallers, goths and punks to find knowledge about their scenes, and to find others who share their interests. The Net has a communicative potential for these subcultures. But its radical potential only goes so far. The freedom that allows 'true' punks to find one another also makes it easier for people to post nonsense about punk. The instrumentalization of popular culture means the metal, goth and punk that people find at the top of a Google search is more often than not mis-identified, sanitized, commercial, (post)modern adaptations of the three subcultures. There is every single black-metal demo from the early 1990s online, but most people surfing the Net for heavy metal stop at the music of the mainstream and the corporate labels. In the conclusion to my paper on the changes in goth and black metal subcultures online, I mourn the absence of an awareness of the radical, political intent of communicative alternativism (Spracklen, 2014, p. 13):

> There may be some spaces where communicative action is possible and is happening – there are new musical scenes and subcultures that are emergent in a Williamsian sense (so new they have yet to be recognized by academics), and these may yet have the potential to break the cycle of appropriation and marginalization described by Hebdige (1979). But the alternative in goth and black metal alternative culture has entropied, and there is a loss of anger and radical ideology. There is a heat death of politics and action.

This conclusion holds more broadly for all three subcultures discussed in this chapter. In each one the idea of a radical subculture rejecting and resisting the mainstream has been lost in a combination of nostalgia, invented tradition and commercialization. Websites that curate and archive a subculture point to its loss in the real world. Websites that provide 'idiot' guides on being alternative point to the commodification of alternative subculture. In today's global society, being alternative is just another lifestyle choice, as safe as choosing to wear clothing from any shopping-mall chain-store. The Net shows people what to wear and how to look, and which bands to listen to, as it does any genre or scene within popular culture. People use the Net to find identity and belonging but that belonging is all-too-often connected to instrumental rationalities and hegemonic power – as we will see in the next chapter.

10
Sex and Romance

Before I commenced the research for this book I had to put the project through my university's research-ethics approval process. Generally the people who have scrutinized my research projects for areas of ethical concern or risk have never had anything to worry about – I do not undertake any invasive procedures such as taking blood, which is usual for my colleagues in sport science – but for this project I had one problem to resolve. I had to make it clear that I was not going to be watching or exploring pornography on the Net. I did not find this a problem as I am morally opposed to it anyway, but it highlights the dilemmas academics have with studying the subject. It is the one of the most significant parts of the leisure industry (Roberts, 2004), but one that carries with it immediate moral and ethical concerns. For my university, they are concerned with their reputation. For me, as a radical feminist, I am concerned with ensuring people know my moral position upfront. The research about pornography, then, is reliant on secondary sources.

In this chapter, I explore the ways in which the Net is used as a source of visceral sexual pleasure and real-world social interactions. The first section of the chapter will examine the growth of pornography online, the commodification of sex and the connection between pornography and pornification of popular culture. I will show that masturbating to pornography is the biggest form of leisure associated with the Net, and will explore the debates around censorship and freedom. I will provide a strong feminist critique of the porn industry, but will also suggest that legislation against porn is not necessarily the solution. Instead, I will argue that the gender order has to be challenged across modern society so that men and women are fully equal, and men learn to treat women as human beings and not sexual objects of desire. In the second section of the chapter, I will examine the growth of dating agencies online, and other websites and spaces that offer single people the chance to meet up with other people. I will argue that such sites make communicative leisure choices much easier, but reduce social interactions to an instrumental gender logic.

Sex, prostitution and pornography

Humans have always lusted after the pleasure of sexual activity, and in one sense such desires must presumably be the result of evolutionary pressures in prehistory, since both sex organs are designed to provide sexual climaxes (Abramson and Pinkerton, 2002; Alexander, 1979; Brundage, 2009; Butler, 2006; Foucault, 2012; Laqueur, 2003). The act of sex, then, was and is more than just a way of sustaining the species or our genes. Sex is a leisure activity that gives pleasure and satisfaction for the person or the people taking part in it (Foucault, 2012; Laquer, 2003). In many cultures, sexual activity is encouraged as a form of communal bonding and exploration (Abramson and Pinkerton, 2002). In the cultures and societies from which Western society emerged, however, sexual activity has been strictly controlled through various taboos and religious laws (Butler, 2006; Foucault, 2012). In the Christian tradition, for example, sex was viewed as an unnatural urge by many philosophers and aesthetic saints, which had to be resisted to be a true Christian (Brown, 1988; Brundage, 2009). In the Classical tradition, sex was something enjoyed by free men (and some elite women) with prostitutes and slaves (female and male), but other people were restricted over what sexual activity they were allowed to engage in (Bartsch, 2006). Sex, then, has always been a problem for communities, cultures and societies around the world, historically and currently – people want to use their communicative rationality to choose sexual activity of some kind, but sexual activity has been controlled and constrained. Furthermore, sexual activity is something that is not engaged in equally by different genders or sexualities or classes: we live in a hegemonically masculine society that normalizes heteromale desire and valorizes a narrow conception of sexual activity (Braidotti, 2013; Butler, 2006; Gagnon and Simon, 2011; Weeks, 2014). All societies to a greater or lesser extent struggle with the social construction of sexuality and gender and the inheritance of our genes.

How to find sexual partners is a problem that has been resolved in number of ways in different cultures and societies. For many women there has been no choice in this matter, and they have been the subject of arbitrary male power (Foucault, 2012). In cultures with strong codes of morality, sexual activity has been restricted to the formal relation-ship of a heterosexual marriage, which has been garlanded with religious imperatives (Butler, 2006). These marriages are usually arranged between families to maintain status and distinction in the wider community, and the young people in the marriage have little if any say in who they marry. The sexual activity in such marriages has been limited to the procreation of children and perpetuating the community, though in the logic of heteronormativity the men in such relationships have the power to enforce their desires on their wives, or elsewhere (Brooke, 1989). Although stories about people falling in love and running away together are very old in many cultures, the idea that people find sexual activity with a life partner of their choosing is a relatively modern one, associated with the rise of individualism and the loosening of religious and conservative constraints (Bauman, 2003; Brogaard, 2014; Giddens, 2013). With modernity has come the idea that people can find sexual partners and sexual activity without any hindrance through the rituals and markets of dating, providing the sexual activity is not deemed too transgressive and the partners are consenting (Foucault, 2012; Gagnon and Simon, 2011). The idea of dating will be discussed in more detail in the next section – both as a way of finding this mythical 'one', this soulmate for life, and as way of finding sex with a temporary consensual partner – but it does seem to be a crucial way in which sexual freedoms are enacted in a communicative way.

Prostitution is one response to the problem of how to satisfy the sexual urges of people unable to find consenting partners. Prostitution is traditionally a form of sexual exploitation based on male power (Carline, 2011; MacKinnon, 1989; Shrage, 2013; Weeks, 2014). It is tied up with the idea of instrumentality, the control of women and the normalization of men's hypersexual activity. The defenders of prostitution say it is a need as old as humanity, the nature of men to want sex without the attachments of family or the emotions of a relationship: men cannot help being driven by their sex organs because it is in their nature to want sex and have sex, it is argued (Shrage, 2013). In some cultures such as those in the Near East, prostitution was associated with religious codes and ceremonies, and young women became associated with temples where they sold their bodies to men until they were given their freedom (Bartsch, 2006). In many other cultures in pre-modern times, prostitutes were slaves, runaway women or women captured in warfare – all were seen as suitable subjects of male sexual dominance (Shrage, 2013). Prostitutes were treated with disdain by ruling elites and priests in ancient Rome and Greece, and though they were not completely outlawed by

Classical authorities they were marginalized and harassed for being visible reminders of the 'laxness' of morals (Bartsch, 2006; Brundage, 2009). Male prostitutes suffered the same pressures and indignities as female prostitutes (Bartsch, 2006).

Pornography is another response to the problem of sexual urges. As soon as human cultures adopted writing and representational art, pornography started to be created. There is evidence of pornography in graffiti from Roman Pompeii, as well as in the countless poems and stories of lust from Greece and Rome that have been nervously catalogued by Victorian puritan scholars (Bartsch, 2006). Masturbation must have taken place by prehistorical humans as a way of finding sexual satisfaction alone, just as happens now, and just as happens in some other mammals (Laquer, 2003). Pornography makes masturbation easier, as it shapes the fantasies that help bring people to sexual climax. Pornography was invented at a time of male power, so it became primarily a device for helping men achieve orgasm (Fredrick, 2002; Nussbaum and Sihvola, 2013; Richlin, 1992). Christian and Muslim rules publicly condemned pornography for being the work of evil, sapping the moral of young men who should be doing good work, but such condemnations did not stop the spread and use of pornography, either in the form of crude sexual cartoons or as stories (Moulton, 2004). With the invention of printing, pornographic stories became common across Europe, sold alongside bibles and almanacs by travelling salesmen (Coopersmith, 1998; Marcus, 2008; Moulton, 2004).

Interest in transgression and deviance in the Academy started with doctors and psychologists, legal experts and philosophers. For doctors and psychologists, transgression of social norms was a failing of deviant people. From the late nineteenth century onwards, the medicalization of deviance saw any transgression of social and cultural boundaries as a mental problem that needed to be cured, and if the person could not be cured then they had to be locked away from society for their own safety. What was deviant was anything that transgressed the norms and values of the polite Christian, West: drinking, gambling, having sex outside of marriage, engaging in radical politics, socializing with different classes or races or genders, engaging in any sexual activity that didn't involve one husband and his wife and their genitals, and breaking the laws of the nation. Legal experts and philosophers argued for the tightening of laws so that they fully reflected the moral values of nations – this was a period in which the United States, for example, prohibited the sale and consumption of alcohol; and we still live in nations that ban the use of other mind-altering substances (Greenaway, 2003). In medical textbooks throughout the twentieth century, people who engaged in such deviant behaviours were identified and described as if they were suffering from a disease like cancer. In the second half of the twentieth century, the rise of cultural studies as an academic discipline saw the ideas of transgression and deviance transformed. Foucault (1973, 2006) argued that madness was a cultural construction, a product of the increasing scientization and rationalization of modern life. For Foucault, and for radical psychologists such as Laing (1990), there was no real deviance, no real mental health problems. These mental problems were only a failure of modern nation states to recognize (or allow) the diversity of human thought and human behaviour. Other academics started to use these insights to explore the construction of deviance and transgression, and the importance of such behaviour in the development of human beings.

Judith Butler's (2006) work on gender and performativity has been very influential among dark leisure researchers interested in sex and sexuality such as Williams (2009). Butler's theories build on the idea of performance associated with Goffman (1971). He argued that individuals follow scripts and stage directions to perform social identity. Butler suggests that gender is itself a performance and it cannot be anything else other than something performed by individuals. Drawing on radical feminist theories, Butler shows that the hegemonic power of heterosexual men is expressed through the performance of heteronormativity. This performance is undertaken by men and by women. For men, being heteronormative is to play a traditionally dominant role, stereotypically articulated through masculine sports and leisure pursuits such as watching football, shooting guns and drinking beer. For women, heteronormativity is to play a traditionally subservient role, domestic, private, being pleasing to men and allowing men to have their fun. Where Butler differs from radical feminist theory is in her belief in the power of individual agency to undermine such performativity. It is perfectly possible, she claims, for individuals to transgress this heteronormative order. Butler uses drag as an example of such transgression: homosexual men and women can and do subvert heteronormative performances by playing grotesque caricatures of the other gender, so lesbian drag kings, for example, smoke pipes and wear moustaches, and drag queens hide behind garish make-up, boas and sequins.

This has a strong bearing on understanding transgression in dark leisure. The norms and values being transgressed are not merely the laws of the land, or the religious norms that bind any given culture. Dark leisure can be and is often a form of leisure that transgresses heteronormative boundaries. So sex is a dark leisure activity when it transgresses the gender order, or the heteronormative order, the prudish-ness of the mainstream. But heteronormative people are also offended by other forms of dark leisure that are not overtly associated with heteronormativity. Young men sitting in a park, smoking cannabis, offend the heteronormative order because they are a threat to the hege-monic power of men: they are not conforming to the correct way for men to behave in public, they are allowing themselves to be transformed by a chemical that 'un-mans' them, makes them lethargic and slow to react. Proper, heterosexual men are supposed to be strong, fast, alert and able to think rationally. It is easier to see the behaviour of women out drinking as a heteronormative transgression. In going into pubs and bars, getting drunk with their friends and chatting up men, women out drinking behave like heterosexual men. They are not being proper het-eronormative women who should stay at home at best, looking after the family, or, if they do go out, they must be out with a male chaper-one to watch their every move. There are still many cultures that frown on women drinking in bars, and many places where women are made to feel uncomfortable if they want to enter a bar alone. Dark leisure, then, has a close connection with Butler's concept of heteronormative transgression: many forms of dark leisure are examples of it.

For Chris Rojek (2000b), dark leisure is associated with intention-ality and agency. Individuals in late modernity have the freedom to choose to reject mainstream leisure forms in favour of ones that disturb the mainstream of society. Dark leisure is the kind of leisure activ-ity that rejects the mainstream, transgresses norms and values, and allows the people undertaking that leisure to identify themselves as liminal, deviant, alternative, rebellious non-conformists. For young peo-ple, this act of intentionality is often associated with illegality: writing graffiti on subway walls, stealing lipstick from a store, smashing the windows of schools and factories. In their development, we can see how children learn to be deceptive and dishonest, breaking the rules they have been given and finding play in things their parents warn them away from (every parent can remember such moments in their young one's lives, though the children themselves may not recall any particular deviant moment). Dark leisure, then, is a form of gratifica-tion. Individuals feel good doing things they know other people do not want them to do. They identify with particular leisure activities that have an uncomfortable but thrilling sensation because these activ-ities mark them out as outsiders, as individuals able to make choices about the things they like regardless of laws and morals. As people become adults, dark leisure becomes less about illegality and more about liminality and resistance to societal norms. Individuals recognize that the intentionality behind choosing dark leisure comes with the feelings of individualism and superiority it evokes, the taboo-breaking and not breaking a particular law.

Bob Stebbins (1997) has suggested that dark leisure is a casual leisure activity – not an activity that could be defined as serious leisure – because it is something associated with gratification: people search for their fix and are satiated by it and turn away. Certainly this is true of some forms of dark leisure – drinking and taking drugs, having sex with strangers – but there are dark leisure forms that demand the same amount of intensity and commitment as playing sports at a competitive level. For instance, sex and death tourism demand considerable forward planning and preparation by the traveller, and create work (paid and unpaid, casual and full-time) for tour guides, prostitutes, museums and so on. Dark leisure forms can be serious leisure, and do offer individuals lasting experiences and long-term personal development even if they also offer short-term gratification. For many adherents of dark leisure forms, the particular activity gives them meaning in a way no other work or leisure activity could ever do. They live for the act of dark leisure, the thrill and the moment, the plan and the experience, the reflection and preparation. In the difficult times of late modernity in particular, when social structures are weak and capitalism has wrecked any sense of belonging and community, dark leisure may be the only escape people have from the uncertainties of such life.

The dark leisure forms are of course different in different cultures and societies – for example, some types of sexual activity or drugs are socially acceptable in some places, but not others. What matters is the way in which different individuals identify with particular dark leisure activities and forms to make similar statements about their social identity and alternative positionality. Dark leisure is the product of an interaction between individuals and the social networks in which they live, the culture and society which determines what is dark and liminal in the first instance. When the United States of America banned the sale and consumption of alcohol it turned bars into illegal speakeasies, places where individuals could drink (against the law) and feel they were being rebellious and bravely individual. Politicians and church leaders condemned the illegal sale of alcohol and warned about the consequences of such depravity: women cavorting with men, races intermingling, unmarried sex, prostitution and violent criminality. But the dark leisure form was a product of the Prohibition. When the laws were relaxed the moral panic about alcohol misuse and depravity lessened, replaced by the moral panic about drugs such as cannabis and cocaine. For individuals choosing to do dark leisure at the high-point of Prohibition, individuality and coolness were bought in a cocktail from some jazz joint in a side-street cellar. For individuals choosing to do dark leisure at the beginning of the twenty-first century, coolness probably came draped in the sneakers and shirt of a gangsta rapper and a wrap of crystal meth. Or dark leisure might be constructed as an adherence to Satanism or some other 'left-hand path', rejecting the mainstream faiths of modern society in favour of a faith that is provocatively oppositional: the prevalence of Satanic symbolism in modern heavy metal sub-genres (black and death metal, and some goth) is proof of the need to use dark leisure to express such transgressive intentionality (even if most heavy metal fans quite correctly take the Satanism as a bit of a joke they are still happy for it being offensive to the morals of the mainstream).

By the age of modernity, pornography was in a contradictory moral position. For right-wing, conservative religious moralists pornography was clearly morally wrong because it encouraged lustful thoughts, which were the work of the Devil (or some other source of evil: Courtwright, 2011; Lottes, Weinberg and Weller, 1993; Thompson, Chaffee and Oshagan, 1990). Their desire to restrict or ban pornography was supported by left-wing feminists who argued that pornography was a product essentially consumed by men, which degraded women and reduced them to sexual objects (Fraterrigo, 2012; Whittier, 2014). But other liberal and left-wing commentators and politicians defended pornography as the product of a free capitalist exchange, and a press that needed to be free from restriction (Kappeler, 2013). This was a powerful argument that gradually eased censorship in some countries and legitimized pornography in others. Conservative and feminist notions that pornography degraded women and harmed sexual relations were dismissed as moral panics, and pornography was deemed to be okay for public consumption so long as its production and sale was regulated – laws were created to try to ensure models were adults and pornography was only sold by licensed dealers. Many feminist campaigners argued that the regulations were regularly breached (Carline, 2011); others said pornography was representative of male violence, male gaze and male power in modern society (Fratterigo, 2012; Kappeler, 2013). But more radical campaigners supporting pornography suggested that pornography could be used to overturn conservative notions of sex and gender roles. Some people suggested that pornography use was recognition that humans were sexual animals with Freudian or Lacanian sexual needs hidden by years of bourgeois repression (McGowan, 2012). Others took a post-feminist line to argue that concerns about pornography were irrational, and as long as women had equal control over the making and selling of pornography then everyone could enjoy the pleasure of its consumption (Attwood, 2010, 2011; Attwood and Walters, 2013).

The availability of pornographic material online has quickened this unresolved moral debate about pornography. Peter Nowak's (2010) analysis of the technological developments on the Net credits the porn industry with forcing the pace of change from dial-up modems through broadband to the latest gadgets and software because the companies involved in the industry need to meet the huge demand for their content from users. Pornography has been shared on the Net almost as long as tips on role-playing games and off-screen gossip about popular television programmes. The spread of pornography with the growth of the early Net was driven by the fact that many of the early adopters were young men: students, soldiers and scientists. This group of users may already have been using pornography at home (reading magazines and watching movies passed between friends), so sharing pornographic stories and images online was a natural progression of their offline habits. The pressure to develop ways of sharing compressed image files was presumably partly driven by an unspoken demand to share pornography. Furthermore, many of the young men involved in the early Net were strongly libertarian, siding with the argument that censorship of pornography was an attack on freedom of speech and freedom of expression, and an outdated move associated with traditional religions and morality. The Net was created in a period of time in the West where the campaign for equal rights had been replaced by the rise of post-feminism, the New Lad and the retrenchment of gender roles. Men's magazines and the New Lad movement normalized pornography and made it a legitimate cultural product, while women were pressured into showing they were cool enough to like pornography (McRobbie, 2011; Ortner, 2014). Porn stars were hailed as feminist icons, men expected women to be like porn stars and women felt obliged. How could anyone complain about the effect of pornography if it was in every man's magazine, and porn stars were given their own awards ceremonies and celebrity status (Brown, 2012)? Pornography, then, became a holy grail of the early Net, searched for by millions of users who became lost and frustrated by the dark swamps of slow download speeds and small memory capacity. But as the technology became more sophisticated, pornography followed. Stories written on message boards were replaced by images scanned from pornographic magazines, which were in turn followed by images created by new online porn corporations behind paywalls, which were then followed by videos, live sex-cams and sex-chats, and streaming (Nowak, 2010).

For many of the makers of pornography, their concern is to maximize their profits by making people pay for digital content. This means using all the commercial tricks of marketing and capitalism to entice potential viewers to pay to subscribe to their websites (Attwood, 2010; Barnett, 2014; Dines, 2010). Pornographers compete with each other to produce new and more extreme sexual content within the bounds of legislation over what is permissible, and recruit ever more hyper-real models (Dines, 2010). At the same time, the commercial producers of porn do what they can to stop non-adults from accessing their content. This may not mean much if all users have to do is click a button to confirm they are over the legal age in their home country, but to become a paid-up subscriber users need to give personal and financial details that might make it more difficult for non-adults to access it without stealing or falsifying such details. Commercial pornography websites also have to be very careful about the home countries of users. Pornography is illegal in some countries, but the Net is a global leisure space. Like the drinks industry and the gambling industry, the pornographic industry tries to be a legally sufficient industry through abiding by local prohibitions and attempting to build websites that are supposedly only accessible from countries where pornography is legal (Barnett, 2014).

The producers of commercial pornography sign up to combat piracy and intellectual property theft in the same way as producers of other forms of popular media, because they are nervous about their profits. Most users of pornography on the Net do not want to sign up to subscriptions to exclusive sites. They are not only wary about handing over their personal details to porn corporations, they also do not feel the need to subscribe to a paywall site when so much pornography exists for free online. After all, all most men want is something that will make them come to a climax reasonably quickly, so viewing times and diversity of content becomes irrelevant (Dines, 2010). What online porn users want is to find their particular sexual fetish quickly, view an image or a video and masturbate. Free pornography on the Net initially emerged through the scanning of copyrighted material, but soon corporations started to offer free pornography on sites that made their money from advertising. The model of commodification and commercialization is similar to many other websites and online industries: people in general online are reluctant to pay for content, and corporations find their profits through the development of targeted ads and the sale of data to other corporations (Attwood, 2010; Berg, 2014).

Pornography has become ubiquitous on the Net, and it is said to be responsible for a majority of the data downloaded or streamed (Attwood, 2010, 2011; Nowak, 2010). In the early years of the Net the mainstream media ran exclusive articles that showed how easy it was to stumble upon pornography accidentally on the Net through the mis-spelling of a URL name, or through searching for something seemingly innocuous on Google. While this still obviously remains the case, and some people do end up on pornographic websites by accident, it is clearly ridiculous to claim that that is how people end up watching online pornography. Most of the people who access pornography online want to find it, and know where to find it. There is free pornography everywhere (Attwood, 2010). Some of this pornography is created by women for women, or by gay men for gay men, but the vast bulk of the free pornography online caters for a heteronormative consumer: the heterosexual man wanting to find satisfaction through watching aggressive, penetrative sex (Dines, 2010; Walter, 2011).

What this excess of heteronormative pornography does is normalize myths of female subservience, the normalization of women as sex objects and the superiority of the voyeuristic, male gaze. Pornography essentializes racial difference through the categorization of models (Brooks, 2010; Vannier, Currie and O'Sullivan, 2014) and normalizes the sexualization of young women through the co-option of markers of young womanhood such as virginity, teens and babes (Dine, 2010; Walter, 2011). The women who perform pornography may well be deluded into thinking they are making the choice to take part in such humiliating acts, and they may well be paid to perform, but their autonomy in choosing to perform is not at work when they are told how to perform. Most heteronormative sex is degrading for its women participants. The women in such pornography are reduced to their bodies, playing the role of the willing whore who allows men to do what they like with her, or the frightened victim forced to accept the demands of the men (Dine, 2010). For the men who watch such pornography on a regular basis, it becomes difficult to think the brutalization and objectification is not normal. When pornography was regulated and restricted, young men and boys could not easily find and consume it, so it was hard for such violent images to shape their ideas about what sex is and what role a woman plays in the sex act.

With the easy availability of porn online, generations of boys become men by masturbating to the free heteronormative porn they find. They do not sign up to pay-sites or porn corporations that are committed to feminist praxis. They just download the porn they have been told about by their mates, or find the first things that come up that are free. There is, then, a real problem with the way in which such pornography has normalized a very restricted notion of masculinity, femininity and sex. Boys learn from porn that to be a man they have to put women in their place and make women do whatever the man wants. Girls learn from porn that to find a boyfriend they need to be as willing to do anything as the women in the pornography. Everyone who watches such pornography thinks it is morally okay to watch it, because if it was so bad, wouldn't it be banned? No one is forced to take part in pornography, the argument goes, and if it is legal to purchase pornography offline then we should not be concerned if it is available online. But pornography has become part of the mainstream of popular culture, changing the way women and men think about their bodies and their relationships – men now think women do not and should not have pubic hair because pornographic models shave, and women are forced to respond to this by shaving their pubic areas; at the same time, men feel pressured to have the six-packs and the shaved chests of the male porn model (Mulholland, 2011; Walter, 2011). Instead of relationships being defined by consensuality and mutual satisfaction and comfort, young men and women – following the example of pornography – think relationships are defined by male aggression, female compliance and anal sex. Pornography's extreme misogyny and abuse has become the new normal in schools, and without proper sex education (by parents and by teachers) countering the effects of this pornification of popular culture, the pressure to be tough men and willing women will dominate. While such pornography is free to use online it will be used by men, and it will affect the way they think in such a sense that it becomes almost impossible to resist and challenge the normalization of heteronormative pornography. Men and women who do object to the pornification of popular culture are ridiculed as old-fashioned conservatives, or naïve idealists trying to stop something that has already changed the world and global society.

Dating

In the rush to modernity, the old ways of finding sexual partners, such as arranged marriages, have been challenged by the rise of the liberal belief that we are all free to choose whatever partners we can find (Bauman, 2003; Giddens, 2013). This is the lie of individualism, the simple imperative that we should all be allowed to act communicatively about our sexual and relationship tastes. No one is allowed to stop us finding as many sexual partners as we desire, so long as we liaise with partners who are consenting (Bauman, 2003). What we do with them is our own affair. Conversely, we are also subject to another myth, that of the soul-mate. We are told by films and television programmes and songs that there is one person out there who is intended to be our life partner, the person we will find who will make our life meaningful (Cover, 2010; Giddens, 2013). The soulmate myth is deliberately magical and spiritual in its construction and reproduction. The idea is that this person shares our soul, is one half of a united spiritual one that will combine both souls. The world becomes a stage in which these two souls are fated to become one. This is of course irrational nonsense, but the myth is deeply influential. So people are torn between two commands from modern culture: to taste everything on offer, and to find their one true love before another pixie dies.

Before the Net, the modern-day problem of finding a partner – someone to marry, someone to love or just someone to find solace in – was difficult to resolve. For students in colleges and schools it was simple enough to bump into potential partners in classes and social events, though the highly gendered subcultures of these spaces made it hard for people to find partners if they did not confirm to rigid stereotypes and behaviours, such as being a cheerleader or a jock. For people who had entered the workplace, finding a date proved more difficult. Offices and other workplaces were not often good places to find dates, especially when relationships were subject to the regulations of modern human resources (Bauman, 2003). People without someone in their lives were told to go to bars and nightclubs to chat up other people, but many suitors were put off by feeling too old or too uncomfortable with their bodies to mimic the dating habits of students (Giddens, 2013). People looking for a date, then, invariably had to fall back on dating agencies, or small adverts in newspapers and magazines (Goodwin, 1990). Dating agencies were and are selective in their work, making clients pay large fees without making any promises of finding a good match – popular cultural representations of such dating agencies always showed the unlucky suitor being set up with dates that have lied about their looks, their politics, their beliefs and their tastes (as the suitor has, too). Adverts in newspapers and magazines could bring the right kinds of people closer together. If one was a middle-class woman who voted Conservative in the United Kingdom, for example, one could use dating adverts posted in a middle-class Conservative newspaper. That way, one could be reasonably sure that the only person responding to your advert was someone who held your political beliefs and views. But adverts in newspapers and magazines relied on people responding to those ads, and finding the time to respond to the interested suitors.

The Net has made it easier to meet more people than ever before, as well as allowing people to meet the right kind of people. Message boards and forums are obviously places where one can interact with people with the same sorts of political views and interests. If admitting to an obsession with science fiction once upon a time made you a social pariah, with the arrival of the Net such obsession can be owned up to in the company of other science-fiction obsessives. Of course one still needs to transform the friendship space of an online forum into a space where one can build relationships. Given the anonymous nature of much interaction on the Net, it might be easy to fall in love with someone who you would never want to meet in the real world, and there are deliberate fakers and manipulative sadists online as well as playful types who are flexible with their gendered and social identities (Cover, 2012). How people behave online is not always an accurate representation of who they are in real life. Someone on a Star Wars fan forum who uses a picture of Luke Skywalker as their avatar and who talks about his belief in everybody having to be understanding about each other's emotional needs may well be someone who looks and behaves like Jabba the Hutt. But there is evidence that such forums of interest do act as spaces where people engage with each other in a reasonably transparent way, which allows deep friendships to be created out of free, communicative discourse (Arora, 2014; Lupton, 2014). So people do find love and relationships through getting to know others on these sites, even if some individuals approach the offline, real-world interactions with caution (Cover, 2012).

Facebook and similar social-media sites are similar online spaces where the communicative leisure habit of finding a date takes place. On these sites people interact through sharing information about themselves with other users, which are limited to those who connect in some way (as friends or followers, for example) or accessible to anyone who wishes to look. While connecting people was always a public aim of every social-media site, the ideas they had in mind when establishing these sites were connecting friends and family, old school classmates and business partners. In fact, many people use social media to advertise their tastes and their interests to those who might be interested in liking such tastes and interests. For some people, Facebook can be a way of seeking out potential partners for relationships, whether it is people nearby who like the same kind of sports, or people far across the globe who might be looking to escape a particularly troubling economic situation. Facebook and similar social media that offer a way of finding old friends inevitably create the moral dilemma of old flames; that is, the user might have dated, or tried to date someone in the past who reappears via social media. Is it polite or impolite to ignore a friend request from someone you once courted? Or someone you rejected? Or someone you had sex with? And should you make friend requests to people with whom you have a dating history? While it is easier to make such moral decisions with people you no longer want to be connected to, Facebook has allowed many people already in relationships to re-ignite sexual activities with someone from their past (Gregg, 2013). It has become a commonplace small scandal of tabloid newspapers to read about the supposedly devoted husbands and wives who run away with someone they have met through Facebook whom they once dated at school. The tabloid ire is directed at Facebook or the Net rather than the agency of the protagonists in the affair, which is ridiculous – the technology is not causing the immoral behaviour. However, the technology does make it easier for people to re-connect with old lovers. But if people seeking affairs are stuck in unhappy relationships, perhaps the affairs serve some moral good.

For young adults and children, the opportunities provided by the Net pose more serious ethical problems. Young people routinely use social media in a naïve and trusting manner, making friends and following users, allowing their pictures to be looked at and sharing other people's content through software such as Instagram and Snapchat. These technologies are the normal spaces in which they communicate with one another and engage in the communicative leisure of bonding and identity-building. But these processes are equally available to be used as spaces to find dates and partners (Michikyan, Subrahmanyam and Dennis, 2014). The moral panic about paedophiles using this software and these social-media sites is part of a wider hyperbole of stranger-fear, but the anonymity of the Net does allow adults to pretend to be young people, and this happens enough (there are real people who try to meet their sexual desires for children through social media, and there are cases all the time when children are chatted up by strangers online who turn out to be paedophiles) for software developers and site owners to make a show of creating greater screening and security protocols – though many of the operators of such technology seem reluctant to try to remove the threat altogether. This may be an effect of the notion that the Net is a space where anonymity and privacy is respected over payments and scrutiny, or it may be an acknowledgement that there is not very much that can be done to stop someone with no criminal record

188 Digital Leisure, the Internet and Popular Culture

from falsifying their identity online, or using darknet systems such as Tor to falsify or hide their unique user identities (Martin, 2014). Educating children to be careful about who they accept as friends on social media might stop some paedophiles from operating but not all young people listen to warnings by their parents and teachers.

The other moral panic about this software around the phenomenon of 'sexting' may be over-played in the minds of concerned parents, but there is no doubt that young people find such technologies useful to explore their sexualities and their choices of partners (Ybarra and Mitchell, 2014). Theoretically the ease with which young people use social media and the Net allows them an easier way of meeting people they might actually like, people who may have the same interests, and the communicative nature of the space means people with the same sexualities can find each other in safe spaces, and women can have the same moral equivalency as men in the pursuit of sexual choices. The problem with such technologies comes with the ease with which older boys can enforce sexual behaviour and take power through persuading young women and girls to perform in a sexual way online (Dine, 2010). Young men are still encouraged to be studs and young women are castigated for being whores, and the Net amplifies these narrow gender roles. Young women looking to demonstrate their status as women are forced to respond in limited number of acceptable ways to such attention, and there is enormous psychological and cultural pressure to comply with the unwritten rules of heteronormativity (Michikyan, Subrahmanyam and Dennis, 2014; Walter, 2011). The same pressure is also placed on young men who may be uncomfortable with the idea of sending sexual messages to prospective partners as a way of proving their manly virility. The behavioural norms of social media make it difficult for young people to have private spaces, difficult not to perform rigid gender roles, and the norms create a space where ever-younger children think it is normal to send and receive such sexual messages. In the public sphere of social media, communicative discourse is replaced by the instrumentality of gender performativity and hyper-sexualization (Ybarra and Mitchell, 2014). Young women perform the role of devoted girlfriend and porn star, and images of their bodies are traded around young men as a way of punishment or a way of embodied objectification.

Away from informal networking spaces, many adults seeking that special person or some company use formal dating sites. These sites have become big business, with millions of users creating income from subscriptions and from ad revenue. Dating sites encourage people to sign up through pop-up ads and directed ads on side-bars, as well as advertising purchased in magazines and on television. For some dating sites the target is lonely men enticed by a photograph of a young, conventionally attractive woman posing seductively. These sites seem to be little more than revenue-generators (what is often called 'click-bait') or scams designed to get men to part with cash. Dating sites that are more legitimate use images of women and men, depending on the sexuality and gender of the intended user, in more romantic or neutral poses. For these sites there is a question about whether to aim for a particular interest group, or class or religion or ethnicity: there are dating sites for heavy metal fans and lovers of opera, Christians and secularists (Aron, 2012).

The biggest dating sites, the ones that have adverts in the mainstream media, pitch towards aspirational classes and tastes, though they do not explicitly use more exclusionary factors (O'Connor, 2014). They want to convince everyone who is looking for their soulmate that they can find them if only they register and pay the appropriate fees. Testimonials from couples who met through the dating site point to their bourgeois lifestyles and their perfect home lives. The sites claim to use more sophisticated, automated algorithms to match up potential dates than the old-fashioned manual labour of the dating agent (Aron, 2012). Users are prompted to reveal as much as possible as they can in an honest way about their interests, politics, work and leisure. They are told to be truthful about their age and use honest images of themselves on the personal pages they create. They are told to be realistic about their expectations of who they might expect to date. But of course internet dating sites follow the rule of performativity on social media and the Net – people lie about what they like and what they do; people post carefully selected or modified images; people have unrealistic expectations (it is said that heterosexual men of any age nearly predominantly express a desire to meet women in their 20s – Burrows, 2013). Users adopt the instrumental logic of neo-liberal capitalism to turn themselves into marketable commodities, massaging the truth to make sure they are in the best position to get the man or woman of their dreams. Then they are brutally dismissive of the people they are matched with, because they have bought into the myth that everybody can have anything they want, and everyone is worth it (Toma and Hancock, 2012). Even where users have rejected the myth of finding their soulmate, and are only looking for company and some kind of pleasure (that may or may not be sexual in variety), dating sites still impose rules and limitations on users. In these situations, users have to pretend that they have incredibly busy and fulfilling lives, and that they are not really so bothered about their alienation and solitude.

Many people seem to use dating sites and other social media as sites to find partners for casual sex. For some dating sites, such users can be removed from their membership databases if they start to pester other users with content of a sexual nature: dating sites that sell themselves as being sites for finding one's true love want the searching and the interactions to be suitably romantic and decorous (Aron, 2012). There are just as many adults as young people using Twitter, Facebook and Instagram to conduct affairs and send images of a sexual nature to one another. The instant, informal nature of these forms of communications make users push their communications from polite discourse to sexual suggestions in a matter of minutes. Indeed, as I was finishing off the writing for this book, a male Conservative Member of Parliament in the United Kingdom has just been tricked by a journalist pretending to be a conventionally attractive woman to send 'her' an image of his penis through social media; he has admitted to pestering other women online for images of them naked (http://www.huffingtonpost.co.uk/2014/10/11/brooks-newmark-sexting-quits-mp_n_5970204.html, posted 11 October 2014, accessed 20 October 2014). But there are sites online that cater specifically for people wanting affairs, and people just wanting casual sex.

Having an affair means knowingly breaking the vows you have made to your life partner. Even if many people live in long-term relationships that do not have the vows of fidelity exchanged in a formal ceremony, there is an implicit understanding that being in a long-term relationship with someone means you are faithful to that person for life. Some cultures and religions give men the power to have more than one wife, and some modern-day sexual radicals live in open or polyamorous relationships (Mitchell, Bartholomew and Cobb, 2014). But affairs are secret acts of infidelity to one's partner. Dating sites that are built to enable users to have affairs with others are clearly taking an ethical position that there is moral legitimacy in enabling such acts: they might think there is a biological need for sexual adventure and diversity, which is limited by the bourgeois conception of the faithful couple; or they might think there is a moral gap between enabling an affair and having an affair. What these sites seem to promise is a way of making infidelity simple. Before the Net, if someone wanted an affair because they felt trapped or dissatisfied in their relationship, they had to find someone with whom they could have such a sexual encounter – and as we have seen, it is difficult enough to find one consensual partner, never mind another. So the existence of sites that promise the chance to buy access to other people who want to have an affair makes breaking the moral contract as simple as filling in a PayPal form.

Having an affair typically means maintaining a secondary sexual relationship with some willing partner over time. What some people want is casual sex with a wide variety of partners. The Net's use as a communicative leisure space allows people to find each other for such casual sex. Swingers and doggers might arrange sexual encounters through social media, sharing tips about safe places to meet up for sex (Hunter, 2014). Gay and bisexual men can use a suite of dating sites, lists and apps to search for potential partners for casual sex nearby (Peterson, 2000). As the technology becomes more sophisticated, the pursuit of casual sex becomes more commodified. The sites become reliant on generating advertising revenue, users learn how to commoditize their bodies and their sexual preferences, and the corporations who own the technology collect the data users leave behind them to sell to other corporations looking to have a share of the sex market.

The pressures of finding a partner in late modernity can be particularly awkward for people who belong to religions or cultures where families have traditionally arranged marriages. Versions of dating sites have appeared that allow single people from these cultural backgrounds to meet people without the involvement of their parents. But the most popular dating sites for cultures with arranged marriages are ones that work as brokers helping clients find a potential husband or wife. When potential and suitable partners are assessed and identified, the client might bring in parents to take control of the negotiations, or parents may be reduced to subsidiary roles. While this is a way of digital technology being co-opted to maintain conservative traditions, those same traditions are subtly transformed by the rhetoric of liberal choice and the real power of women to use these sites to control the traditions in their favour: the discourse of the sites is about finding husbands and wives, but the use of the sites allows women to bypass stern parental guardians and introduce an element of the Western search for a soulmate into their decision-making (Giddens, 2013).

Dating sites force people to deny the simple truth: these sites exist because the condition of late modernity has made people work too long and has atrophied the social and cultural bonds of communicative leisure where people usually meet other people. We are told we all need to focus on self-advancement and careers, our material wealth and our status as transient professionals. Or we are told we are failures, outcasts who do not consume the products of global capitalism correctly, people who have failed to become full-time professionals, members of the urban elites with their mortgaged homes (Bauman, 2003). The marginalized classes lose the cultural and economic capital needed to build social bonds with others – and become literally and symbolically removed from the dating scene. Online dating sites reinforce the inequities and hegemonic power of late modernity, while simultaneously constructing the myth that we can be liberated from our loneliness if we only pay our money, smarten up and get bought at the slave-auction.

Conclusion

The Net has provided an important leisure space for the development of sexual and romantic interactions. It provides a communicative space for people to find others with similar interests, and has given gay men and women (of a number of sexualities) ways to resist and circumvent the restrictions imposed on their sexuality by the hegemonic gender order of heteronormativity (Butler, 2006). People who challenge such heteronormativity are right to do so, and we should celebrate any attempt to subvert norms and conservative traditions in favour of freedom of action and freedom of speech. The lifeworld cannot be maintained without liberal politics and ethics, and the dangers of allowing censorship and taste to restrict leisure spaces and activities should be clear. That said, the Net has failed to stop the hegemonic power structures of the real world from replicating inside the virtual world. Pornography is mainly consumed by heterosexual men and designed for heterosexual men, especially the pornography that is readily available and free online. Such pornographic content makes men treat women as inferior, and puts women in their place, reaffirming the gender order that makers of feminist porn would try to fight. This is the dark side of dark leisure: its way of reproducing discourses of privilege and Othering. Such pornography commodifies bodies and sex, tainting human interactions in the world of dating, romance and relationships. Both online pornography and dating sites are leisure spaces where the primary mode of rationality is instrumentalization, albeit spaces where some communicative rationality operates on the margins.

11
Conclusions

There are people in the world who have got bored with the Digital Age. There are people who have rejected the Net altogether, being fearful of the way in which governments and corporations routinely monitor us and our personal data (McChesney, 2013; Petley, 2014). It is quite clear that both hegemons are colluding with one another to go beyond the boundaries of what most citizens would think is reasonable, invading our private leisure spaces and taking our private and personal information in the name of counter-terrorism or just profiteering. Quite rightly, people are choosing to reduce or eliminate their digital presence: in my own use of Facebook, for example, I have made a point about lying about my age, just to throw out any algorithms and person-matching that might be taking place. For governments, the rise of the Digital Age has frightened them with its utopian ethic and its piracy and its freedoms and its claims to be ushering in a new world of transparency and knowledge. They have responded, as we have seen, with fears about terrorism and extremism that give them what they claim to be a just cause to abandon centuries-long, hard-earned human rights. They routinely intercept digital data and routinely check it, finding loopholes and permissions in long-winded regulations and laws to breach the privacy of millions of Net users around the world (McChesney, 2013). For corporations, the rise of the Digital Age frightened them with its copyright infringements and its utopian commitment to limit the ability of anyone to make a profit out of the use of the Net. But they have responded by turning every website into an advertising opportunity, taking over online rivals and shutting them down, becoming enormous transnational corporations with no accountability other than the bottom line. If you buy a smartphone you might think it's cool to have instant GPS, instant weather forecasts and easy-to-use apps that allow you to surf social media and buy things. But look closely at the software and the permissions, and by allowing Google or Apple to run their fancy products you are allowing them access to everything of yours: your personal data, the sites you might wish to browse, your account details and your location in the real world in perpetuity (so long as the GPS is on). Does Google really need to know that you have recently visited New York? That you have purchased a book on Bulgarian folk customs under the rule of the Ottoman Empire? It is no wonder that many people around the world are fed up with this imposition of instrumental control and have rejected digital technology for a less-tracked, hard-to-monetize, real-world leisure life.

There are many older people who have tried it once or twice but have not really seen the point of it (Bonfadelli, 2002). There are many people in the global South and in marginalized communities elsewhere who cannot afford to be on the Net, who continue to live their work and leisure lives in the real world. There are people who have gone completely 'off-grid' from modern technology as an attempt to return to supposedly more pristine rural, pre-modern life (McChesney, 2013). As I write this in 2014, it seems like Facebook may well be losing its popularity – people do not seem to be posting to it as regularly as they used to. Similarly, online forums do not have as many posts and users. Many people are making a point of interacting and doing communicative leisure offline in the real world, face-to-face with others, and digital technologies are only used as a way of arranging and remembering such social interactions. The idea that the Net is a font of all knowledge is also being challenged in a number of ways: people no longer contribute information to sites such as Wikipedia to the same extent (Jemielniak, 2014); users of the Net are becoming uninterested in looking beyond the immediate sites they use (McNair, 2014); and hopefully people are realizing that the Net is not as good as a good reference book, available in a library.

The prediction that the arrival of e-books and Amazon would mean the end of traditional publishing and book-selling has not come true yet, and looks unlikely to become true as people still prefer to read proper, traditional books they have bought in bookshops. It has become a marker of distinction to prefer books bought and consumed in this way, a rejection of the commerciality and plasticity of the digital and virtual (Finkelstein and McCleery, 2012). In various music subcultures the only record sales that are increasing are for vinyl releases – and many bands, musicians, producers and fans have rejected the clean sounds of digital audio for the warm, imperfect fuzziness of analogue.

In alternative music, for example, there has been since the 2000s a rise in bands playing occult rock and doom metal, genres predicated on attempts to reproduce the imperfect analogue sounds of the 1970s. This might be branded as superficial, hipsterish nostalgia, the re-invention of a musical decade that never really happened in the way it is remembered, but even if that is true the analogue turn represents a conscious rejection of the superficial, ersatz digital copy. Staying with alternative music, print-only fanzines have made a return in the extreme metal underground. As the editor of one fanzine explains:

> Some of you may be wondering why I chose to resurrect a dinosaur in today's technological age and I am only too happy to elaborate. Having spent almost a decade working with online zines I began to notice a general apathy in viewing habits, regardless of content or style. If you aren't bombarding the various online platforms with information and constantly plugging away in order to bring your work to people's attentions then frankly the hits dropped and if for example you are offline for two or three days I noticed a complete drop-off in activity. Now I didn't live through the glory days of the 80s metal scene ... but it seems to me that whilst everyone has any information at their fingertips, it doesn't have to be this way!
>
> (Hayhurst, 2014, p. 2)

This is not the voice of someone who grew up in the age before the Net became commonplace in people's everyday leisure habits; this is not someone who still thinks of the Digital Age as a new age in any way at all. This is someone who has grown up thinking the Net is a normal part of everyday life, a place that exists as a leisure space and a work space. Yet he has realized the limitations of this space – the inadequacies of it as a way of sharing opinions and information, and the inadequacies of it as a space for finding information. For the extreme metal underground musicians, the problem is finding ways to let anyone know they exist. The notion that it is possible to simply post music online and wait for people to find it and rave about it is erroneous, because people do not look for new music in that way. Most of the people who use the Net find music they already like, or find music they have been told to like by their peers or by the mainstream media. Even in relatively obscure underground genres such as death metal and black metal, subcultural fans have a problem with finding new music on the Net: how is it possible to filter through everything that might have been posted on YouTube, and how do you find the music that is authentically underground? The temptation is to remain with the bands that have a modicum of celebrity in those genres, such as Cannibal Corpse, Carcass, Emperor or Mayhem. Print fanzines allow extreme metal fans to read interviews with bands who do not have contracts with bigger independent labels, or any contracts with any label. They allow fans to read reviews written by critical experts who are not trying to make or follow a fashionable trend. Print, then, is the future for extreme metal. In the same way, specialist music, culture, politics and sports magazines continue to provide the lengthy features and reviews that one cannot find on the Net (McChesney, 2013; McNair, 2014).

People, then, are rejecting the Net as a primary or dominant leisure space. Does this mean that the Net will disappear altogether as a leisure space? The answer from the rest of this book is so far there is no evidence that this will happen, and plenty of evidence to suggest that lots of people around the world are still using the Net as an important leisure space, and lots of evidence to suggest that numbers of people using the Net are increasing year-on-year with the spread of cheaper and more reliable technologies. It might be possible that the Net will disappear in some imagined future. It is quite possible, for example, to imagine a world where some environmental or economic catastrophe has reversed technological progress to a world of distant, unconnected communities reliant on books for knowledge. It is possible to follow the trends of nostalgic hipsterism and suggest a world where people reject social media and online retailing, choosing to interact in small communities and streets rather than in virtual spaces. It is equally possible to imagine a world where people become physically connected to the Net through bioengineering and cybernetic technologies, becoming watched around the clock by global dictatorships to make sure we buy the things we are told to buy. This final, 11th chapter is a relatively short conclusion that sketches out a research programme for digital leisure, and for the exploration of the interaction between the Net and other parts of our world, as a means of trying to predict what might happen in the future about that interaction without looking foolish.

A research programme for digital leisure

Inter-disciplinarity

One of the current weaknesses of research on the Net is the lack of sustained inter-disciplinarity. There are sociologies of the Net, and anthropologies of the Net and social psychologies of the Net. There are research projects that explore the legal and political implications of the Net, and books that explore the history of the Net and the supposed postmodern nature of the Net (Arora, 2014; Lupton, 2014). There are research projects that explore the interactions between the technological materialities and the humans who use them (Mahoney and Haigh, 2011; McGillivray, 2014). There are specific research projects that explore parts of what I have identified as the leisure spaces of the Net, for example, work on gaming (Crawford, 2011) or work on social media, or work on online pornography (Attwood, 2010, 2011). While all this research has value, and it all contributes to knowledge, the Net is so vast and so complex that to truly make sense of it we need to have an inter-disciplinary lens. We need to be able to draw upon specific knowledge and methodological tools from a range of disciplines to begin to make sense of the bigger pictures, the ways in which our interactions (as agents) with the Net are shaped and constrained and the ways in which the Net shapes and constrains us.

Leisure studies as a subject field has a long history of being multi-disciplinary, that is, accepting work that focuses on management or history or sociology or philosophy or psychology or economics or geography or cultural studies, and encouraging work that might draw on a couple of those disciplines at the same time. Leisure studies as a subject field, then, has progressed because it has championed multi-disciplinary work. In recent years, this has allowed for a more critical inter-disciplinary leisure studies to emerge. That is, this critical inter-disciplinary leisure studies uses whatever is necessary to solve the problem of what the meaning and purpose of leisure is in any given space or time (Spracklen, 2009, 2011a). Inter-disciplinary studies of leisure allow researchers and theorists to think of how leisure spaces and activities might be constructed by societies and cultures at given moments in their history, and how these spaces and activities might be shaped by moralities, ethics, laws, policies, politics, power, prejudices, structures, habits, tastes, ontologies, beliefs, mind-sets, bodies, symbols, myths, materialities and technologies. To think in that way we have to be able to read across disciplines and understand their epistemologies and assumptions, their debates and their key ideas. It is not an easy task, and not one encouraged by the instrumentality of academic life, with its units of research assessment and its metrics that force people to become narrowly focused on disciplines and subject fields. But to understand and do work on digital leisure studies, it is not enough to be multidisciplinary. We have to engage in inter-disciplinary studies of digital leisure because that is the most successful way of doing leisure studies.

The uniqueness of the Net as a leisure space

The conflation of societal change and cultural change that gave rise to modern sports at the end of the nineteenth century was not a necessary condition for the emergence of such leisure, merely a sufficient one. That is, there was nothing in the changing conditions that allowed the emergence and development of modern sports as a global phenomenon to be predicted. But they did emerge and they did leave a lasting impression on global society – and the reasons they emerged and developed can be understood as part of a wider societal shift to modernity, rationality, instrumentality and global capitalism. Modern sports, we know now, are seen as a normal and inevitable part of modernity, an everyday part of popular culture and leisure, whether we play sports or watch sports as a spectator (Spracklen, 2011a, 2013a). They have existed for more than a hundred years and seem to have reached just about every locality on the planet with greater or lesser levels of interaction and engagement. Modern sports were an innovation that changed the ways people did leisure. They have been incredibly influential in shaping modern societies, reproducing the hegemonic gender order, capitalism, racial hierarchies and nationalism; while at the same time selling a myth of individual agency and choice. Modern sports changed leisure spaces and activities so completely that we can say with the evidence before us that their appearance is a marker or an effect of those deep socio-cultural transformations. Furthermore, the rise of modern sports in turn caused an acceleration of those transformations that had initially caused the rise of modern sports: modernity and sports were caught in what we might call a positive feedback loop, resulting in a form of leisure and a form of society that was almost incommensurable (Kuhn, 1957) with the forms that existed beforehand. It would be inappropriate to talk about a paradigm shift, but modern sports are practices and ideologies associated with the appearance of a brave new world.

Can we say the same thing about the Net? It is still too early to make a prediction about the lasting effects of the Net, but we can see from earlier in this book that many scholars argue its creation is caused by another socio-cultural transformation or transformations: the shift to globalization, interculturalism, cosmopolitanism, postmodernity and/or posthumanity. The Net does seem to be having a dramatic impact on the way in which people think about their identity, their community and their place in the world. As we have seen in this book, people do seem to think that the Net is more powerful as a source of their social identity than the real world, and being on the Net itself gives a strong sense of belonging to a global community of Net-citizens. People can play with multiple identities and bond with like-minded explorers. The community and knowledge of the Net is de-centred, allowing people to find things and resist things even if some parts of the Net are taken over or closed down. Many people think the Net has already transformed them into engaged citizen-activists, acting in a communicative way to challenge the structures of the world that keep people constrained. Governments and corporations are so afraid of transformative, global power of the Net that they work to control it where they can. The Net, then, has enormous transformative potential. It has already changed the way people think about their place in the world and their identities. We are in the 1870s and 1880s, when people were literally running around proclaiming the amazing life-affirming nature of sports. The Net has made the world shrink, given people new knowledge and new ways of thinking. As such, the Net is a unique leisure space, and our research programme has to start with the assumption that we are dealing with something that is so novel that it might become something like modern sports.

The ordinariness of the Net as a leisure space

At the same time, we must not take the analogies too far. Advocates of the Net want us to think it is transformative and ushering in a new world, a Netopia, where governments and corporations and all forms of powers are eliminated. But most people who use the Net do not think they are becoming part of a utopian web of significance. Most people who logon to the Net do so for mundane reasons. As we have seen throughout this book, the Net is just another leisure space, one that sometimes intersects with offline leisure spaces (such as when someone watches a sports event then talks about it in a blog), but one that often does not. If we follow the arguments of the Netopians too far we lose sight of the simple truth that most people just use the Net to look at stupid videos, to buy things or to masturbate. This is not a complaint about the moral wrongness of most people's digital leisure activities, it is just a fact we need to be clear about before we go out to do more research.

Any research programme on digital leisure has to understand the way in which this particular leisure space is just like every other leisure space. Most of the time, people use such spaces because they are bored or unwilling to take part in anything that feels like work or deep thought (Roberts, 2011). That is, for most people such spaces are entered into in a passive, careless manner, and the Net allows people to act easily in this way. For some people, leisure spaces are spaces that are actively entered and engaged with, and in the habits around the Net we can see such activity and agency at work. The Net, then, is just an ordinary leisure space and an ordinary space of leisure activity; a mundane leisure form that just so happens to operate in this weird global and virtual way.

The communicative rationality and action at work

People make decisions about their leisure lives all the time. These decisions and those lives and actions often begin with communicative rationality. As discussed earlier, I have written extensively about applying Jurgen Habermas' ideas to leisure (Habermas, 1984, 1987; Spracklen, 2006, 2009, 2011a, 2011b, 2013a, 2013b). For Habermas, communicative rationality emerges in a dominant form with the onset of the Enlightenment, when enough people have the education and the wealth to contribute to debates about society, ethics, natural philosophy and politics. The rules of communicative rationality are that everybody has to be allowed a free choice to accept or not to accept someone else's claim about the world, and everybody has the freedom to put their own claims forward, knowing that they will be judged by others on the merits of the evidence and the argument – and not the status or importance of the person making such a claim. It is this communicative rationality operating in salons and cafes that leads to modern democracy, liberalism and the end of autocracy and feudalism. Communicative rationality, then, is a marker of the emergence of the modern public sphere, of modernity and of the lifeworld. I have argued, following Habermas, that communicative leisure is the form of leisure that reproduces communicative rationality: it is leisure that is chosen freely, without constraint, which allows us to be human, to explore our relationship with our inner selves and with others (Spracklen, 2009, 2011a). All types of leisure have the potential to be communicative and to maintain the integrity of the lifeworld, but all leisure spaces have the potential to be colonized by the instrumental rationality of the systems of modernity: hegemonic powers and global capitalism.

In our research programme on digital leisure we have to acknowledge this paradoxical nature of leisure spaces, forms and activities. In its purest sense, the Net is a communicative leisure space. Throughout this book I have shown how people actively use their agency to shape meaning for themselves and their relations with others in virtuality. In the early years of the Net, scientists and engineers found a sense of community and solidarity, space to share ideas but share pleasure and fun. With the arrival of bulletin boards and newsgroups, others could join in the communicative interactions and communicative leisure taking place. People could establish codes of etiquette and Net ethics among one another, which allowed them to get pleasure and purpose from discussions and website building. Even now, people use their serious leisure time and skills to volunteer to help build websites, databases and forums. People volunteer as moderators. The Net does still have its own rules and norms of behaviour. There is still a communicative core to digital leisure. Social media creates communities and counter-hegemonic activism. People find knowledge and safe spaces to talk about freedoms and difference. It is still something that one enters into using one's own agency. No one is compelled to use the Net: everybody chooses to login. In any research programme on digital leisure, its communicative value has to be recognized. We have to understand the communicative rationality and action that is at work in digital leisure. But that value, as we have seen, has his limits. So we have to explore those limits, and that exploration becomes the rationale for our research project: how much does digital leisure allow us to be free. And how much does it constrain us?

The instrumental rationality and action at work

The constraints at work in digital leisure are the same that constrain other forms of leisure. Modern sports, for example, have become completely professionalized, commercialized and commodified. People do not play sports because they get satisfaction from the company and the physical activity – they sit at home and buy subscriptions to television channels so they can watch big events in between watching adverts, while wearing their official sportswear covered in the logos of sponsors. Modern sports have become a product of the instrumentality of global capitalism, turning active participation into passive consumption. Simultaneously, modern sports serve the instrumental interests of nation states and hegemonies, stirring people up to support the country or the team while keeping them subdued and in check. Similarly, cultural forms such as plays, books and newspapers, which at least attempted to create a communicative space free from government control, have been replaced in popular culture by the instrumental products Adorno (1991) warned us about: the television shows, the trashy Hollywood movies and the pop songs that are sold through them. All modern leisure is the site for the contestation of meaning and purpose, between people who want to be free and the powers that want to stop people from being truly autonomous agents. As work and family have become routinely instrumentalized and co-opted into the

202 *Digital Leisure, the Internet and Popular Culture*

systems, leisure spaces and activities remain sites where the lifeworld and communicative rationality can still survive. But every year the struggle to save the lifeworld of leisure from colonization becomes harder and harder.

How much instrumentality is at work in digital leisure? In this book, I hope I have made it clear that there is a dangerously dominant amount of instrumentality associated with digital leisure. There is the fact that the Net has always served the purposes of the military–industrial complex, and the fact that governments routinely use the Net to monitor and control their citizens. There is the fact that corporations have taken over most of the systems, software and hardware of the Net, and users have to routinely pay to access it. There is the fact that personal data is routinely converted into monetized advertising. There is the fact that individuals are commodified by the Net, and the Net supports and reproduces the heteronormative, elitist, racist hierarchies of the real world. Any research programme on digital leisure has to be a way of helping us map out in specific places and spaces the ways in which such instrumentality operates. How do people begin to resist such instrumentality on the Net? Is it possible to compromise and allow oneself to be a part of an instrumental leisure space, if that then allows one to find a communicative space beyond the adverts and the paywalls? These questions can only be answered by actually doing inter-disciplinary research that problematizes leisure, digital leisure, agency and constraint.

The future of the Net and final conclusions

Assuming humans manage to overcome the destructive tendencies at play in society, and we manage to tackle the huge environmental problems and problems of inequality that threaten to set us back, there is no reason to think that the Net will not continue to be a part of everyday leisure and work lives. We have become so used to using the technology that it is as normal to us as libraries and newspapers. But it is quite possible to envisage a future popular culture that perceives our version of the Net, with its utopian ethics and communicative ideals, as hopelessly antiquated. This future version of the Net will inevitably be shaped by the instrumental power of corporations and nation states, as all the indicators point to an increase in instrumentality across leisure to join the instrumentality of the late modern workplace. Corporations will get better at removing content that is unlicensed, small businesses will be consumed by transnational businesses, and nation states will become more effective at collecting and controlling information. Whether users will feel the need to resist this is debatable, though there are signs that people are beginning to wake up to the ways in which we sign our rights to privacy away when we sign up to services online. The technological changes that are inevitable may make it possible for alternative Nets to appear that bypass the physical restraints of telecommunications networks, but I am not so sure that such developments would be allowed by nation states' paranoid about terrorists and other supposed threats to security.

Like it or not, then, the Net is here to stay for at least as long as we allow technological capitalism to be the driver of human endeavour, human work and human leisure. As such, it is our duty as leisure researchers to understand it and make sense of our place in it.

References

Abramson, P. R. and Pinkerton, S. D. (2002) *With Pleasure: Thoughts on the Nature of Human Sexuality* (Oxford: Oxford University Press).

Adorno, T. (1947) *Composing for the Films* (New York: Oxford University Press).

Adorno, T. (1967) *Prisms* (London: Neville Spearman).

Adorno, T. (1991) *The Culture Industry* (London: Routledge).

Adorno, T. and Horkheimer, M. (1992) *Dialectic of Enlightenment* (London: Verso).

Aitchison, C. (2000) 'Poststructural Feminist Theories of Representing Others: A Response to the "Crisis" in Leisure Studies' Discourse', *Leisure Studies*, 19, 127–144.

Aitchison, C. (2013) *Gender and Leisure: Social and Cultural Perspectives* (Abingdon: Routledge).

Alderman, J. (2008) *Sonic Boom: Napster, MP3, and the New Pioneers of Music* (New York: Basic Books).

Alexander, R. D. (1979) 'Sexuality and Sociality in Humans and Other Primates', in A. Katchadourian (ed.) *Human Sexuality: A Comparative and Developmental Perspective* (Berkeley: University of California Press).

Allen, C. (2011) 'Opposing Islamification or Promoting Islamophobia? Understanding the English Defence League', *Patterns of Prejudice*, 45, 279–294.

Anderson, B. (1983) *Imagined Communities* (London: Verso).

Anderson, T. J. (2013) *Popular Music in a Digital Music Economy* (New York: Routledge).

Antonio, R. J. and Brulle, R. J. (2011) 'The Unbearable Lightness of Politics: Climate Change Denial and Political Polarization', *The Sociological Quarterly*, 52, 195–202.

Appadurai, A. (1996) *Modernity at Large: Cultural Dimensions of Globalization* (Minneapolis: University of Minnesota Press).

Arceneaux, N. and Weiss, A. S. (2010) 'Seems Stupid until You Try It: Press Coverage of Twitter, 2006–9', *New Media and Society*, 12, 1262–1279.

Arditi, D. (2012) *The State of Music: Cultural, Political and Economic Transformations in the Music Industry* (Fairfax: George Mason University).

Aron, A. (2012) 'Online Dating: The Current Status – and Beyond', *Psychological Science in the Public Interest*, 13, 1–2.

Arora, P. (2014) *The Leisure Commons: A Spatial History of Web 2.0* (New York: Routledge).

Arsel, Z. and Thompson, C. J. (2011) 'Demythologizing Consumption Practices: How Consumers Protect Their Field-Dependent Identity Investments from Devaluing Marketplace Myths', *Journal of Consumer Research*, 37, 791–806.

Aspray, W. and Ceruzzi, P. E. (2010) *The Internet and American Business* (Cambridge: MIT Press).

Åström, J. and Karlsson, M. (2013) 'Blogging in the Shadow of Parties: Exploring Ideological Differences in Online Campaigning', *Political Communication*, 30, 434–455.

Attwood, F. (ed.) (2010) *Porn.com: Making Sense of Online Pornography* (Oxford: Peter Lang).

Attwood, F. (2011) 'The Paradigm Shift: Pornography Research, Sexualization and Extreme Images', *Sociology Compass*, 5, 13–22.

Attwood, F. and Walters, C. (2013) 'Fifty Shades and the Law: Regulating Sex and Sex Media in the UK', *Sexualities*, 16, 974–979.

Aupers, S. (2012) 'Trust No One: Modernization, Paranoia and Conspiracy Culture', *European Journal of Communication*, 27, 22–34.

Bainbridge, W. (2011) *The Virtual Future* (New York: Springer).

Balsdon, J. (2004) *Life and Leisure in Ancient Rome* (London: Phoenix).

Banks, J. (2014) *Online Gambling and Crime: Causes, Controls and Controversies* (Farnham: Ashgate).

Barnett, J. (2014) 'The British Porn Industry's Ambiguity towards Opposing Censorship', *Porn Studies*, 1, 321–325.

Bartsch, S. (2006) *The Mirror of the Self: Sexuality, Self-knowledge, and the Gaze in the Early Roman Empire* (Chicago: University of Chicago Press).

Baudrillard, J. (1986) *America* (London: Verso).

Baudrillard, J. (1988) *Selected Writings* (Cambridge: Polity).

Baudrillard, J. (1994) *Simulacra and Simulation* (Ann Arbor: University of Michigan Press).

Baudrillard, J. (1995) *The Gulf War Did Not Take Place* (Sydney: Power Publications).

Baudrillard, J. (2002) *Screened Out* (London: Verso).

Baulch, E. (2003) 'Gesturing Elsewhere: The Identity Politics of the Balinese Death/Thrash Metal Scene', *Popular Music*, 22, 195–215.

Bauman, Z. (1992) *Intimations of Postmodernity* (London: Routledge).

Bauman, Z. (2000) *Liquid Modernity* (Cambridge: Polity).

Bauman, Z. (2002) *Society under Siege* (Cambridge: Polity).

Bauman, Z. (2003) *Liquid Love: On the Frailty of Human Bonds* (Cambridge: Polity).

Bauman, Z. (2004) *Wasted Lives: Modernity and Its Outcasts* (Cambridge: Polity).

Bauman, Z. (2005) *Liquid Life* (Cambridge: Polity).

Bauman, Z. (2006a) *Liquid Fear* (Cambridge: Polity).

Bauman, Z. (2006b) *Liquid Times: Living in an Age of Uncertainty* (Cambridge: Polity).

Beck, U., Giddens, A. and Lash, S. (1994) *Reflexive Modernization. Politics, Tradition and Aesthetics in the Modern Social Order* (Cambridge: Polity).

Bell, D. and Bennion-Nixon, L. J. (2000) 'The Popular Culture of Conspiracy/The Conspiracy of Popular Culture', *The Sociological Review*, 48, 133–152.

Benkler, Y. (2002) 'Coase's Penguin, or, Linux and the Nature of the Firm', *Yale Law Journal*, 112, 369–446.

Bennett, A. (2000) *Popular Music and Youth Culture: Music, Identity and Place* (London: Macmillan).

Bennett, A. (2001) *Cultures of Popular Music* (Buckingham: Open University Press).

Bennett, A. (2002) 'Researching Youth Culture and Popular Music: A Methodological Critique', *The British Journal of Sociology*, 53, 451–466.

Bennett, A. (2006) 'Punk's Not Dead: The Continuing Significance of Punk Rock for an Older Generation of Fans', *Sociology*, 40, 219–235.

Bennett, A. and Peterson, R. A. (eds) (2004) *Music Scenes: Local, Translocal and Virtual* (Nashville: Vanderbilt University Press).

Bennett, W. (2003) 'Communicating Global Activism', *Information, Communication and Society*, 6, 143–168.

Benson-Allott, C. (2013) *Killer Tapes and Shattered Screens: Video Spectatorship from VHS to File Sharing* (Sacramento: University of California Press).

Berg, H. (2014) 'Labouring Porn Studies', *Porn Studies*, 1, 75–79.

Berners-Lee, T. and Fischetti, M. (2000) *Weaving the Web* (London: Harper).

Best, S. (2013) *Zygmunt Bauman: Why Good People Do Bad Things* (Farnham: Ashgate).

Bettig, R. V. (1992) 'Critical Perspectives on the History and Philosophy of Copyright', *Critical Studies in Media Communication*, 9, 131–155.

Bhambra, G. (2011) 'Historical Sociology, Modernity, and Postcolonial Critique', *American Historical Review*, 116, 653–662.

Billings, A. C. (ed.) (2012) *Sports Media: Transformation, Integration, Consumption* (New York: Taylor and Francis).

Billows, R. A. (2004) *Julius Caesar: The Colossus of Rome* (Abingdon: Routledge).

Bishop, J. (2014) 'Representations of "Trolls" in Mass Media Communication: A Review of Media-Texts and Moral Panics relating to Internet Trolling', *International Journal of Web Based Communities*, 10, 7–24.

Blackshaw, T. (2010) *Leisure* (London: Routledge).

Blackshaw, T. (2014) 'The Crisis in Sociological Leisure Studies and What to Do about It', *Annals of Leisure Research*, 17, 127–144.

Boellstorff, T. (2008) *Coming of Age in Second Life* (Princeton: Princeton University Press).

Bohman, J. (2004) 'Expanding Dialogue: The Internet, the Public Sphere and Prospects for Transnational Democracy', *The Sociological Review*, 52, 131–155.

Bonfadelli, H. (2002) 'The Internet and Knowledge Gaps: A Theoretical and Empirical Investigation', *European Journal of Communication*, 17, 65–84.

Booth, P. (2013) 'Reifying the Fan: Inspector Spacetime as Fan Practice', *Popular Communication*, 11, 146–159.

Borsay, P. (2005) *A History of Leisure* (Basingstoke: Palgrave).

Bos, L., Van der Brug, W. and De Vreese, C. (2011) 'How the Media Shape Perceptions of Right-Wing Populist Leaders', *Political Communication*, 28, 182–206.

Bottomore, S. (1999) 'The Panicking Audience? Early Cinema and the Train Effect', *Historical Journal of Film, Radio and Television*, 19, 177–216.

Bourdieu, P. (1986) *Distinction* (London: Routledge).

Bourke, J. (2005) *Fear: A Cultural History* (London: Virago).

Brah, A. (1996) *Cartographies of the Diaspora* (London: Routledge).

Braidotti, R. (2013) *Nomadic Subjects: Embodiment and Sexual Difference in Contemporary Feminist Theory* (New York: Columbia University Press).

Bramham, P. (2006) 'Hard and Disappearing Work: Making Sense of the Leisure Project', *Leisure Studies*, 25, 379–390.

Brandimarte, L., Acquisti, A. and Loewenstein, G. (2013) 'Misplaced Confidences: Privacy and the Control Paradox', *Social Psychological and Personality Science*, 4, 340–347.

Brandt, R. L. (2011) *One Click: Jeff Bezos and the Rise of Amazon.com* (London: Penguin).

Brenner, R. (1990) *Gambling and Speculation: A Theory, a History, and a Future of Some Human Decisions* (Cambridge: Cambridge University Press).

Briggs, A. and Burke, P. (2009) *A Social History of the Media* (Cambridge: Polity).

Brill, D. (2008) *Goth Culture: Gender, Sexuality and Style* (Oxford: Berg).

Brogaard, B. (2014) *On Romantic Love: Simple Truths about a Complex Emotion* (Oxford: Oxford University Press).

Brooke, C. N. L. (1989) *The Medieval Idea of Marriage* (Oxford: Oxford University Press).

Brooks, S. (2010) 'Hypersexualization and the Dark Body: Race and Inequality among Black and Latina Women in the Exotic Dance Industry', *Sexuality Research and Social Policy*, 7, 70–80.

Brown, J. C. (1970) *The Troika Incident: A Tetralogue in Two Parts* (New York: Doubleday).

Brown, J. J. (2008) 'From Friday to Sunday: The Hacker Ethic and Shifting Notions of Labour, Leisure and Intellectual Property', *Leisure Studies*, 27, 395–409.

Brown, M. C. (2012) 'The Price of Pleasure: Pornography, Sexuality and Relationships', *Teaching Sociology*, 40, 83–85.

Brown, P. (1988) *The Body and Society: Men, Women, and Sexual Renunciation in Early Christianity* (New York: Columbia University Press).

Brulle, R. J. (2014) 'Institutionalizing Delay: Foundation Funding and the Creation of US Climate Change Counter-Movement Organizations', *Climatic Change*, 122, 681–694.

Brundage, J. A. (2009) *Law, Sex, and Christian society in Medieval Europe* (Chicago: University of Chicago Press).

Bryce, J. and Rutter, J. (2003) 'Gender Dynamics and the Social and Spatial Organization of Computer Gaming', *Leisure Studies*, 22, 1–15.

Bryman, A. (2004) *The Disneyization of Society* (London: Sage).

Buckingham, D. and Willett, R. (eds) (2013) *Digital Generations: Children, Young People, and the New Media* (New York: Routledge).

Bull, M. (2005) 'No Dead Air! The iPod and the Culture of Mobile Listening', *Leisure Studies*, 24, 343–355.

Burgess, J. and Green, J. (2013) *YouTube: Online Video and Participatory Culture* (New York: John Wiley & Sons).

Burrows, K. (2013) 'Age Preferences in Dating Advertisements by Homosexuals and Heterosexuals: From Sociobiological to Sociological Explanations', *Archives of Sexual Behavior*, 42, 203–211.

Butler, J. (2006) *Gender Trouble: Feminism and the Subversion of Identity* (London: Routledge).

Caillois, R. (2001) *Man and the Sacred* (Champaign: University of Illinois Press).

Cameron, A. (1976) *Circus Factions* (Oxford: Clarendon).

Campbell-Kelly, M. and Garcia-Swartz, D. D. (2013) 'The History of the Internet: The Missing Narratives', *Journal of Information Technology*, 28, 18–33.

Carline, A. (2011) 'Criminal Justice, Extreme Pornography and Prostitution: Protecting Women or Promoting Morality?', *Sexualities*, 14, 312–333.

Carnegie, E. and McCabe, S. (2008) 'Re-enactment Events and Tourism: Meaning, Authenticity and Identity', *Current Issues in Tourism*, 11, 349–368.

Caruso, R. (2009) 'The Basic Economics of Match Fixing in Sport Tournaments', *Economic Analysis and Policy*, 39, 355.

Castells, M. (1996) *The Information Age Volume One: The Rise of the Network Society* (Oxford: Blackwell).

Castells, M. (1997) *The Information Age Volume Two: The Power of Identity* (Oxford: Blackwell).

Castells, M. (1998) *The Information Age Volume Three: End of Millennium* (Oxford: Blackwell).

Castells, M. (2000) 'Toward a Sociology of the Network Society', *Contemporary Sociology*, 29, 693–699.

Castells, M. (2001) *The Internet Galaxy: Reflections on the Internet, Business and Society* (Oxford: Oxford University Press).

Castells, M. (2007) 'Communication, Power and Counter-Power in the Network Society', *International Journal of Communication*, 1, 238–266.

Castells, M. (2009) *Communication Power* (New York: Oxford University Press).

Castells, M. (2011) 'Network Theory: A Network Theory of Power', *International Journal of Communication*, 5, 773–787.

Castells, M. (2012) *Networks of Outrage and Hope: Social Movements in the Internet Age* (Cambridge: Polity).

Cavanagh, A. (2010) *Sociology in the Age of the Internet* (London: McGraw-Hill Education).

Chadwick, A. and Howard, P. N. (eds) (2010) *Routledge Handbook of Internet Politics* (New York: Taylor and Francis).

Chambers, D. (2012) 'Wii Play as a Family: The Rise in Family-Centred Video Gaming', *Leisure Studies*, 31, 69–82.

Chatterton, P. (2008) 'Demand the Possible: Journeys in Changing Our World as a Public Activist-Scholar', *Antipode*, 40, 421–427.

Cheng, S. and Missari, S. (2014) 'The Effects of Internet Use on Adolescents' First Romantic and Sexual Relationships in Taiwan', *International Sociology*, 29, 324–347.

Clarke, A. C. (2002) 'Dial F for Frankenstein', in A. C. Clarke *The Collected Stories* (London: Orb).

Cloonan, M. (2013) *Popular Music and the State in the UK: Culture, Trade or Industry?* (Farnham: Ashgate).

Coalter, F. (2000) 'Public and Commercial Leisure Provision: Active Citizens and Passive Consumers?', *Leisure Studies*, 19, 163–181.

Cohen, A. P. (1985) *The Symbolic Construction of Community* (London: Tavistock).

Cohen, S. A. (2010) 'Personal Identity (De)formation among Lifestyle Travellers: A Double-edged Sword', *Leisure Studies*, 29, 289–301.

Consalvo, M. and Paasonen, S. (2002) *Women and Everyday Uses of the Internet* (New York: Peter Lang).

Coopersmith, J. (1998) 'Pornography, Technology and Progress', *Icon*, 4, 94–125.

Corneliussen, H. and Rettberg, J. W. (eds) (2008) *Digital Culture, Play, and Identity: A World of Warcraft Reader* (Cambridge: MIT Press).

Cotte, J. (1997) 'Chances, Trances and Lots of Slots: Gambling Motives and Consumption Experiences', *Journal of Leisure Research*, 29, 380–406.

Courtwright, D. T. (2011) 'Perversion for Profit: The Politics of Pornography and the Rise of the New Right', *Journal of American History*, 98, 907–908.

Cover, R. (2010) 'Object(ive)s of Desire: Romantic Coupledom versus Promiscuity, Subjectivity and Sexual Identity', *Continuum: Journal of Media and Cultural Studies*, 24, 251–263.

Cover, R. (2012) 'Performing and Undoing Identity Online: Social Networking, Identity Theories and the Incompatibility of Online Profiles and Friendship

Regimes', *Convergence: The International Journal of Research into New Media Technologies*, 18, 177–193.

Crain, M. (2014) 'Financial Markets and Online Advertising: Re-evaluating the Dotcom Investment Bubble', *Information, Communication and Society*, 17, 371–384.

Crawford, G. (2005) 'Digital Gaming, Sport and Gender', *Leisure Studies*, 24, 259–270.

Crawford, G. (2011) *Video gamers* (Abingdon: Routledge).

Crawford, G. and Gosling, V. (2009) 'More than a Game: Sports-themed Video Games and Player Narratives', *Sociology of Sport Journal*, 26, 50–66.

Crawford, G., Gosling, V. K. and Light, B. (eds) (2013) *Online Gaming in Context: The Social and Cultural Significance of Online Games* (New York: Routledge).

Critcher, C. (2008) 'Moral Panic Analysis: Past, Present and Future', *Sociology Compass*, 2, 1127–1144.

Crosby, S. L. (2014) 'Beyond Ecophilia: Edgar Allan Poe and the American Tradition of Ecohorror', *Interdisciplinary Studies in Literature and Environment*, 21, 513–525.

Crouch, D. (2011) 'Book Review: The Tourist Gaze 3.0', *Tourist Studies*, 11, 291–295.

Dahlberg, L. (2005) 'The Corporate Colonization of Online Attention and the Marginalization of Critical Communication', *Journal of Communication Inquiry*, 29, 160–180.

Dahlgren, P. (2005) 'The Internet, Public Spheres, and Political Communication: Dispersion and Deliberation', *Political Communication*, 22, 147–162.

Daniels, J. (2013) 'Race and Racism in Internet Studies: A Review and Critique', *New Media and Society*, 15, 695–719.

Daschuk, M. and Popham, J. (2013) 'Music Identities, Individualization, and Ownership Shifts: Empowering a Litigious Paradigm of Copyright Protection', *Sociology of Crime Law and Deviance*, 18, 59–78.

d'Astous, A. and Gaspero, M. D. (2013) 'Explaining the Performance of Online Sports Bettors', *International Gambling Studies*, 13, 371–387.

Davis, D. (2013) *A History of Shopping* (Abingdon: Routledge).

Davis, T. (2010) 'Third Spaces or Heterotopias? Recreating and Negotiating Migrant Identity Using Online Spaces', *Sociology*, 44, 661–677.

Dean, J. (1998) *Aliens in America: Conspiracy Cultures from Outerspace to Cyberspace* (Ithaca: Cornell University Press).

Deazley, R. (2006) *Rethinking Copyright: History, Theory, Language* (London: Edward Elgar).

Debord, G. (1995) *The Society of the Spectacle* (London: Zone Books).

Delanty, G. (2010) *Community* (London: Routledge).

Delanty, G. (2011) 'Cultural Diversity, Democracy and the Prospects of Cosmopolitanism: A Theory of Cultural Encounters', *British Journal of Sociology*, 62, 633–656.

Delanty, G. (ed.) (2012a) *Handbook of Cosmopolitanism Studies* (London: Routledge).

Delanty, G. (2012b) 'A Cosmopolitan Approach to the Explanation of Social Change', *Sociological Review*, 62, 333–354.

Descartes, R. (1998) 'Meditations on First Philosophy, 1641', in R. Descartes *Meditations and other metaphysical writings* (Harmondsworth: Penguin).

Dick, P. K. (1968) *Do Androids Dream of Electric Sheep?* (New York: Doubleday).

Dick, P. K. (1969) *Ubik* (New York: Doubleday).

Dilmperi, A., King, T. and Dennis, C. (2011) 'Pirates of the Web: The Curse of Illegal Downloading', *Journal of Retailing and Consumer Services*, 18, 132–140.

Dines, G. (2010) *Pornland: How Porn Has Hijacked Our Sexuality* (Boston: Beacon Press).

Dodds, K. (2006) 'Popular Geopolitics and Audience Dispositions: James Bond and the Internet Movie Database (IMDb)', *Transactions of the Institute of British Geographers*, 31, 116–130.

Donovan, T. (2010) *Replay: The History of Video Games* (Lewes: Yellow Ant).

Dourish, P. and Bell, G. (2014) 'Resistance Is Futile: Reading Science Fiction Alongside Ubiquitous Computing', *Personal and Ubiquitous Computing*, 18, 769–778.

Downs, C. (2010) 'Mecca and the Birth of Commercial Bingo 1958–70: A Case Study', *Business History*, 52, 1086–1106.

Drew, R. (2014) 'New Technologies and the Business of Music: Lessons from the 1980s Home Taping Hearings', *Popular Music and Society*, 37, 253–272.

Drushel, B. E. and German, K. (eds) (2011) *The Ethics of Emerging Media: Information, Social Norms, and New Media Technology* (London: Bloomsbury Publishing).

Ducheneaut, N., Yee, N., Nickell, E. and Moore, R. J. (2006) 'Building an MMO with Mass Appeal: A Look at Gameplay in World of Warcraft', *Games and Culture*, 1, 281–317.

Duncombe, S. and Tremblay, M. (eds) (2011) *White Riot: Punk Rock and the Politics of Race* (London: Verso).

Dunn, K. (2008) 'Never Mind the Bollocks: The Punk Rock Politics of Global Communication', *Review of International studies*, 34, 193–210.

Dunn, K. (2011) 'Anarcho-punk and Resistance in Everyday Life', *Punk and Post Punk*, 1, 201–218.

Durham, M. (2003) 'The American Far Right and 9/11', *Terrorism and Political Violence*, 15, 96–111.

Eckart, G. (2005) 'The German Gothic Subculture', *German Studies Review*, 28, 547–562.

Edmond, M. (2014) 'Here We Go Again Music Videos after YouTube', *Television and New Media*, 15, 305–320.

Eisenstein, E. (1983) *The Printing Revolution in Early Modern Europe* (Cambridge: Cambridge University Press).

Elias, N. (1978) *The Civilizing Process: Volume One* (Oxford: Blackwell).

Elias, N. (1982) *The Civilizing Process: Volume Two* (Oxford: Blackwell).

Elliott, A. and Urry, J. (2010) *Mobile Lives* (London: Routledge).

Elovaara, M. (ed.) (2013) *Fan Phenomena: Star Wars* (Bristol: Intellect).

Eschenfelder, K. R., Desai, A. C. and Downey, G. (2011) 'The Pre-Internet Downloading Controversy: The Evolution of Use Rights for Digital Intellectual and Cultural Works', *The Information Society*, 27, 69–91.

Ewalt, D. M. (2013) *Of Dice and Men: The Story of Dungeons and Dragons and the People Who Play It* (New York: Scribner).

Fairchild, C. (2012) 'Alan Freed Still Casts a Long Shadow: The Persistence of Payola and the Ambiguous Value of Music', *Media, Culture and Society*, 34, 328–342.

Faust, K., Meyer, J. and Griffiths, M. D. (2013) 'Competitive and Professional Gaming: Discussing Potential Benefits of Scientific Study', *International Journal of Cyber Behavior, Psychology and Learning*, 3, 67–77.

Featherstone, M. (1991) *Consumer Culture and Postmodernism* (London: Sage).

Ferrarese, M. (2014) 'Kami Semua Headbangers: Heavy Metal as Multiethnic Community Builder in Penang Island, Malaysia', *International Journal of Community Music*, 7, 153–171.

Fillis, I. and Mackay, C. (2014) 'Moving beyond Fan Typologies: The Impact of Social Integration on Team Loyalty in Football', *Journal of Marketing Management*, 30, 334–363.

Fine, G. A. (2002) *Shared Fantasy: Role Playing Games as Social Worlds* (Chicago: University of Chicago Press).

Finkelstein, D. and McCleery, A. (2012) *An Introduction to Book History* (Abingdon: Routledge).

Fischer, S. R. (2003) *History of Writing* (London: Reaktion Books).

Fitri, N. (2011) 'Democracy Discourses through the Internet Communication: Understanding the Hacktivism for the Global Changing', *Online Journal of Communication and Media Technologies*, 1, 1–20.

Foley, C., Holzman, C. and Wearing, S. (2007) 'Moving Beyond Conspicuous Leisure Consumption: Adolescent Women, Mobile Phones and Public Space', *Leisure Studies*, 26, 179–192.

Forrest, D. (1999) 'The Past and Future of the British Football Pools', *Journal of Gambling Studies*, 15, 161–176.

Foucault, M. (1973) *The Birth of the Clinic* (London: Tavistock).

Foucault, M. (1986) 'Other Spaces and the Principles of Heterotopia', *Lotus International*, 48, 9–17.

Foucault, M. (1991) *Discipline and Punish: The Birth of the Prison* (Harmondsworth: Penguin).

Foucault, M. (2006) *The History of Madness* (London: Routledge).

Foucault, M. (2012) *The History of Sexuality* (New York: Random House).

Fox, R. (2005) *The Classical World* (Harmondsworth: Penguin).

Franklin-Reible, H. (2006) 'Deviant Leisure: Uncovering the "Goods" in Transgressive Behaviour', *Leisure/Loisir*, 30, 55–71.

Fraterrigo, E. (2012) 'Carolyn Bronstein. Battling Pornography: The American Feminist Anti-Pornography Movement, 1976–1986', *The American Historical Review*, 117, 1262–1263.

Fredrick, D. (ed.) (2002) *The Roman Gaze: Vision, Power, and the Body* (Baltimore: Johns Hopkins University Press).

Frith, S. (ed.) (2004) *Popular Music: Critical Concepts in Media and Cultural Studies* (New York: Psychology Press).

Frost, C. (2006) 'Internet Galaxy Meets Postnational Constellation: Prospects for Political Solidarity after the Internet', *The Information Society: An International Journal*, 22, 45–49.

Fuchs, C. (2010) 'Labor in Informational Capitalism and on the Internet', *The Information Society*, 26, 179–196.

Fuchs, C. (2013) 'Societal and Ideological Impacts of Deep Packet Inspection Internet Surveillance', *Information, Communication and Society*, 16, 1328–1359.

Fuchs, C. (2014) *Digital Labour and Karl Marx* (Abingdon: Routledge).

Fuchs, C. and Dyer-Witheford, N. (2014) 'Karl Marx @ Internet Studies', *New Media and Society*, 15, 782–796.

Fukuyama, F. (2006) *The End of History and the Last Man* (New York: Simon and Schuster).

Fuller, S. (2000) *Thomas Kuhn: A Philosophical History for Our Times* (Chicago: University of Chicago Press).

Fuller, S. (2012) 'CSI: Kuhn and Latour', *Social Studies of Science*, 42, 429–434.

Gagnon, J. H. and Simon, W. (2011) *Sexual Conduct: The Social Sources of Human Sexuality* (New York: Transaction Publishers).

Gainsbury, S. M., Hing, N., Delfabbro, P. H. and King, D. L. (2014) 'A Taxonomy of Gambling and Casino Games via Social Media and Online Technologies', *International Gambling Studies*, published on-line at DOI: 10.1080/14459795.2014.890634.

Garland, J. (2010) 'It's a Mosher Just Been Banged for No Reason: Assessing Targeted Violence against Goths and the Parameters of Hate Crime', *International Review of Victimology*, 17, 159–177.

Geertz, C. (1973) *The Interpretation of Cultures* (New York: Basic).

Gibson, W. (1984) *Neuromancer* (London: Collins).

Giddens, A. (1981) *Capitalism and Modern Social Theory* (Cambridge: Cambridge University Press).

Giddens, A. (1990) *The Consequences of Modernity* (Cambridge: Polity).

Giddens, A. (1991) *Modernity and Self-Identity: Self and Society in the Late Modern Age* (Cambridge: Polity).

Giddens, A. (1999) *Runaway World: How Globalization Is Reshaping Our Lives* (London: Profile).

Giddens, A. (2005) *The New Egalitarianism* (Cambridge: Polity).

Giddens, A. (2013) *The Transformation of Intimacy: Sexuality, Love and Eroticism in Modern Societies* (London: John Wiley).

Giesler, M. (2006) 'Consumer Gift Systems', *Journal of Consumer Research*, 33, 283–290.

Gilchrist, P. and Ravenscroft, N. (2008) 'Power to the Paddlers? The Internet, Governance and Discipline', *Leisure Studies*, 27, 129–148.

Giulianotti, R. (1999) *Football* (Oxford: Blackwell).

Giulianotti, R. (2002) 'Supporters, Followers, Fans, and Flaneurs: A Taxonomy of Spectator Identities in Football', *Journal of Sport and Social Issues*, 26 25–46.

Giulianotti, R. and Robertson, R. (2007) 'Forms of Glocalization: Globalization and the Migration Strategies of Scottish Football Fans in North America', *Sociology*, 41, 133–152.

Goffman, E. (1971) *The Presentation of Self in Everyday Life* (Harmondsworth: Penguin).

Goodwin, R. (1990) 'Dating Agency Members: Are They Different?', *Journal of Social and Personal Relationships*, 7, 423–430.

Goulding, C. and Saren, M. (2009) 'Performing Identity: An Analysis of Gender Expressions at the Whitby Goth Festival', *Consumption Markets and Culture*, 12, 27–46.

Gramsci, A. (1971) *Selections from Prison Notebooks* (London: Lawrence and Wishart).

Green, E. and Adam, A. (1998) 'On-line Leisure: Gender, and ICTs in the Home', *Information Communication and Society*, 1, 291–312.

Greenaway, J. (2003) *Drink and British Politics since 1830* (Basingstoke: Palgrave).

Gregg, M. (2013) 'Spouse-busting: Intimacy, Adultery, and Surveillance Technology', *Surveillance and Society*, 11, 301–310.

Gunter, B. (1998) *The Effects of Video Games on Children: The Myth Unmasked* (London: Bloomsbury).

Gustafsson, N. (2012) 'The Subtle Nature of Facebook Politics: Swedish Social Network Site Users and Political Participation', *New Media and Society*, 14, 1111–1127.

Habermas, J. (1984) *The Theory of Communicative Action, Volume One: Reason and the Rationalization of Society* (Cambridge: Polity).

Habermas, J. (1987) *The Theory of Communicative Action, Volume Two: The Critique of Functionalist Reason* (Cambridge: Polity).

Habermas, J. (1989) *The Structural Transformation of the Public Sphere* (Cambridge: Polity).

Habermas, J. (1990) *The Philosophical Discourse of Modernity* (Cambridge: Polity).

Habermas, J. (1998) *The Inclusion of the Other* (Cambridge: Polity).

Habermas, J. (2000) *Post-National Constellation* (Cambridge: Polity).

Habermas, J. (2002) *Religion and Rationality: Essays on Reason, God, and Modernity* (Cambridge: Polity).

Habermas, J. (2006) 'Political Communication in Media Society: Does Democracy Still Enjoy an Epistemic Dimension? The Impact of Normative Theory on Empirical Research', *Communication Theory*, 16, 411–426.

Habermas, J. (2008) *Between Naturalism and Religion* (Cambridge: Polity).

Habermas, J. (2014) 'Internet and Public Sphere: What the Web Can't Do', interview by Markus Schwering, http://www.resetdoc.org/story/00000022437, posted 24 July 2014, accessed 3 September 2014.

Haenfler, R. (2006) *Straight Edge: Hardcore Punk, Clean Living Youth, and Social Change* (New Brunswick: Rutgers University Press).

Hall, S. (1993) 'Culture, Community, Nation', *Cultural Studies*, 7, 349–363.

Hammett, D. (2014) 'Understanding the Role of Communication in Promoting Active and Activist Citizenship', *Geography Compass*, 8, 617–626.

Hanegraaff, W. J. (1999) 'New Age Spiritualities as Secular Religion: A Historian's Perspective', *Social Compass*, 46, 145–160.

Harambam, J., Auters, S. and Houstman, D. (2011) 'Game Over? Negotiating Modern Capitalism in Virtual Game Worlds', *European Journal of Cultural Studies*, 14, 299–319.

Haraway, D. J. (1991) *Simians, Cyborgs, and Woman: The Reinvention of Nature* (London: Free Association Books).

Harcourt, W. (ed.) (1999) *Women@ Internet: Creating New Cultures in Cyberspace* (Basingstoke: Palgrave Macmillan).

Hark, I. R. (2008) *Star Trek* (Basingstoke: Palgrave).

Harriman, A. and Bontje, M. (2014) *Some Wear Leather, Some Wear Lace: A Worldwide Compendium of Postpunk and Goth in the 1980s* (Bristol: Intellect).

Harris, K. (2000) 'Roots? The Relationship between the Global and the Local within the Extreme Metal Scene', *Popular Music*, 19, 13–30.

Harris, L. and Rae, A. (2011) 'Building a Personal Brand through Social Networking', *Journal of Business Strategy*, 32, 14–21.

Harrison, H. (1961) *The Stainless Steel Rat* (New York: Pyramid).

Harvey, D. (2011) *The Enigma of Capital: and the Crises of Capitalism* (London: Profile Books).

Hayhurst, L. (2014) 'Introduction', *Northern Darkness*, 1, 2.

Hebdige, D. (1979) *Subcultures: The Meaning of Style* (London: Routledge).

Held, D., McGrew., Goldblatt, D. and Perraton, J. (1999) *Global Transformation: Politics, Economics and Culture* (Cambridge: Polity).

Herrmann, A. F. (2012) 'Never Mind the Scholar, Here's the Old Punk: Identity, Community, and the Aging Music Fan', *Studies in Symbolic Interaction*, 39, 153–170.

Hesmondhalgh, D. (2010) 'User-generated Content, Free Labour and the Cultural Industries', *Ephemera*, 10, 267–284.

Hesmondhalgh, D. (2013) *Why Music Matters* (London: John Wiley & Sons).

Hetherington, K. (1997) *The Badlands of Modernity: Heterotopia and Social Ordering* (London: Psychology Press).

Hilderbrand, L. (2009) *Inherent Vice: Bootleg Histories of Videotape and Copyright* (Durham: Duke University Press).

Hill, K. A. and Hughes, J. E. (1997) 'Computer-mediated Political Communication: The USENET and Political Communities', *Political Communication*, 14, 3–27.

Hillygus, D. S. and Shields, T. G. (2014) *The Persuadable Voter: Wedge Issues in Presidential Campaigns* (Princeton: Princeton University Press).

Hine, C. (2005) 'Internet Research and the Sociology of Cyber-Social-Scientific Knowledge', *The Information Society*, 21, 239–248.

Hobsbawm, E. (1987) *The Age of Empire* (London: Abacus).

Hobsbawm, E. and Ranger, T. (1983) *The Invention of Tradition* (Cambridge: Cambridge University Press).

Hodge, B. (2013) 'Nonlinear Causality in Castells's Network Society: Disorder as Problem and Opportunity under Globalization', *Global Networks*, 13, 330–344.

Hodkinson, P. (2002) *Goth: Identity, Style and Subculture* (Oxford: Berg).

Hodkinson, P. (2005) 'Insider Research in the Study of Youth Cultures', *Journal of Youth Studies*, 8, 131–149.

Hodkinson, P. (2011) 'Ageing in a Spectacular Youth Culture: Continuity, Change and Community amongst Older Goths', *The British Journal of Sociology*, 62, 262–282.

Hodkinson, P. (2013) 'Family and Parenthood in an Ageing "Youth" Culture: A Collective Embrace of Dominant Adulthood?', *Sociology*, 47, 1072–1087.

Holland, S. (2004) *Alternative Femininities: Body, Age and Identity* (Oxford: Berg).

Holland, S. (ed.) (2008) *Remote Relationships in a Small World* (New York: Peter Lang).

Holt, R. (1989) *Sport and the British: A Modern History* (Oxford: Clarendon).

Holton, R. J. (2005) 'Network Discourses: Proliferation, Critique and Synthesis', *Global Networks*, 5, 209–215.

Horne, J. (2006) *Sport in Consumer Culture* (Basingstoke: Palgrave).

Hourani, A. (2005) *A History of the Arab Peoples* (London: Faber and Faber).

Huang, C. Y. (2003) 'File Sharing as a Form of Music Consumption', *International Journal of Electronic Commerce*, 9, 37–55.

Huizinga, J. (2003) *Homo Ludens: A Study of the Play-Element in Culture* (London: Taylor and Francis).

Hunter, I. Q. (2014) 'Naughty Realism: The Britishness of British Hardcore R18s', *Journal of British Cinema and Television*, 11, 152–171.

Hutchins, B. and Rowe, D. (eds) (2012) *Sport beyond Television: The Internet, Digital Media and the Rise of Networked Media Sport* (New York: Routledge).

Jackson, E. L. (1999) 'Leisure and the Internet', *Journal of Physical Education, Recreation and Dance*, 70, 18–22.

James, M. L., Wotring, C. E. and Forrest, E. J. (1995) 'An Exploratory Study of the Perceived Benefits of Electronic Bulletin Board Use and Their Impact on Other Communication Activities', *Journal of Broadcasting and Electronic Media*, 39, 30–50.

Jeffreys, S. (1999) 'Globalizing Sexual Exploitation: Sex Tourism and the Traffic in Women', *Leisure Studies*, 18, 179–196.

Jemielniak, D. (2014) *Common Knowledge? An Ethnography of Wikipedia* (Stanford: Stanford University Press).

Jewkes, Y. and Yar, M. (eds) (2013) *Handbook of Internet Crime* (New York: Routledge).

Jhally, S. (1984) 'The Spectacle of Accumulation: Material and Cultural Factors in the Evolution of the Sports/media Complex', *Critical Sociology*, 12, 41–57.

Jin, S. A. A. and Phua, J. (2014) 'Following Celebrities' Tweets about Brands: The Impact of Twitter-Based Electronic Word-of-Mouth on Consumers' Source Credibility Perception, Buying Intention, and Social Identification with Celebrities', *Journal of Advertising*, 43, 181–195.

Johnson, N. F. (2012) *The Multiplicities of Internet Addiction: The Misrecognition of Leisure and Learning* (Farnham: Ashgate).

Johnson, P. (2006) 'Unravelling Foucault's "Different Spaces"', *History of the Human Sciences*, 19, 75–90.

Jolly, M. (2011) 'Lamenting the Letter and the Truth about Email', *Life Writing*, 8, 153–167.

Jones, L. (2012) 'The Commonplace Geopolitics of Conspiracy', *Geography Compass*, 6, 44–59.

Jones, S. (2002) 'Music That Moves: Popular Music, Distribution and Network Technologies', *Cultural Studies*, 16, 213–232.

Jones, S. G. (1984) 'The Economic Aspects of Association Football in England, 1918–39', *The British Journal of Sports History*, 1, 286–299.

Kahn-Harris, K. (2007) *Extreme Metal* (Oxford: Berg).

Kappeler, S. (2013) *The Pornography of Representation* (New York: John Wiley & Sons).

Kayany, J. M. (1998) 'Contexts of Uninhibited Online Behavior: Flaming in Social Newsgroups on Usenet', *Journal of the American Society for Information Science*, 49, 1135–1141.

Kelly, J. R. (1983) *Leisure Identities and Interactions* (London: George Allen and Unwin).

Kelly, J. R. (2012) *Leisure* (Urbana: Sagamore Publishing).

Kim, J. (2012) 'The Institutionalization of YouTube: From User-Generated Content to Professionally Generated Content', *Media, Culture and Society*, 34, 53–67.

Kim, S. W. and Douai, A. (2012) 'Google vs. China's "Great Firewall": Ethical Implications for Free Speech and Sovereignty', *Technology in Society*, 34, 174–181.

King, C. R. and Leonard, D. J. (2014) *Beyond Hate: White Power and Popular Culture* (Farnham: Ashgate).

Kirsh, S. J. (2011) *Children, Adolescents and Media Violence: A Critical Look at the Research* (London: Sage).

Kjølsrød, L. (2013) 'Mediated Activism: Contingent Democracy in Leisure Worlds', *Sociology*, 47, 1207–1223.

Klausen, J. (2014) 'Tweeting the Jihad: Social Media Networks of Western Foreign Fighters in Syria and Iraq', *Studies in Conflict and Terrorism*, published on-line at DOI: 10.1080/1057610X.2014.974948.

Knight, C. (2011) 'In Defence of Cosmopolitanism', *Theoria*, 58, 19–34.

Knight, P. (ed.) (2002) *Conspiracy Nation: The Politics of Paranoia in Postwar America* (New York: New York University Press).

Kraidy, M. (2005) *Hybridity: Or the Cultural Logic of Globalization* (Philadelphia: Temple University Press).

Kuhn, T. (1957) *The Copernican Revolution* (Chicago: University of Chicago Press).

Kunhibava, S. (2011) 'Reasons on the Similarity of Objections with Regards to Gambling and Speculation in Islamic Finance and Conventional Finance', *Journal of Gambling Studies*, 27, 1–13.

Kuwahara, M. (2005) *Tattoo: An Anthropology* (Oxford: Berg).

Laing, A. and Royle, J. (2013) 'Bookselling Online: An Examination of Consumer Behaviour Patterns', *Publishing Research Quarterly*, 29, 110–127.

Laing, R. D. (1990) *The Divided Self* (Harmondsworth: Penguin).

Lampe, M. and Ploeckl, F. (2014) 'Spanning the Globe: The Rise of Global Communications Systems and the First Globalisation', *Australian Economic History Review*, 54, 242–261.

Landon, B. (2014) *Science Fiction after 1900: From the Steam Man to the Stars* (New York: Routledge).

Langford, D. (ed.) (2000) *Internet Ethics* (New York: Macmillan).

Laqueur, T. W. (2003) *Solitary Sex: A Cultural History of Masturbation* (New York: Zone Books).

Latour, B. (1987) *Science in Action* (Cambridge: Harvard University Press).

Lauria, R. (2001) 'In Love with Our Technology: Virtual Reality, a Brief Intellectual History of the Idea of Virtuality and the Emergence of a Media Environment', *Convergence: The International Journal of Research into New Media Technologies*, 7, 30–51.

Lawrence, L. (2003) 'These Are the Voyages...: Interaction in Real and Virtual Space Environments in Leisure', *Leisure Studies*, 22, 301–315.

Lebow, R. N. (2012) *The Politics and Ethics of Identity: In Search of Ourselves* (Cambridge: Cambridge University Press).

Ledbetter, J. (2011) *Unwarranted Influence: Dwight D. Eisenhower and the Military Industrial Complex* (New York: Yale University Press).

Lee, T. J. and Byun, W. H. (2014) 'Issues and Impacts of Internet Gambling: The Case of Australia', *Tourism Analysis*, 19, 361–368.

Leiss, W. (2013) *Social Communication in Advertising: Consumption in the Mediated Marketplace* (New York: Routledge).

Leonelli, S. (2013) 'Why the Current Insistence on Open Access to Scientific Data? Big Data, Knowledge Production, and the Political Economy of Contemporary Biology', *Bulletin of Science, Technology and Society*, 33, 6–11.

LeVine, M. (2008) *Heavy Metal Islam* (New York: Random House).

Lewenstein, B. V. (1995) 'Do Public Electronic Bulletin Boards Help Create Scientific Knowledge? The Cold Fusion Case', *Science, Technology and Human Values*, 20, 123–149.

Lewis, T. and Kahn, R. (2005) 'The Reptoid Hypothesis: Utopian and Dystopian Representational Motifs in David Icke's Alien Conspiracy Theory', *Utopian Studies*, 16, 45–74.

Lincoln, S. (2005) 'Feeling the Noise: Teenagers, Bedrooms and Music', *Leisure Studies*, 24, 399–414.

Linderoth, J. (2012) 'Why Gamers Don't Learn More: An Ecological Approach to Games as Learning Environments', *Journal of Gaming and Virtual Worlds*, 4, 45–62.

Liptrot, M. (2014) 'Different People with Different Views but the Same Over-All Goals: Divisions and Unities within the Contemporary British DIY Punk Subcultural Movement', *Punk and Post Punk*, 2, 213–229.

Long, N. J. (2012) 'Utopian Sociality: Online', *Cambridge Anthropology*, 30, 80–94.

Lottes, I., Weinberg, M. and Weller, I. (1993) 'Reactions to Pornography on a College Campus: For or against?', *Sex Roles*, 29, 69–89.

Löwy, M. (2014) 'A Common Banner: Marxists and Anarchists in the First International', *Socialism and Democracy*, 28, 107–114.

Lucas, C., Deeks, M. and Spracklen, K. (2011) 'Grim Up North: Northern England, Northern Europe and Black Metal', *Journal for Cultural Research*, 15, 279–296.

Lumby, C. and Funnell, N. (2011) 'Between Heat and Light: The Opportunity in Moral Panics', *Crime, Media, Culture*, 7, 277–291.

Lupton, D. (2014) *Digital Sociology* (New York: Routledge).

Lynch, P. and Whitaker, R. (2013) 'Rivalry on the Right: The Conservatives, the UK Independence Party (UKIP) and the EU Issue', *British Politics*, 8, 285–312.

Lyotard, J. F. (1984) *The Postmodern Condition: A Report on Knowledge* (Manchester: University of Manchester Press).

MacKinnon, C. (1989) *Toward a Feminist Theory of the State* (Cambridge: Harvard University Press).

MacKinnon, R. (2012) *Consent of the Networked: the World-Wide Struggle for Internet Freedom* (New York: Basic Books).

Maffesoli, M. (1996) *The Time of the Tribes: The Decline of Individualism in Mass Society* (London: Sage).

Magliocco, S. (2011) *Witching Culture: Folklore and Neo-paganism in America* (Philadelphia: University of Pennsylvania Press).

Mahoney, M. S. and Haigh, T. (2011) *Histories of Computing* (Cambridge: Harvard University Press).

Mammone, A., Godin, E. and Jenkins, B. (eds) (2013) *Varieties of Right-Wing Extremism in Europe* (Abingdon: Routledge).

Marcus, S. (2008) *The Other Victorians* (New York: Transaction Publishers).

Marshall, L. (2002) 'Metallica and Morality: The Rhetorical Battleground of the Napster Wars', *Entertainment Law*, 1, 1–19.

Martin, J. (2014) *Drugs on the Dark Net: How Cryptomarkets Are Transforming the Global Trade in Illicit Drugs* (Basingstoke: Palgrave Macmillan).

Marx, K. (1963) *The Eighteenth Brumaire of Louis Bonaparte* (New York: International Publishers).

Mattar, Y. (2003) 'Virtual Communities and Hip-Hop Music Consumers in Singapore: Interplaying Global, Local and Subcultural Identities', *Leisure Studies*, 22, 283–300.

McChesney, R. W. (2013) *Digital Disconnect: How Capitalism Is Turning the Internet against Democracy* (New York: The New Press).

McChesney, R. W. (2014) 'Be Realistic, Demand the Impossible: Three Radically Democratic Internet Policies', *Critical Studies in Media Communication*, 31, 92–99.

McCosker, A. (2014) 'Trolling as Provocation: YouTube's Agonistic Public', *Convergence: The International Journal of Research into New Media Technologies*, 20, 201–217.

McCright, A. M. and Dunlap, R. E. (2011) 'Cool Dudes: The Denial of Climate Change among Conservative White Males in the United States', *Global Environmental Change*, 21, 1163–1172.

McGillivray, D. (2014) 'Digital Cultures, Acceleration and Mega Sporting Event Narratives', *Leisure Studies*, 33, 96–109.

McGowan, T. (2012) *The End of Dissatisfaction? Jacques Lacan and the Emerging Society of Enjoyment* (Albany: SUNY Press).

McGrath, A. E. (2012) *Historical Theology: An Introduction to the History of Christian Thought* (London: John Wiley & Sons).

McManus, P. and Graham, R. (2014) 'Horse Racing and Gambling: Comparing Attitudes and Preferences of Racetrack Patrons and Residents of Sydney, Australia', *Leisure Studies*, published ahead of print at DOI: 10.1080/02614367.2012.748088.

McNair, B. (2014) 'News 2.0: Can Journalism Survive the Internet?', *Journalism Studies*, 15, 116–117.

McNamee, M. J., Sheridan, H. and Buswell, J. (2000) 'Paternalism, Professionalism and Public Sector Leisure Provision: The Boundaries of a Leisure Profession', *Leisure Studies*, 19, 199–209.

Mcquire, S. (2010) 'Rethinking Media Events: Large Screens, Public Space Broadcasting and Beyond', *New Media and Society*, 12, 567–582.

McRobbie, A. (2011) 'Beyond Post-Feminism', *Public Policy Research*, 18, 179–184.

Merrin, W. (2005) *Baudrillard and the Media: A Critical Introduction* (Cambridge: Polity).

Messner, M. A. and De Oca, J. M. (2005) 'The Male Consumer as Loser: Beer and Liquor Ads in Mega Sports Media Events', *Signs*, 30, 1879–1909.

Miah, A. (2000) 'Virtually Nothing: Re-evaluating the Significance of Cyberspace', *Leisure Studies*, 19, 211–225.

Michikyan, M., Subrahmanyam, K. and Dennis, J. (2014) 'Can You Tell Who I Am? Neuroticism, Extraversion, and Online Self-presentation among Young Adults', *Computers in Human Behavior*, 33, 179–183.

Milne, E. (2012) *Letters, Postcards, Email: Technologies of Presence* (Abingdon: Routledge).

Mitchell, M. E., Bartholomew, K. and Cobb, R. J. (2014) 'Need Fulfillment in Polyamorous Relationships', *The Journal of Sex Research*, 51, 329–339.

Moore, R. (2004) 'Postmodernism and Punk Subculture: Cultures of Authenticity and Deconstruction', *The Communication Review*, 7, 305–327.

Morris, R. G. and Higgins, G. E. (2010) 'Criminological Theory in the Digital Age: The Case of Social Learning Theory and Digital Piracy', *Journal of Criminal Justice*, 38, 470–480.

Moulton, I. F. (2004) *Before Pornography: Erotic Writing in Early Modern England* (Oxford: Oxford University Press).

Muir, A. (2013) 'Online Copyright Enforcement by Internet Service Providers', *Journal of Information Science*, 39, 256–269.

Mullany, L. (2004) 'Become the Man That Women Desire: Gender Identities and Dominant Discourses in Email Advertising Language', *Language and Literature*, 13, 291–305.

Mulholland, M. (2011) 'When Porno Meets Hetero: SEXPO, Heteronormativity and the Pornification of the Mainstream', *Australian Feminist Studies*, 26, 119–135.

Murdock, G. (1994) 'New Times/Hard Times: Leisure Participation and the Common Good', *Leisure Studies*, 13, 239–248.

Murthy, D. (2011) 'Twitter: Microphone for the masses?', *Media, Culture and Society*, 33, 779–789.

Nip, J. Y. (2004) 'The Queer Sisters and Its Electronic Bulletin Board: A Study of the Internet for Social Movement Mobilization', *Information, Communication and Society*, 7, 23–49.

Norgaard, K. M. (2011) *Living in Denial: Climate Change, Emotions, and Everyday Life* (Cambridge: MIT Press).

Nowak, P. (2010) *Sex, Bombs and Burgers* (London: Allen and Unwin).

Nunn, H. (2013) *Reality TV: Realism and Revelation* (New York: Columbia University Press).

Nussbaum, M. C. and Sihvola, J. (eds) (2013) *The Sleep of Reason: Erotic Experience and Sexual Ethics in Ancient Greece and Rome* (Chicago: University of Chicago Press).

O'Connor, P. (2014) 'Watched and Watching', *Cultural Studies*, 28, 352–355.

Ogden, J. R., Ogden, D. T. and Long, K. (2011) 'Music Marketing: A History and Landscape', *Journal of Retailing and Consumer Services*, 18, 120–125.

Oliver, K. (2014) 'The Excesses of Earth in Kant's Philosophy of Property', *The Comparatist*, 38, 23–40.

O'Neill, O. (2013) *Acting on Principle: An Essay on Kantian Ethics* (Cambridge: Cambridge University Press).

Orford, J., Wardle, H. and Griffiths, M. (2013) 'What Proportion of Gambling Is Problem Gambling? Estimates from the 2010 British Gambling Prevalence Survey', *International Gambling Studies*, 13, 4–18.

Orlikowski, W. J. (2007) 'Sociomaterial Practices: Exploring Technology at Work', *Organization Studies*, 28, 1435–1448.

Ortner, S. B. (2014) 'Too Soon for Post-Feminism: The Ongoing Life of Patriarchy in Neoliberal America', *History and Anthropology*, 25, 530–549.

Paasonen, S. (2005) *Figures of Fantasy: Internet, Women and Cyberdiscourse* (New York: Peter Lang).

Palan, R., Murphy, R. and Chavagneux, C. (2010) *Tax Havens: How Globalization Really Works* (London: Cornell University Press).

Panek, E. T., Nardis, Y. and Konrath, S. (2013) 'Mirror or Megaphone? How Relationships between Narcissism and Social Networking Site Use Differ on Facebook and Twitter', *Computers in Human Behavior*, 29, 2004–2012.

Palme, J. (2011) 'Before the Internet: Early Experiences of Computer Mediated Communication', in J. Impagliazzo, P. Lundin and B. Wangler (eds) *History of Nordic Computing 3* (Berlin: Springer).

Papacharissi, Z. (2002) 'The Virtual Sphere: The Internet as a Public Sphere', *New Media and Society*, 4, 9–27.

Pariser, E. (2011) *The Filter Bubble: What the Internet Is Hiding from You* (London: Penguin).

Parke, J., Wardle, H., Rigbye, J. and Parke, A. (2013) *Exploring Social Gambling: Scoping, Classification and Evidence Review* (London: Report Commissioned by the UK Gambling Commission, The Gambling Lab).

Parlett, D. (1999) *The Oxford History of Board Games* (New York: Oxford University Press).

Pavlidis, A. (2012) 'From Riot Grrrls to Roller Derby? Exploring the Relations between Gender, Music and Sport', *Leisure Studies*, 31, 165–176.

Peck, B. M., Ketchum, P. R. and Embrick, D. G. (2011) 'Racism and Sexism in the Gaming World: Reinforcing or Changing Stereotypes in Computer Games?', *Journal of Media and Communication Studies*, 3, 212–220.

Peterson, L. W. (2000) 'The Married Man On-line', *Journal of Bisexuality*, 1, 191–209.

Petley, J. (2014) 'The State Journalism Is In: Edward Snowden and the British Press', *Ethical Space*, 11, 9–18.

Pilkington, H. (2010) 'No longer "on Parade": Style and the Performance of Skinhead in the Russian Far North', *The Russian Review*, 69, 187–209.

Pilkington, H. (2014) 'Sounds of a "Rotting City": Punk in Russia's Arctic Hinterland', in B. Lashua, K. Spracklen and S. Wagg (eds) *Sounds and the City: Popular Music, Place and Globalization* (Basingstoke: Palgrave).

Pinch, T. (2010) 'The Invisible Technologies of Goffman's Sociology from the Merry-go-round to the Internet', *Technology and culture*, 51, 409–424.

Plato (2007) *The Republic*, translated by H.D.P. Lee and D. Lee (Harmondsworth: Penguin).

Porter, D. (1997) *Internet Culture* (London: Routledge).

Possamai, A. and Lee, M. (2011) 'Hyper-Real Religions: Fear, Anxiety and Late-Modern Religious Innovation', *Journal of Sociology*, 47, 227–242.

Postigo, H. (2003) 'From Pong to Planet Quake: Post-industrial Transitions from Leisure to Work', *Information Communication and Society*, 6, 593–607.

Potter, R. H. and Potter, L. A. (2001) 'The Internet, Cyberporn, and Sexual Exploitation of Children: Media Moral Panics and Urban Myths for Middle-class Parents?', *Sexuality and Culture*, 5, 31–48.

Putnam, R. (2000) *Bowling Alone: The Collapse and Revival of American Community* (New York: Simon & Schuster/Touchstone).

Rafaeli, S. and LaRose, R. J. (1993) 'Electronic Bulletin Boards and "Public Goods" Explanations of Collaborative Mass Media', *Communication Research*, 20, 277–297.

Rak, J. (2005) 'The Digital Queer: Weblogs and Internet Identity', *Biography*, 28, 166–182.

Ramirez, M. (2013) 'You Start Feeling Old: Rock Musicians Reconciling the Dilemmas of Adulthood', *Journal of Adolescent Research*, 28, 299–324.

Rankin, B., Ergin, M. and Gökžen, F. (2014) 'A Cultural Map of Turkey', *Cultural Sociology*, 8, 159–179.

Raphael, D. D. (2013) *Hobbes: Morals and Politics* (Abingdon: Routledge).

Rawls, J. (1971) *A Theory of Justice* (New York: Routledge).

Richlin, A. (ed.) (1992) *Pornography and Representation in Greece and Rome* (Oxford: Oxford University Press).

Ritzer, G. (2004) *The McDonaldization of Society* (Pine Oaks: Sage).

Ritzer, G. and Jurgenson, N. (2010) 'Production, Consumption, Prosumption: The Nature of Capitalism in the Age of the Digital Prosumer', *Journal of Consumer Culture*, 10, 13–36.

Robbins, B. (2012) *Perpetual War: Cosmopolitanism from the Viewpoint of Violence* (Durham: Duke University Press).

Robbins, J. (2004) 'The Globalization of Pentecostal and Charismatic Christianity', *Annual Review of Anthropology*, 33, 117–143.

Roberts, K. (1997) 'Same Activities, Different Meanings: British Youth Cultures in the 1990s', *Leisure Studies*, 16, 1–15.

Roberts, K. (1999) *Leisure in Contemporary Society* (Wallingford: CAB International).

Roberts, K. (2004) *The Leisure Industries* (Basingstoke: Palgrave).

Roberts K. (2011) 'Leisure: The Importance of Being Inconsequential', *Leisure Studies* 30, 5–20.

Robinson, D. and Gibson, C. (2011) 'Governing Knowledge: Discourses and Tactics of the European Union in Trade-Related Intellectual Property Negotiations', *Antipode*, 43, 1883–1910.

Rohn, J. (2013) 'Science Fiction: Broken Brains and Runaway Technology', *Nature*, 498, 432.

Rojek, C. (2000a) 'Leisure and the Rich Today: Veblen's Thesis after a Century', *Leisure Studies*, 19, 1–15.

Rojek, C. (2000b) *Leisure and Culture* (London: Sage).

Rojek, C. (2005a) 'P2P Leisure Exchange: Net Banditry and the Policing of Intellectual Property', *Leisure Studies*, 24, 357–369.

Rojek, C. (2005b) 'An Outline of the Action Approach to Leisure Studies', *Leisure Studies*, 24, 13–25.

Rojek, C. (2006) 'Sports Celebrity and the Civilizing Process', *Sport in Society*, 9, 674–690.

Rojek, C. (2010) *The Labour of Leisure* (London: Sage).

Rojek, C. (2013) 'Is Marx still Relevant to the Study of Leisure?', *Leisure Studies*, 32, 19–33.

Rojek, C. and Urry, J. (1997) *Touring Cultures* (London: Routledge).

Rosa, H. (2013) *Social Acceleration: A New Theory of Modernity* (New York: Columbia University Press).

Rosen, L. D., Whaling, K., Rab, S., Carrier, L. M. and Cheever, N. A. (2013) 'Is Facebook Creating "iDisorders"? The Link between Clinical Symptoms of Psychiatric Disorders and Technology Use, Attitudes and Anxiety', *Computers in Human Behavior*, 29, 1243–1254.

Rosenthal, M. (2014) 'The Lesser Known Business Models of Online Copyright Infringement', *Journal of Information Ethics*, 23, 55–64.

Rountree, K. (2012) 'Neo-paganism, Animism, and Kinship with Nature', *Journal of Contemporary Religion*, 27, 305–320.

Ryan, S. (2002) Cyborgs in the Woods', *Leisure Studies*, 21, 265–284.

Sabin, R. (ed.) (2002) *Punk Rock: So what? The Cultural Legacy of Punk* (New York: Routledge).

Salter, A. and Blodgett, B. (2012) 'Hypermasculinity and Dickwolves: The Contentious Role of Women in the New Gaming Public', *Journal of Broadcasting and Electronic Media*, 56, 401–416.

Sanders, G. (2013) 'Punk May Just Be Dead', *Critical Sociology*, 39, 295–301.

Satterthwaite, A. (2001) *Going Shopping: Consumer Choices and Community Consequences* (New York: Yale University Press).

Savage, J. (2002) *England's Dreaming, Revised Edition: Anarchy, Sex Pistols, Punk Rock, and Beyond* (Basingstoke: Macmillan).

Scase, R. (1992) *Class* (Buckingham: Open University Press).

Schiermer, B. (2014) 'Late-Modern Hipsters: New Tendencies in Popular Culture', *Acta Sociologica*, 57, 167–181.

Scholz, T. (ed.) (2013) *Digital Labor: The Internet as Playground and Factory* (New York: Routledge).

Schwabach, A. (2011) *Fan Fiction and Copyright: Outsider Works and Intellectual Property Protection* (Farnham: Ashgate).

Seargeant, P. and Tagg, C. (eds) (2014) *The Language of Social Media: Identity and Community on the Internet* (New York: Palgrave Macmillan).

Shaw, S. M. (1999) 'Men's Leisure and Women's Lives: The Impact of Pornography on Women', *Leisure Studies*, 18, 197–212.

Shields, R. M. and Shields, R. (eds) (1996) *Cultures of the Internet: Virtual Spaces, Real Histories, Living Bodies* (London: Sage).

Shrage, L. (2013) *Moral Dilemmas of Feminism: Prostitution, Adultery and Abortion* (Abingdon: Routledge).

Sicart, M. (2014) *Play Matters* (Cambridge: MIT Press).

Silver, B. J. (2003) *Forces of Labor: Workers' Movements and Globalization since 1870* (Cambridge: Cambridge University Press).

Sivan, S. (2003) 'Has Leisure Got Anything to Do with Learning? An Exploratory Study of the Lifestyles of Young People in Hong Kong Universities', *Leisure Studies*, 22, 129–146.

Skeggs, B. (2013) *Class, Self, Culture* (Abingdon: Routledge).

Smigel, E. (1963) *Work and Leisure: A Contemporary Social Problem* (New Haven: College and University Press).

Smith, A. (1993) 'The Nation: Invented, Imagined, Reconstructed?', in M. Ringrose and A. J. Lerner (eds) *Reimagining the Nation* (Buckingham: Open University Press).

Southern, P. (2014) *Augustus* (London: Routledge).

Spracklen, K. (2006) 'Leisure, Consumption and a Blaze in the Northern Sky: Developing an Understanding of Leisure at the End of Modernity through the Habermasian Framework of Communicative and Instrumental Rationality', *World Leisure Journal*, 48, 33–44.

Spracklen, K. (2007) 'Negotiations of Belonging: Habermasian Stories of Minority Ethnic Rugby League Players in London and the South of England', *World Leisure Journal*, 49, 216–226.

Spracklen, K. (2009) *The Meaning and Purpose of Leisure* (Basingstoke: Palgrave).

Spracklen, K. (2011a) *Constructing Leisure* (Basingstoke: Palgrave).

Spracklen, K. (2011b) 'Dreaming of Drams: Authenticity in Scottish Whisky Tourism as an Expression of Unresolved Habermasian Rationalities', *Leisure Studies*, 30, 99–116.

Spracklen, K. (2013a) *Whiteness and Leisure* (Basingstoke: Palgrave).

Spracklen, K. (2013b) 'Nazi Punks Folk Off: Leisure, Nationalism, Cultural Identity and the Consumption of Metal and Folk Music', *Leisure Studies*, 32, 415–428.

Spracklen, K. (2014) 'There Is (Almost) No Alternative: The Slow "Heat Death" of Music Subcultures and the Instrumentalization of Contemporary Leisure', *Annals of Leisure Research*, 17, 252–266.

Spracklen, K. (2015) *Exploring Sports and Society* (London: Palgrave).

Spracklen, K. and Henderson, S. (2013) 'Oh! What a Tangled Web We Weave: Englishness, Communicative Leisure, Identity Work and the Cultural Web of the English Folk Morris Dance Scene', *Leisure/Loisir*, 37, 233–249.

Spracklen, K., Richter, A. and Spracklen, B. (2013) 'The Eventization of Leisure and the Strange Death of Alternative Leeds', *City*, 17, 164–178.

Spracklen, K. and Spracklen, B. (2012) 'Pagans and Satan and Goths, Oh My: Dark Leisure as Communicative Agency and Communal Identity on the Fringes of the Modern Goth Scene', *World Leisure Journal*, 54, 350–362.

Spracklen, K. and Spracklen, B. (2014) 'The Strange and Spooky Battle over Bats and Black Dresses: The Commodification of Whitby Goth Weekend and the Loss of a Subculture', *Tourist Studies*, 14, 86–102.

Stebbins, R. (1982) 'Serious Leisure: A Conceptual Statement', *Pacific Sociological Review*, 25, 251–272.

Stebbins, R. (1997) 'Casual Leisure: A Conceptual Statement', *Leisure Studies*, 16, 17–25.

Stebbins, R. (2009) *Leisure and Consumption* (Basingstoke: Palgrave Macmillan).

Stebbins, R. (2010) 'The Internet as a Scientific Tool for Studying Leisure Activities: Exploratory Internet Data Collection', *Leisure Studies*, 29, 469–475.

Stephens, D. (2013) *The Retail Revival: Reimagining Business for the New Age of Consumerism* (New York: John Wiley & Sons).

Sterne, J. (2012) *MP3: The Meaning of a Format* (Durham: Duke University Press).

Storey, D. (2012) *Territories: The Claiming of Space* (Abingdon: Routledge).

Streeter, T. (2010) *The Net Effect: Romanticism, Capitalism, and the Internet* (New York: NYU Press).

Sutton-Smith, B. (2009) *The Ambiguity of Play* (Cambridge: Harvard University Press).

Szablewicz, M. (2010) 'The Ill Effects of "Opium for the Spirit": A Critical Cultural Analysis of China's Internet Addiction Moral Panic', *Chinese Journal of Communication*, 3, 453–470.

Tatarchevskiy, T. (2011) 'The Popular Culture of Internet Activism', *New Media and Society*, 13, 297–313.

Thacker, S. and Griffiths, M. D. (2012) 'An Exploratory Study of Trolling in Online Video Gaming', *International Journal of Cyber Behavior, Psychology and Learning*, 2, 17–33.

Thomes, T. P. (2013) 'An Economic Analysis of Online Streaming Music Services', *Information Economics and Policy*, 25, 81–91.

Thompson, M. E., Chaffee, S. H. and Oshagan, H. H. (1990) 'Regulating Pornography: A Public Dilemma', *Journal of Communication*, 40, 73–83.

Thoreau, E. (2006) 'Ouch! An Examination of the Self-Representation of Disabled People on the Internet', *Journal of Computer-Mediated Communication*, 11, 442–468.

Tkach-Kawasaki, L. M. (2003) 'Politics@ Japan Party Competition on the Internet in Japan', *Party Politics*, 9, 105–123.

Toma, C. L. and Hancock, J. T. (2012) 'What Lies Beneath: The Linguistic Traces of Deception in Online Dating Profiles', *Journal of Communication*, 62, 78–97.

Toner, J. P. (1999) *Leisure and Ancient Rome* (Cambridge: Polity).

Travers, A. (2003) 'Parallel Subaltern Feminist Counterpublics in Cyberspace', *Sociological Perspectives*, 46, 223–237.

Tripp, L. M. and Herr-Stephenson, R. (2009) 'Making Access Meaningful: Latino Young People Using Digital Media at Home and at School', *Journal of Computer-Mediated Communication*, 14, 1190–1207.

Turkle, S. (1995) *Life on the Screen: Identity in the Age of the Internet* (New York: Simon and Schuster).

Turkle, S. (2011) *Alone Together* (New York: Basic Books).

Turner, G. (2013) *Understanding Celebrity* (London: Sage).

Turner, V. (1969) *The Ritual Process: Structure and Anti-structure* (Ithaca: Cornell University Press).

Urry, J. (1990) *The Tourist Gaze* (London: Sage).

Urry, J. (1995) *Consuming Places* (London: Routledge).

Urry, J. (2000) *Sociology beyond Societies* (Abingdon: Routledge).

Urry, J. (2003) *Global Complexity* (Cambridge: Polity).

Urry, J. (2007) *Mobilities* (Cambridge: Polity).

Urry, J. (2011) *Climate Change and Society* (Cambridge: Polity).

Van Dijck, J. (2011) 'Tracing Twitter: The Rise of a Microblogging Platform', *International Journal of Media and Cultural Politics*, 7, 333–348.

Van Dijck, J. (2013) 'You Have One Identity: Performing the Self on Facebook and LinkedIn', *Media, Culture and Society*, 35, 199–215.

Vannier, S. A., Currie, A. B. and O'Sullivan, L. F. (2014) 'Schoolgirls and Soccer Moms: A Content Analysis of Free "Teen" and "MILF" Online Pornography', *The Journal of Sex Research*, 51, 253–264.

Veblen, T. (1970) *The Theory of the Leisure Class* (London: Unwin).

Wajcman, J. (2002) 'Addressing Technological Change: The Challenge to Social Theory', *Current Sociology*, 50, 347–363.

Wallach, J. and Clinton, E. (2013) 'History, Modernity, and Music Genre in Indonesia: Popular Music Genres in the Dutch East Indies and Following Independence', *Asian Music*, 44, 3–23.

Walser, R. (1993) *Running with Devil: Power, Gender and Madness in Heavy Metal Music* (Hanover: Wesleyan University Press).

Walter, N. (2011) *Living Dolls: The Return of Sexism* (New York: Redress).

Wardle, H., Moody, A., Griffiths, M., Orford, J. and Volberg, R. (2011) 'Defining the Online Gambler and Patterns of Behaviour Integration: Evidence from the British Gambling Prevalence Survey 2010', *International Gambling Studies*, 11, 339–356.

Warr, R. and Goode, M. M. (2011) 'Is the Music Industry Stuck between Rock and a Hard Place? The Role of the Internet and Three Possible Scenarios', *Journal of Retailing and Consumer Services*, 18, 126–131.

Washington, H. (2013) *Climate Change Denial: Heads in the Sand* (Abingdon: Routledge).

Weaver, J. (2013) 'Making a Scene: The Female Punk Narrative in Lou Adler's Ladies and Gentlemen, The Fabulous Stains and Susan Seidelman's Smithereens', *Punk and Post Punk*, 2, 179–195.

Weber, M. (1992) *Economy and Society* (Sacramento: University of California Press).

Weber, M. (2001) *The Protestant Ethic and the Spirit of Capitalism* (London: Routledge).

Webster, F. (1997) 'Is This the Information Age? Towards a Critique of Manuel Castells', *City*, 2, 71–84.

Weeks, J. (2014) *Sex, Politics and Society: The Regulations of Sexuality since 1800* (London: Routledge).

Weinstein, D. (2000) *Heavy Metal: The Music and Its Culture* (New York: Dacapo Press).

Wellman, B. and Haythornthwaite, C. (eds) (2008) *The Internet in Everyday Life* (London: John Wiley & Sons).

Wenner, L. A. (ed.) (1989) *Media, Sports, and Society* (London: Sage).

West, M. D. (2013) 'Is the Internet an Emergent Public Sphere?', *Journal of Mass Media Ethics*, 28, 155–159.

Wheaton, B. (2007) 'Identity, Politics, and the Beach: Environmental Activism in Surfers against Sewage', *Leisure Studies*, 26, 279–302.

White, M. (2006) *The Body and the Screen: Theories of Internet Spectatorship* (Cambridge: MIT Press).

Whittier, N. (2014) 'Rethinking Coalitions: Anti-Pornography Feminists, Conservatives, and Relationships between Collaborative Adversarial Movements', *Social Problems*, 61, 175–193.

Wilkinson, D. and Thelwall, M. (2010) 'Social Network Site Changes over Time: The Case of MySpace', *Journal of the American Society for Information Science and Technology*, 61, 2311–2323.

Williams, D. (2009) 'Rethinking Deviant Leisure', *Leisure Sciences*, 31, 207–213.

Williams, R. (1977) *Marxism in Literature* (Oxford: Oxford University Press).

Williams, R. (1981) *Culture* (London: Fontana).

Williams, R. (ed.) (2013) *Torchwood Declassified: Investigating Mainstream Cult Television* (London: IB Tauris).

Wilson, A. and Ashplant, T. (1988) 'Whig History and Present-Centred History', *The Historical Journal*, 31, 1–16.

Wilson, B. (2007) 'New Media, Social Movements, and Global Sport Studies: A Revolutionary Moment and the Sociology of Sport', *Sociology of Sport Journal*, 24, 457–477.

Witte, J. C. and Mannon, S. E. (2010) *The Internet and Social Inequalities* (Abingdon: Routledge).

Wittgenstein, L. (1968) *Philosophical Investigations* (Oxford: Blackwell).

Wood, S. and Tirone, S. (2013) 'The Leisure of Women Caring for People Harmfully Involved with Alcohol, Drugs, and Gambling', *Journal of Leisure Research*, 45, 583–601.

Wood, R. T. and Griffiths, M. D. (2008) 'Why Swedish People Play Online Poker and Factors That Can Increase or Decrease Trust in Poker Web Sites: A Qualitative Investigation', *Journal of Gambling Issues*, 21, 80–97.

Wood, R. T. and Williams, R. J. (2007) 'Problem Gambling on the Internet: Implications for Internet Gambling Policy in North America', *New Media and Society*, 9, 520–542.

Woodworth, G. M. (2004) 'Hackers, Users, and Suits: Napster and Representations of Identity', *Popular Music and Society*, 27, 161–184.

Ybarra, M. L. and Mitchell, K. J. (2014) ' "Sexting" and Its Relation to Sexual Activity and Sexual Risk Behavior in a National Survey of Adolescents', *Journal of Adolescent Health*, 55, 757–764.

Zaidman, N. (2003) 'Commercialization of Religious Objects: A Comparison between Traditional and New Age Religions', *Social Compass*, 50, 345–360.

Zeff, R. L. and Aronson, B. (1999) *Advertising on the Internet* (New York: John Wiley & Sons).

Zhao, S. (2006) 'The Internet and the Transformation of the Reality of Everyday Life: Toward a New Analytic Stance in Sociology', *Sociological Inquiry*, 76, 458–474.

Žižek, S. (2010) *Living in the End Times* (London: Verso).

Zoonen, L. V. (2001) 'Feminist Internet Studies', *Feminist Media Studies*, 1, 67–72.

Zukin, S. (2004) *Point of Purchase: How Shopping Changed American Culture* (New York: Psychology Press).

Index

Aitchison, Cara, 45–6
alternative culture, 22–3, 153–72
alternativism, 154–6
Amazon, 4, 139–42
Americanization, 85–6
AOL, 25
Apple, 14, 194
ARPANET, 23, 25

Baudrillard, Jean, 54–5
Bauman, Zygmunt, 57–9, 82
belonging, 82–6, 94–112
Bramham, Peter, 3
Brown, James C., 20
bulletin boards, 21–5

Cambridge (UK), 1
Castells, Manuel, 4–5, 15, 27, 38,
    61–9, 76–7, 105–6
Clarke, Arthur C., 20
Cold War, The, 13
commodification, 4, 30, 54, 86,
    117–19, 133–52, 172
communicative rationality, 21, 24,
    30–1, 64–5, 77–9, 82–3, 112, 119,
    153–72, 200–1
CompuServe, 25
conservative ideology, 22
conspiracy theories, 109–12
control, 80–2
cosmopolitanism, 60–1
cricket, 3

dating, 184–92
Delanty, Gerard, 60–1
Dick, Philip K., 20

email, 1, 28–9, 36–7, 87–8

Facebook, 4, 57, 98–102, 104,
    186–7, 194
feminism and the Net, 35–6, 55–6,
    174–6, 181–4

file sharing, 40, 113–32
Foucault, Michel, 55
France, 25
Freedom, 77–9

gambing, 134–8
gaming, 14, 24, 37–8, 90, 147–51
Gibson, William, 20
Giddens, Anthony, 59–60
Giulianotti, Richard, 2–3, 46–7
globalization, 2–4, 29–30, 49, 54, 58,
    59–60, 66, 146–7, 157–8, 165
glocalization, 2
Google, 4, 139, 194
goths, 161–8

Habermas, Jürgen, 2, 18, 31, 64, 67,
    69–73, 74–6, 82, 116–17, 155,
    200–1
Habermasian leisure, 74–6
hackers, 22
heavy metal, 157–61
hegemony, 15, 31, 66–7, 75, 80, 201–2
hobbyists, 14
home computers, 24
homogenization, 85
Horne, John, 3
hyper-reality, 54–5

identity, 82–6, 94–112
inconsequential leisure, 89–91
instrumental rationality, 31, 69–73,
    75–6, 80, 90–3, 112, 116–17,
    201–2
internet sociology, 33

Leeds (UK), 1, 142
liquid modernity, 58

marketization, 15
masculinity, 83, 85, 174–6
mass media, 13, 63–5, 69–73
Miah, Andy, 36–7

Microsoft, 30
middle classes, 15, 21–2, 103–4, 140
Minitel, 25
Misogyny, 150, 181–4
Mobilities, 50–1, 56–7
modernity, 12–13, 27, 58, 62, 140, 155
MySpace, 5–6, 98

PCs, 14–15
Plato, 18–19
pop music industry, 114–15, 117–18
pornography, 14, 22, 35–6, 55, 173–92
postmodernity, 33–5, 37, 44–8, 57, 62
public sphere, 67, 69–73, 75–6
punks, 169–71

radical (far) right activism, 107–9
radical left activism, 105–7
Roberts, Ken, 3, 35, 44–5, 89
Rojek, Chris, 4, 36, 40–1, 47–8, 178–9

science-fiction computers, 16–19,
    39–40
serious leisure, 24–5, 49–50, 87–9
sex, 173–92
shopping, 138–43
social media, 94–112
sport, 3–4, 13, 143–7

Stainless Steel Rat, The (book
    series), 17
Star Trek, 17–18, 101, 104
Star Wars, 20–1
Stebbins, Robert, 49–50, 87
subcultures, 38–9, 153–72

television, 12, 86, 134, 144–5
tourism studies, 3, 43–4
Turkle, Sherry, 55–6
Twitter, 86, 98–9

United Kingdom, 94, 105–6, 108
United States of America, 13–14, 23,
    25, 31, 107–10
Urry, John, 50–1, 56–7, 82

video games (history), 14
virtuality, 18–20, 44–5

webcam, 1
Welles, Orson, 19
whisky, 44
Wikipedia, 4, 194
World of Warcraft, 6, 149–51
World Wide Web (history), 15, 23,
    26–31

YouTube, 123–5, 143

GPSR Compliance
The European Union's (EU) General Product Safety Regulation (GPSR) is a set
of rules that requires consumer products to be safe and our obligations to
ensure this.

If you have any concerns about our products, you can contact us on

ProductSafety@springernature.com

In case Publisher is established outside the EU, the EU authorized
representative is:

Springer Nature Customer Service Center GmbH
Europaplatz 3
69115 Heidelberg, Germany